More Years for the Locust: The Origins of the SWP was first published in London, Great Britain in 1997 by the IS Group (ISBN 0-9530607-0-5)

This edition published in Great Britain in 2011 by Unkant Publishers, First Floor Offices, Hoxton Point, 6 Rufus Street, London N1 6PE

Designed by Keith Fisher & Andy Wilson
Cover by Ben Watson & Andy Wilson
Cartoons by Phil Evans

British Library Cataloguing-in-Publication Data
A CIP catalogue record for this book is available from the British Library
A Paperback Original

ISBN 978-0-9568176-3-1
1 3 5 7 9 10 8 6 4 2

Set in Unkant Jensen
www.unkant.com

More Years for the Locust
The Origins of the SWP

Jim Higgins

Unkant Publishers

London, UK

Contents

Jim Higgins

Jim Higgins (December 2, 1930–October 13, 2002) was a political militant and an organic working class intellectual. Having joined the Communist Party as a teenager, he became a Trotskyist in the Socialist Labour League and then an early member of the Socialist Review Group–forerunners of the International Socialists and Socialist Workers Party.

Dedication

This book is dedicated
to the memory of
Harry Wicks
(1905–1989)
revolutionary communist
and a real working class hero

Acknowledgements

Unkant publishers would
like to thank Jane Allen
for her help and encouragement
in republishing
More Years for the Locust.

Every individual, every organisation, every movement should be aware of their own history. In the case of individuals and most organisations and movements it is quite possible for them to live out their existence with a history built on myths, half-truths and plain untruths, indeed, in the case of many individuals and political organisations an objective and impartial history would be an absolute bar to further existence. For the socialist movement history as a collection of sustaining myths is possible but undesirable.

Jim Higgins, 'The Origins of the Communist Party', *International Socialism* (1st series), No.40, October/November 1969, pp.33-36.

Andy Wilson: Preface to the Unkant Edition

I first met Jim Higgins at a fringe meeting at the Socialist Workers Party's (SWP) annual Marxism event sometime in the mid-90s. The IS Group (ISG), of which I was a founder member, had organised the meeting to discuss the SWP's peculiar idea of party democracy, and Jim had agreed to speak on our platform about his own experiences in the International Socialists (IS–forerunners of the SWP). Perhaps tellingly I don't remember much about the meeting itself but I still have vivid memories of Jim's performance in the bar afterwards, reliving past battles and spinning pitch-perfect character portraits of the various sinners involved. Here in the flesh was one of those fantastic beasts that Marxist theory had prepared us young communists for but which our party experience had been rather shy of delivering (give or take Duncan Hallas)–a genuine, old-school working-class revolutionary leader. Anyone who ever met Jim is bound to mention his scabrous wit, but he combined this with a vast knowledge of Marxism, revolutionary history and much else besides, and he brought all of it to bear in argument, making him a truly formidable figure who was nevertheless not in the least forbidding... as long as you weren't up to no good.

Some time after this first meeting the ISG offered to publish the first edition of this book, Jim's political memoirs, in which he sets out to paint a picture of the prehistory of the SWP, its origins in the Socialist Review Group and International Socialists, culminating in the dispute this book focuses on, which led to the formation of the IS Opposition and Jim's eventual departure from the group he had spent years building, alongside many other leading industrial militants and senior members of the IS.

As to the rights and wrongs of the debate and the split–which, in any case, should surely be regarded as calamitous for the IS tradition–the fact is that most SWP members today will know very little about it, which is reason enough for us to want to make the book available again. The particular circumstances which inspired the dispute are long gone, along with many of those who took part, but the need to rethink and refocus the revolutionary Marxist tradition remains pressing, and Jim has more than earned a place in that discussion. I consider Jim's airbrushing out of IS/SWP history to be scandalous, and one of my hopes in republishing the book is that it will help introduce Jim to supporters of the IS tradition who may never have heard of him.

For this edition of the book we have followed the original except that obituaries by Roger Protz and Nigel Fountain have been added, some typos corrected, chapter titles have been concocted in order to make it easier to identify the various parts of Jim's argument, and an index has been added in order, we hope, to make the book easier to use as a reference and in debate. We have also added an introduction by John Game, which stakes out the continued relevance of Jim's book for a new generation of radicals, and specifically to members of the SWP as their organisation tries to rebuild itself after jettisoning the core of the leadership that had effectively directed the party after Cliff's death.

John Game: The Trouble With Jim Higgins

L ike many comrades I first read *More Years for the Locust* on the internet.[1] It was for anyone who had hung around the Revolutionary Left in Britain a bit of a guilty pleasure. It was not reviewed by the SWP, the assumption being that it was of interest only to bitter sectarians.

The reception on the rest of the revolutionary left (the bitter sectarians) was no better. Here the abuse of important figures in the SWP leadership (particularly Cliff) and the disparagement of the organisation that emerged out of the 1970s were seen as key merits and much dwelt on. They tended to pass over in silence the far more insulting things he had to say about them and their organisations. Insofar as the book was noticed, the consensus seemed to be that it was apolitical and, in contested ways, disreputable. In short the SWP didn't like his judgements whilst their opponents didn't like his politics. The majority of course were indifferent to debates about the post-war revolutionary left.

This was in the far off 1990s when capitalism was unexpectedly confident, and the SWP, by way of a response, confidently deranged. The publishers of the book had just been expelled in circumstances so farcical that the expulsions have long since been quietly disowned, even by some who voted for them. Large num-

1. Thanks to Einde O'Callaghan, Ted Crawford and the inspirational Marxist Internet Archive (*marxists.org*).

bers of comrades were dropping out of activity, remaining attached to the politics but finding the organisation uninhabitable. The early 1980s had bought a new generation of activists into the organisation, radicalised by Thatcherism and the Miner's strike of 1984, and strengthened by what seemed a coherent account of the difficulties socialists faced during that decade. They were shaped by very different circumstances to that of the comrades of the 1970s and in some senses the world which Higgins was to portray would have seemed quite alien to them. By the end of the 1990s the darker prognosis of Jim seemed to be coming true. Despite high hopes at the beginning of that decade, by its end there was no new levy of cadre and recruitment to make up for what had been lost. Despite this the audience for the book was small. A beleaguered left organisation is not the best place for a free and open exchange of ideas and there was no particular reason for anyone outside of it to pay too much attention.

More than a decade later and the context has changed in a number of important ways. Between that period and this lie the highs of the great mobilisations of the anti-war movement and the lows of the splits that followed the collapse of the SWP's engagement with the Respect coalition. One consequence of this was a series of very public and unpleasant rows on the left which made the allegedly bitter account of Higgins seem positively bucolic. The return of real political struggles which revolutionaries could play a meaningful role in, led to the return of real and meaningful political controversy. Unfortunately it rapidly became obvious that much of the organisational framework inherited from the 1990s, as well as a large section of the existing leadership, could not cope with this. Rigidity and an inability to admit mistakes gave way to fragmentation and the majority of the older leadership simply peeled away, uncomfortable working with a cadre that had begun to answer back. The resulting argument and debate inside the organisation represented not only an attempt to recover some sense of political coherence but linked this struggle to restoring confidence in a layer of militants and activists who had been dismayed by these disasters and the role of the SWP in them. Hence the discussions of democracy, organisation and perspective could no longer be treated as purely internal matters, leading to calls for considerable changes in the culture of the organisation.

If this was and is an uneven and controversial process it was given urgency by the development of the most serious crisis of capitalism seen since the 1970s. This has meant that questions of organisation, strategy and tactics have once again become debates for larger groups of activists. Debates have raged across the internet on the nature and respective merits of Leninism, Vanguardism, Trotskyism, Stalinism, Maoism, Autonomism, and Anarchism, often quite independently of official representatives of these doctrines or deviations. There has also been a more academic re-examination of the tradition as Lenin's *What is to be Done?* is subjected to a new translation and books written about the Comintern in French in the 1970s are republished in translation and we find out what Paul Levi of the KPD really had to say about the March Action: if we can afford it.

In the meantime we are rapidly moving into the kind of social turbulence which make the debates of this period seem of more than historical relevance perhaps for the first time in living memory. With something like a visceral shock we suddenly meet our first real centrist, or on the other hand, find ourselves debating the popular front government of Leon Blum as a practical exercise in political fortune telling. If much of this does recall what Higgins saw as a tendency to reach for the wrong maps at the first sign of crisis it's also true that it might reasonably be asked why we should concern ourselves with the long forgotten doings of a small revolutionary socialist organisation over the post-war period which, for much of the time, spent its time informing people why the crisis of capitalism *wasn't* happening, recruiting people on the basis of an understanding that there was not a lot going on.

The first reason is that many of the debates we are having today are not in fact new. There is a tendency as there always is in these situations to re-invent the wheel. Higgins provides an account of the emergence of a form of politics which rejected the dogma's of much of the far left, not only in relationship to the Soviet Union, but also in terms of distortions involved in the transmission of the Bolshevik tradition itself. Intellectually we can discover from a historian like Broué that one source of the dogmatism of Trotskyism was that it had to present itself as orthodox, precisely when new thinking was necessary. This was because the left opposition had to present themselves as the *real* Bolsheviks in front of the insane tribunal of the Stalinists. The result, put rather diplomatically by the Trotskyist historian Broué, was that they became a bit mad as well as dogmatic.[1] Higgins is of course less diplomatic. One finds in the first part of the book the history of a group of activists who consciously began to break away from this gnawing of the locusts. Whether this involved explanations of Stalinism, the nature of the vanguard party, Trotsky's prognosis about capitalism, or just about anything else, the evolution of the IS tradition which Higgins describes as a kind of lived experience in these pages re-examined just about every question currently being debated on the left.

It's precisely because these discussions are presented here as the property of activists with all their flaws and colour as opposed to a set of icons or the result of the scourings of an intrepid archivists that this account remains so important. It gives a real sense of traditions on the far left which still exist and reproduce themselves (sometimes within our selves, so it's always handy to know what to look out for!). There is a human scale to the story so often missing in the more staid accounts of the left and its history which often create an artificial barrier between readers and the activists being written about, who were after all, people much like them. This dimension of the book which, to put it bluntly, makes it such a good laugh, also provides a great store of what Aristotle would have called practical wisdom. The laughter and the *nous* are here very closely related and impossible to summarise, they must be read. But if revolutionaries are great iconoclasts they are also great respecters of tradition (as opposed to personal dignity) and the detailed discussions of what it was actually like to be an entryist in the labour party, to try and set up a rank and file movement or to merge with other organisations are gold dust politically whatever one makes of particular judgements of this or that controversy (I personally found the unforgettable accounts of Cliff's recruiting techniques rather impressive). There is much to learn here that one simply can't learn anywhere else. In the proper sense it gives wisdom to those capable of receiving it.

The second reason we should pay attention is that some of the books reputation as a jaundiced and bitter account of the doings

---

1. These and many other insights can be found in Pierre Broué's *The German Revolution 1917-1923*, London: Haymarket Press , 2006.

of the left stem from a genuine anger on Higgins part about what he took to be a retreat from this tradition in circumstances which more closely resemble contemporary crisis of both capitalism and the left than when it was first published. If some of us debate the early 1920s in Germany or the Blum government in France, others are thinking of Chile and Portugal in the 1970's. The crisis of that decade feels much closer now than it did when the book was first published in the 1990s long before the economic turmoil of the last few years or the dramatic social and political struggles that have followed it. Jim believed that the International Socialists had made the most serious attempt in the post war period to build a mass socialist current inside the British working class, an attempt which reached its high point in the early 1970s. He also believed that they blew it when they were at their peak and just when the game got serious. Whatever the differences comrades may have with his account, given recent experiences and future dilemmas it's not really possible to read it without thinking of parallels, even if we're free to decide to reject some of them. There are two dimensions to the account he gives of this crisis which seem very relevant for us today.

The first reflects the shift from small group politics to larger mass organisations and the debates about how to embody these shifts in organisational forms. Again, one can't help be struck by some rather familiar themes even if we, like Jim, are sometimes a little unsure about what conclusions to draw. All the familiar problems of relating the efficiency said to flow from discipline and centralism to the development of a strong cadre capable of thinking for itself, without which all this is empty playacting, appear here. Socialists do of course want their organisation to be effective. They also want their organisation to be accountable. Higgins gives no easy answers here save to stress and re-stress the basic principle that leadership divorced from the building of a working class cadre always ends in disaster. If the book appears to end with an extremely caustic take on the far left's obsession with democratic centralism the account he offers of the choices involved is not straightforward. One might conclude that democratic centralism is not a magical incantation but an outline which requires thinking through rather than parroting.

A weakness of the book is often thought to be an exaggerated emphasis on Cliff's personal failings (and a tendency to read these failings back to a period when Jim was in agreement with them). My own sense is that there are points in the book where Jim seems to paint earlier incidents in darker hues than they probably deserve. This seems true regarding the aforementioned recruiting techniques, or Cliff's somewhat casual approach to referencing and/or changing his mind (I'd declare an interest here) with the possibly borderline case of someone being expelled for being an idiot, perhaps understandable if not commendable when the membership comprises thirteen people. Despite a few teleological failings of this kind, one can also gather that Cliff was a pretty impressive character to most, including Jim, who one might safely conclude wasn't easily impressed. If Cliff's 'whim of iron' was often erratic, such failings could be seen as an asset by many comrades for much of the time when he was getting things right, it's just that like most people, he could be wrong. Socialist organisations ought to be able to contain as well as utilize the most talented in their ranks and a kind of exaggerated deference by many seems to have been a problem here (occasionally shared by Jim himself as far as one can work out).

Higgins is of course ultimately utterly unforgiving about Cliff (in a way he is not about others who disappointed him from Harman to Hallas) but it's possible to conclude that the real problem can be giving people more authority than is actually good for them. Perhaps it was inevitable that smaller organisations would assume the personalities of their founders as Higgins argues (rather entertainingly for those of us familiar with them), but this surely ought to be a passing phase. Recent events suggest that Higgins may have had a point about the difficulties associated with too loose and slapdash an attitude to formal procedures, an objection that led to early clashes with Cliff who found Higgins too bureaucratic. There is a wonderful account in the book of the democratic practice of the organisation in the early 1960s where a kind of 'free-wheeling informality' set the tone. It's easy to imagine how this works with a hundred people but with a couple of thousand one can see how freedom of action for some might seem alarmingly arbitrary to others. If this problem in 'small mass parties' expresses itself in internal crisis and much frustration, one might conclude that if these problems aren't addressed we'll never see what it produces in the proper kind of mass party, no matter how favourable the circumstances.

These difficulties all came to a head in the early 1970s during a period when the International Socialists were in the process of successfully turning themselves from a body composed largely of radicalised students into a serious proletarian organisation with a base in some of the most advanced sections of the industrial working class at a time of unparalleled trade union militancy.[1] This was no flash in the pan but, as Higgins recounts, had been the product of a sustained industrial orientation and perspective that in many ways marked off the organisation from all others. It is important to stress here that Jim was himself a key participant in the development of this general orientation and the working out of the specific perspectives associated with it, especially given the very formative influence these perspectives were to have on the general politics of both the IS tradition and the later SWP. It was in the midst of the realisation of these endeavours that serous clashes occurred around the relative priorities of Party building and the building of rank and file organisation inside the class, between relating to older and more established militants, and relating to the 'youth', and, it's possible retrospectively to understand, what sort of organisation we were to become (as well as understanding some of the contemporary lefts fears and obsessions). As part of the Miners Strike levy of comrades I had tended to see comrades like Higgins as understandably disorientated by the decline in trade union militancy but wrongly blaming the SWP in general and Cliff in particular for what we called the downturn. This objective shift in the balance of class forces was held responsible for the disintegration of mass rank and file organisations

---

1. In this context it's been suggested that the trouble with Higgins was that he was a workerist. I've always found this an odd allegation to make in the context of a book which begins with a discussion of Palestine and contains reflections on the slowness of his generation on questions of sexuality and Women's struggles. Such allegations seem to confuse having a working class base with workerism which seems a bit self defeating.

and the end of the most ambitious form of transitional politics we had ever embarked on.[1]

Today it's possible to see that this isn't a suggestion which completely fit's the sequence of events or the time frame. Ian Birchall's excellent biography of Cliff[2] demonstrates that when these arguments actually occurred Cliff was no prophet of the downturn and the position of Higgins and much of the industrial base around him was designated as 'conservative'. As Ian seems to conclude, both Higgins and Cliff were as mistaken as each other about the actual outcome of the events they disagreed about.

It would be foolish to attempt to deliberate on what might have been the perfect perspective for 1975 (well let's say I don't really feel qualified to; a larger discussion amongst more informed comrades might come in handy) but the wider interest for the contemporary reader is that here were a set of dilemmas and problems experienced by a revolutionary organisation with a serious implantation inside the class in the midst of a crisis of capitalism: the shape of the controversies, mistakes and occasional sheer foolishness of our predecessors is surely of some interest in a period like this one. It's also true that if lessons from the 1920s might seem more edifying because it's a long time ago and far away, it's surely useful to look at more recent examples if the examination of history is to serve larger purposes than edification. For it was out of this contested history and out of these contested questions that the SWP as we know it emerged (it's why the book is subtitled the 'origins of the SWP').

Higgins was one of those members of the IS tradition, along with those like Peter Sedgwick who thought that declaring ourselves a party was a terrible mistake, a concession to the kind of ludicrous self importance and self delusion our tradition had always eschewed, made in the aftermath of the failures of perspective that had led to splits and the beginning of the crisis of the organisation which was eventually to issue in the downturn analyses. This is also the context for his great dislike of Cliff's volumes on Lenin (which rather interestingly are creating a similarly acerbic

---

1. A contemporary statement of this form of transitional politics can be found at *marxists.org/history/etol/newspape/isj/1975/no076/jeffreys.htm*.
2. Ian Birchall, *Tony Cliff: A Marxist for His Time*, London: Bookmarks, 2011.

debate amongst activists today).[1] It's also perhaps the source of
his too dismissive remarks about the ANL of this period. As well
as comrades of the calibre of a Higgins or a Sedgwick (and not a
few others) who thought declaring ourselves a Party was a mistake, there were also some people who were complete idiots who
thought it was a mistake, so it's hard today to be sure who was
right in all this. But we do know that the split documented in this
book was a terribly serious one, even more serious than the ones
we have recently been afflicted with. It seems hard to believe that
there are not some things we can learn from it, and some things,
one hopes, we can avoid through a re-examination of this period.
It's true that in the 1980s many in the SWP continued to learn
and profit from the lessons that those like Higgins had taught
us in ways which to some degree contradict Higgins judgements
here it's also true that the recent crisis has opened up again in new
ways some of the questions debated in the 1970s.

I've always felt that this book is incomprehensible outside of
the framework of the IS tradition and should indeed be seen as
part of that tradition. Some may find some of the content overly
negative and bitter. I was struck by the general optimism about
the future of revolutionary politics and the surprising warmth
and inclusiveness in his judgement that lessons can be learnt
from all varieties of socialist endeavour. Given some of what is
described this seems more than generous. Despite this there are
points where the narrative is very bitter indeed. My sense is that
this is understandable and that our tradition should take some
responsibility for that bitterness. The trouble with Higgins is ultimately our own trouble. The reward for recognising this is to
be able to rehabilitate and nourish a part of ourselves. The IS
tradition is broader than the latest line or missive from the latest
CC. This may seem a problem to some but it ought to be seen
as a great resource. Revolutionaries too have traditions. Perhaps
we are now in a position to learn from Higgins even if we were
sadly a bit too stupid to do so before. I can remember meeting
Andy Wilson in a pub five years ago where he suggested that this
book ought to be sold on SWP bookstalls – a suggestion which at
the time I didn't know how to respond to. Now it just seems like
common sense. This introduction is partly an argument in favour

---

1. *links.org.au/taxonomy/term/665.*

of such a proposal. It surely is a nonsense that a revolutionary of Higgins calibre remained unread by generations of revolutionaries simply because of a disagreement in 1975. Hopefully such things will never happen again.

John Game, May 2012

Roger Protz: Preface to the 1997 Edition

I have a rendezvous with Death
At some disputed barricade
Alan Seeger

Jim Higgins has written a witty and wise book about the dashed hopes of revolutionary socialists in the 1960s and 1970s. In a cynical age, when we are told by such gurus of New Labour as Will Hutton that *"socialism is dead"*, it is worth recalling those days of heady activism, mass demonstrations and latent working class power, when it seemed not only desirable but possible that British society could be remodelled in a truly democratic and egalitarian fashion. The need remains and it is worth pointing out to Mr Hutton and his ilk that the 'socialism' they so earnestly despatch to the knacker's yard comes in the twin form of social democracy and Stalinism, over which we shed no tears. In a vulgar, tawdry and increasingly squalid society, where millions live in deepening poverty, a minority stick their trotters and snouts in the privatised troughs, and a manufacturing base is destroyed in a rush to base an economy on service industries and hamburger restaurants, the case for root and branch social change has never been greater.

The main purpose of Jim's book is to paint a picture of the recent past in the hope that the mistakes of that period will not be repeated. Some readers will bridle at the caustic tone and harsh humour. But it must be stressed that the participants in the struggles recorded here made enormous self sacrifice for the movement and found themselves cast aside by 'comrades' who did not give a fig for the distress they caused. Jim plays down his own central role in the events he describes, but I recall how a man plucked from a key position in his trade union to become national secretary of the International Socialists was sidelined within less than a year, the victim of dishonourable, sectarian manoeuvring and back-stabbing. As a result of the bitter and unprincipled infighting within IS, a whole cadre of fine and committed people were lost to the cause of socialism, reduced to working at the margins of the struggle instead of being centrally involved.

It has been said many times that revolutions devour their children. Less attention has been paid to the ability of small revolutionary groups to ingest their offspring long before the first barricade has been built. The high hopes of the members of the International Socialists were smashed as the result of many factors: a lack of a coherent long-term strategy, wild changes of tack by Tony Cliff, with blatant disregard for democratic structures that would leave Tony Blair breathless with admiration, the advancement of place-men and opportunists at the expense of experienced members and a ruthless and savage demonising of opponents of the latest 'line'.

The tragedy of what happened to IS is that it did not start out that way. As Jim graphically records, the early group was based upon a genuine comradeship and shared intellectual abilities. I had spent my formative years in Gerry Healy's Socialist Labour League and was in urgent need of a political oil change and decoke when I joined IS. I was impressed and enthused by the wide-ranging, open debates, the lack of tin-pot dictators, the intellectual rigour of *International Socialism*, good humour and good beer after meetings and, above all, a decent humility about the potential of a group with just a few hundred members. What a difference from the later IS that drew the conclusion that its lack of success demanded not retrenchment and self-criticism but the absurd leap into the crassly named 'mini mass party' of the Socialist Workers Party, with the expulsion of those who objected to the very type of 'substitutionism' that the early IS had always ridiculed.

It is not just water under the bridge. The case for socialism remains unaltered. In reviewing and analysing the mistakes of the past, Jim Higgins' aim is a simple one: to avoid those mistakes in the future, to hope that a younger generation will build a movement based upon democracy and tolerance, and, in so doing, will pick up our guttering torch and blow on the flame.

Roger Protz
July 1996

Roger Protz

Jim Higgins: Journalist and Revolutionary Socialist

Obituary, *The Guardian*, Oct 21 2002

James Robert Higgins, December 2, 1930 – October 13, 2002

Jim Higgins, who has died aged 71 from an aneurysm, was one of the most remarkable and didactic figures in the British revolutionary socialist movement of his time, someone who drew generations of people to independent, libertarian Marxism. He was also the best read and most truly scholarly person I have known.

Higgins was born in Harrow and educated at Harrow County School for Boys. He joined the Young Communist League at fourteen and left school at sixteen. Two years later he was apprenticed to the Post Office as a telecommunications engineer. As a national serviceman in the early 1950s he served with the Royal Signals in Hong Kong – which reinforced his political beliefs.

Back in Britain he became active in both the Communist Party and the Post Office Engineering Union. He broke with the Communist Party in 1956 following the Soviet leader Nikita Krushchev's 'secret speech' denouncing Stalin, and the Soviet invasion of Hungary. These events, plus the Suez crisis, were catalysts in the New Left's birth, but alongside that was a renewed interest in Trotskyism. Higgins read Trotsky voraciously and joined a small group – which was to become the Socialist Labour League and later the Workers Revolutionary Party – led by the pugnacious Irishman Gerry Healey, who brooked no opposition. Higgins quickly found himself in an opposing faction.

By the end of the 1950s he had joined the Socialist Review Group. This was then a forcing ground for new ideas in Marxism, where Tony Cliff and the economist Michael Kidron had devel-oped the theories of the permanent arms economy – an explanation for the post-war boom – and state capitalism, categorising the Soviet Union as another variant of class society.

Higgins became secretary of what became the International Socialists. His conviviality, which mixed theoretical discussion, raucous laughter and a gener-

Jim Higgins

ous consumption of beer, meant that he was at home with trade unionists, Young Socialists and, as the 1960s progressed, revolutionary students.

His small home in Kenton, north-west London, where he lived with his second wife Marion, filled with meetings and parties – there was an almost invisible dividing line between the two. He lectured endlessly to Young Socialists branches and was probably the first man on the left to advocate the causes of women's liberation and gay rights.

He also developed a friendship with Harry Wicks, one of the founders in the 1930s of the tiny, revolutionary socialist and anti-Stalinist Balham Group. Higgins became the acknowledged expert and historian of British Trotskyism.

By the 1960s he was Post Office Engineering Union (POEU) branch secretary and was elected to the union's national executive. There was a strong possibility that, as the broad left's chosen candidate, he would have gone on to become POEU general secretary, but, fatefully, he was encouraged to give up his union work to become IS's full-time national secretary in the early 1970s.

As a result of the French and Czechoslovak events of 1968, and, domestically, the growth of the Vietnam Solidarity Campaign and the growing wave of industrial unrest, by the early 1970s IS had picked up support from both students and trade unionists, while it's monthly paper had been transformed into the weekly *Socialist Worker*.

Higgins used his trade union experience to refashion the organisation. But the group was about to embark on a bout of infighting. In 1973 Higgins resigned and moved to *Socialist Worker*, which I was then editing. He found no respite there. Those of us who opposed the policies of the new leadership were removed from the paper. In 1977, when IS was renamed the Socialist Workers Party – which Higgins opposed – we left.

Higgins had lost both his political organisation and his trade union role. Attempts to form a new group, the Workers' League, foundered. He built a career as a journalist on *Arabia*, a Middle East news magazine, and then a short-lived news weekly, *Events*, where he met Jane Allen, who became his partner and later his third wife. He also wrote for the *New Statesman* and the *Spectator*.

Jane and he set up Greenwood Communications in the early 1980s. This was a specialist magazine design house, which operated from the Angel Islington, with a second office in the bar of the Old Red Lion.

In the 1990s they took the business with them to north Norfolk. Higgins continued to debate, lecture and contribute to leftwing journals. His homes – including that one – overflowed with books, classics of Marxism, Shakespeare, modern poetry and Raymond Chandler and Dashiell Hammett's novels. He fell in love with Norfolk and its bird life, and raised Rhodesian Ridgeback dogs that made visits to his home a daunting experience. Like their owner, their bark was far worse than their bite.

In 1997, he published a political memoir, *More Years for the Locust*. His last article was an obituary, for this newspaper, of his old comrade, Duncan Hallas. He is survived by his third wife, Jane, and his three daughters, Rachel, Julie and Judith, from his previous marriages.

Roger Protz

Nigel Fountain

Jim Higgins: Journalist and Revolutionary Socialist

Obituary, *The Guardian*, Oct 21 2002

James Robert Higgins, December 2, 1930 – October 13, 2002

It was Angel Islington International Socialists at the turn of the 1960s and 70s; darkness and drizzle in the Liverpool Road, draughts, rickety chairs and anaemic overhead lighting in the George's 'functions' room, and the speaker hadn't turned up.

I can't remember why Jim Higgins was there, it wasn't his branch, or why Jim began talking about 14th-century religious schisms. But he did, and the handful of us in that dank pub followed him into late feudalism and the Albigensians in the foothills of the Pyrenees, and concepts of heaven and hell, until the speaker did show up and we returned, reluctantly, to wage freezes, the rank and file movement – and to secular concepts of heaven and hell.

Jim, with an eye for the weak spot and a sometimes savage wit, was possessed of a wonderful, throaty, crackling laugh. He was serious about socialism, but – or maybe and – he was also much taken by lunacies, contradictions, unforeseen consequences, and unpredictable outcomes. Such traits did not always endear him to his erstwhile comrades, but they did make him part of a great, radical, and London, lineage.

Nigel Fountain

More Years for the Locust

Introduction

I will restore to you the years
that the locust has eaten...
The Bible, Joel 14

In that great and profoundly subversive picaresque novel, *The Good Soldier Svejk*, there is a section which details Svejk's anabasis around the ruined Austro-Hungarian empire. The Good Soldier wanders hopefully, but hopelessly lost, all the while maintaining his unfailing good humour while looking for his regiment, from which he was accidentally separated as it set off for the Russian front. By some quirk of a malignant fate that invariably afflicts him, it transpires he is walking in the wrong direction. In my own even less purposeful anabasis along the scenic route to the barricades I have, on occasion, felt that Jaroslav Hašek, rather than some higher power, was writing the script. As I emerged blinking from yet another blind alley, or myopically confusing, for the second or third time, a narrow cul de sac for the broad, straight highway to the socialist commonwealth, I have sworn that next time I would acquire better maps and more reliable guides. Unfortunately, the maps are old and seem to chart only the Petrograd of 1917, and the guides are mostly unreliable and habituated to blind alleys, while the broad, straight highway has yet to be constructed.

None of that should surprise or upset us. It has always been like that, or we would have made the revolution these many years ago and we would, today, in Ian Birchall's phrase, *"be lying in the long grass eating peaches"*. For myself I would require one or two extra little goodies, like permanent sunshine and a big box of Liquorice

Allsorts, to be certain that workers' power was a fact, but I know what he meant. Marx did not envisage the commune until Parisian workers actually formed one. Lenin was deeply suspicious of the soviets until he saw their intrinsically socialist character. This is a rather neat reversal of his 1903 formulation, in *What is to be Done?*, that socialist consciousness is brought to the workers by socialist intellectuals. In fact, we find that socialist organisation of society is revealed to the intellectuals by the workers who actually build it.

How the workers, in what remains of the 20th Century and the untouched 21st, will set about their tasks is not yet known and what is certain is that the current coven of gurus have not got a clue either. What we can be sure of is that it will not be a straight repetition of the past and that it will surprise those fortunate enough to be around at the time. In the meanwhile, there is still plenty to be done. Only the congenitally faint-hearted will conclude that, because there have been some bloody awful socialist organisations, we should withdraw from the struggle, plant a peach tree and then hide in the long grass until the crop falls into our nerveless fingers. To plead that some groups have not lived up to our expectations or, worse still, have exceeded our most lurid nightmares, is merely to describe capitalism's ability to impose its authoritarian values even on those whose intention, at least, was to destroy capitalism itself. All of the groups, without exception, have something to offer, something to teach, something to fill one or other of the gaps in our understanding of socialism.

As a schoolboy during the Second World War, I remember reading the *Daily Worker* under my desk and feeling cheered as the tide of battle turned and all that tank-borne Russian infantry advanced on a 3,000 mile front. It was a time when the Communist Party of Great Britain (CPGB), operating very much as auxiliaries to Mrs Churchill's Aid to Russia Committee, achieved 60,000 members. This truly impressive increase, known as the 'Stalingrad levy', was composed in large measure of patriotic Britons thrilled by Russia's war effort, the Communist Party's no-strike pledge and the cut of Joe Stalin's jib. They disappeared like snowballs on a hot stove as soon as the war ended.

Impressed by the Russian peoples' sacrifices, I was well prepared to believe that their fortitude was due to the socialist spirit engendered by the 1917 revolution. It seemed to me that the defence of October was also the defence of our Russian allies and I became adept at turning history, geography and religious knowledge lessons into a dialogue about soviet power. Mathematics and science were altogether less easy to subvert into this sort of discussion, although I do recall a fairly lively debate on Pavlov's dogs during a physics class. With my friend Zammit – totally non-political but game for anything – we painted 'Open the Second Front Now' in very large letters on the quadrangle wall. I was under suspicion for this outrage, but I had chosen well; Zammit would not peach even under torture. Some years later I met an ex-Communist Party member who told me of his sister, an art teacher at a country school during the war, who was also in the party. She and her friend chose a nice large wall surrounding a church to paint their slogan. The letters were beautifully formed and artistically spaced: 'Open the Second Font Now' it demanded. It may be a measure of the lack of class consciousness among the English peasantry, for the slogan was not thought to be the work of a dyslexic Marxist, but a wry comment on the presence of American airmen at a nearby air base.

With the end of the war and the election of the first majority Labour government, it seemed, for a short time, not only to me but also to a lot of wiser heads, that socialism might be ushered in through the ballot box. The enthusiasm for far reaching social change certainly existed in the working class and especially in the millions mobilised in the armed forces. The Labour Party, however, far from wishing to encourage this enthusiasm and channelling it to effective action, saw a landslide parliamentary majority as quite enough popular support to carry through the reforms necessary to set British capitalism back on its feet again; anything more would not only be immoderate, and Labour prided itself on its moderation, but also very dangerous. By 1947, I was sixteen and eligible to join the Communist Party, and it was very clear that there was going to be no socialism forthcoming from the Attlee administration. At this time, the beginning of the Cold War, the CPGB was reverting to a policy of industrial militancy after its wartime social pacifism.

Having left school and become a Post Office Engineer I was pleased to find that in my branch of the Post Office Engineering

Union (POEU) there was a thriving cell of the Communist Party. Without too much delay I found myself a fully paid up member of both the POEU and the CPGB. At that time in the Post Office Engineering Department, everybody earned very little, but apprentices' pay was so bad it was almost Dickensian. For the princely sum of 14 shillings (70p) I put in a 48 hour, five and a half day week for my first six months on the job. If we had had to work all that time I am not sure it would have been bearable. Fortunately, there were some exceptionally long tea breaks, some marathon snooker sessions and, in the summer, sun-bathing on the Telephone Exchange roof.

At one stage in my training, I was attached to a Heavy Overhead Gang, traditionally a collection of very large and tough chaps who nipped up and down 80 foot telegraph poles with all the noise and agility of howler monkeys. In the mornings I was instructed in the mysteries of an overhead wireman's job and, in the afternoons, taken off to the Frognal area of Hampstead, where our long ladders and climbing skills were perfectly adapted for cleaning the windows of the very large Hampstead mansions. In this way we more than trebled our wages. Rich beyond the dreams of avarice, I took to smoking rolled up Nosegay or Boar's Head and, on Fridays after pay, drinking a few brown ales. This ill paid but relaxed working environment gave me plenty of time for political discussion and agitation – at one time I was the champion collector of signatures for the Stockholm Peace Appeal.

I was conscripted into the army in 1949, but several of the comrades wrote to me in Hong Kong, where I was stationed. Sid Gregory, the branch literature secretary – lit-sec in the party patois – was kind enough to send me copies of the Communist Party's *London District Bulletin* and *World News and Views*.The magazines were wrapped in a carefully recycled Co-op paper bag in such a way that the imprint was clear for all to see: *"Printed and Published for the Communist Party by Farleigh Press (TU All Depts)"*. On mail parades the officiating sergeant would pass over my rolled up bundle like a Field Marshal passing on his baton, with the words: *"And 'ere, Signalman 'Iggins, is your letter from the Kremlin"*. Unmasked as a Red, it was decreed that I should not be allowed into the cipher room. This represented a problem because I was trained at some expense to the army as a cipher mechanic. For the next year and a bit I spent my time in the workshop trying to turn out one serviceable teleprinter from two duff ones. I never succeeded but it filled in the time until I got on a boat and came home to resume my work in the CPGB.

Life in an industrial branch of the Communist Party was more pleasant and more productive than in a branch based on geography. In the latter there was a lot more time for extirpating heresy, precisely because there were fewer meaningful things to do. Once a year, however, we did have an event in our branch called the 'Purge' in which we all sat around engaging in a joyful session of self and mutual criticism.

In Engineering No 2 (the name of our branch) we discussed the party policy and how most effectively to introduce it to the workplace and the union. We held education classes and we invited speakers. Our meetings were held weekly, usually in the West Hampstead flat of one of the comrades. The room was large, with plenty of chairs and a double bed for the comrades to sit on. I recall one meeting at which the speaker was considerably delayed. Our chairman, who had no watch, asked, *"Has any comrade got the time?"* With a happy squeal I fell back on the bed, legs akimbo, crying, *"Anything for the party, comrade chairman"*. I paid for this sally for some years; at the annual purge I was commended for hard work and dedication but invariably castigated for 'light-mindedness'.

It was a branch of people with ages ranging from 16 to 60. Just to engage in casual conversation was to learn a great deal about the British labour movement during the course of this century. It was to be shown, if not immediately accepted, that there was a need for patience and for consistent and steady propaganda and agitation. In a telephone area containing three POEU branches and about 2,000 members we had 20-odd party members, virtually all of whom held some lay office in the branches, the region or, in a couple of cases, on the National Executive. It was a place to learn the essentials of trade unionism and to relate that experience to politics. It was also where you were trained to take on the various representative jobs in the union.

To be a member of the CPGB engaged in industry was to suffer a sort of schizophrenia. On the one hand was the Stalinist line of peaceful coexistence and on the other there was the Foreign Languages Publishing House, churning out translations of Marx, Engels and Lenin and selling them at genuinely bargain prices. It was possible to think Joe Stalin was jolly nice and that peace was the paramount consideration and at the same time pursue the class struggle with the utmost vigour. My affection for Stalin was somewhat reduced when I was elected to lead a discussion of the 'father of socialism's' last work, *The Economic Problems of Socialism in the USSR*. It was bad enough having to read it once, but imagine the horror if you had to read it several times to make notes. It was a truly grisly experience, Stalin having a style that Max Shachtman compared to, *"a sandbag dragged through a puddle of glue"*.

One of the lessons you had to learn was the importance of communications. The rank and file leader has to keep his members informed and to do it regularly. We produced two union branch journals that discussed local and national issues, both as far as the union and the employer was concerned, and suggested the way forward and reported progress. We developed a programme for the union that was regularly publicised in other branches where the left had some influence. We vigorously criticised the bureaucracy of the union and were sometimes subjected to its disciplinary powers. Even at the height of the Cold War, with Catholic Action operating at full blast, Communist Party members were re-elected to local office, although there was a pretty comprehensive clear-out on the executive council.

Like most working class organisations the Communist Party made its demands upon your time and your pocket, but did offer in return the comradeship that goes beyond mere friendship because it involves shared experience and commitment. The essentially reactionary character of Stalinism, its profound exploitation of the working class in Russia and the satellites, was quite difficult to discern from a small ginger group in a middling sized union in Britain. The bombshell landed in 1956. I was attending a POEU annual conference and on the Sunday morning before the start I purchased my copy of the *Observer*. The entire paper was given over to Kruschev's speech to the 20th Congress of the CPSU(B). It was a long catalogue of Stalin's crimes, virtually devoid of any Marxist explanation, but for all that an effective condemnation. If it specifically excluded the various Left and Right oppositions of the 1920s and 1930s from pardon, it posthumously absolved those Stalinists who had incurred Uncle Joe's wrath. Kruschev did not apologise. How could he find the words – he too was a Stalinist – for the millions of innocent workers and peasants who were executed or died miserably in some isolator? He did reveal that so vile was Stalin that, presumably in his cups, he had made Mikoyan – a man of advancing years and poor health – dance the gopak (a rather lively Caucasian folk-romp). Can swinishness go any further?

That was the breaking of the monolith. The ferment in the party did not die down. The cat was out of the bag and there was no way of putting the creature back. Harry Pollitt and Palme Dutt did their best, but everybody knew that they had been privy to at least some of the crimes that Kruschev had brought to light. Both of these men, Pollitt the ace mass agitator, and Dutt the ace theoretician, toured the country attempting to mitigate the effects of the 20th Congress speech. Dutt developed the telling analogy that although the sun had spots it nevertheless was the fountain of all life. Well Joe Stalin was like that. I attended a couple of meetings Dutt addressed along these lines and he was almost totally rejected and abused. The second time I saw him he looked what he was, a tired old man whose lies and evasions had caught up with him; it was not a pretty sight.

I was the secretary of the party branch and, after a deal of heart-searching, called on the branch chairman to tell him that I was resigning from the party. He seemed unsurprised by this, and sympathised with my position. Unfortunately, without saying anything to anyone, he also resigned. The net result was that I received an angry letter from the lit-sec suggesting that I *"make a self critical analysis of my gross failure to call a party meeting for two months"*. For a while I toyed with the idea of calling a meeting and not attending myself but I finally let it rest and did nothing.

Without much expectation and largely to fill the meeting gap, I joined the Labour Party. At the time I was living in Wembley North constituency, in the area covered by the Preston ward. That ward Labour Party really was strange in its political composition. There was a couple who had been in the Austrian Social Democracy when Dolfuss attacked the Vienna workers' flats in 1934. There was a German chap who had worked for the Comintern, and Lottie, a German lady, who had been engaged to Ernst Toller, a poet and Red army commander during the Bavarian Soviet in 1920. Among all this exotica my particular chums were Len and Freda Knight. Like me they were ex-members of the Communist Party. Freda had had a particularly hard time working in a company founded by CPers to trade with China, which apparently did a thriving business importing pig bristle and tung oil. The company recruited through the party, but did not permit its office staff either to join a union or form a party unit. This led to no end of aggravation, not least, I trust, for the party, because Freda was an extremely strong minded person with an acute sense of justice and fair play.

It was the Knights who first introduced me to world of Trotskyism. They had been converted by Cyril Smith, who lived on the other side of Wembley. Cyril was a man of seemingly inexhaustible energy and an enviable ability to keep plugging away at whatever was his appointed task. He was much aided in his work of conversion by the fact that he had access to a number of Trotsky's pamphlets and an edition of *The Revolution Betrayed*. In addition there was the *Labour Review*, his group's excellent theoretical magazine, and also the agitational paper, the *Newsletter*, edited by Peter Fryer. For a man like myself, who not too long before had suffered the cruel compulsion of reading *Economic Problems of Socialism in the USSR*, the chance to read Trotsky, a genuine Marxist who could also write with tremendous style and great clarity, was indeed a privilege. In much the same way, I imagine, as prehistoric man was especially grateful to the unknown genius who discovered fire, or the other chap who invented the wheel, I felt an obligation to sign up. Thus it was that I became a member of the Wembley branch of the 'Club'.

If the Bolshevik party was, 'a party of a new kind' then the Club was, 'a party of an even newer kind'. Meeting followed meeting, paper sales abounded, you found yourself attending ward, constituency and borough Labour Party meetings in addition, if only to make up your paper sales. *Newsletter* public meetings were held addressed by the likes of Peter Fryer and Brian Behan (with John Lawrence and John Palmer, Behan was one of the finest stump orators I ever heard).

Central London education lectures on the history of 'Our Movement' were conducted by Gerry Healy. One such series was held in a quite large room above a pub, which had been booked in the name of a non-existent travel club. During the day the room was obviously a restaurant and you could hear the sounds of dish-washing behind the wooden serving hatch. On these occasions Gerry would start off mumbling into his chest in a very soft voice that was almost inaudible to all but the people in the front rows. The comrades leaned forward, ears straining to catch the pearls he cast before them. Suddenly, without warning, he would switch to full bellow and the comrades recoiled, suffering from acoustic shock. This time, the unfortunate dishwasher dropped a pile of plates. Healy's strength-five oration, containing as it does blood curdling threats, dire warnings and accounts of past mayhem, convinced the publican that this was no normal travel club and that it could well prove costly in the delft department. We were no longer welcome at that particular hostelry.

The high point of my membership was the strike at McAlpine's South Bank site. The dispute started when Brian Behan, who had been a leading dissident in the AUBTW the building workers' union, got a job at the site. After a little while, the manager realised that this Behan could damage his mental health, so he fired him.

This was a mistake, because there were a number of other serious militants on the South Bank, among them Hugh Cassidy. In short order there was a strike and the Club was put on a war footing. All the resources of the group were available to the strike. It was one of the first picket lines composed of building workers and revolutionaries. Healy occupied the cafe over the road from the site and meetings were in session there practically all the time. At one stage there was a bit of a fracas outside the gate and Brian Behan was arrested, subsequently getting three months in Shepton Mallett.

For Healy the strike represented a qualitative change in the class struggle. He saw, arrayed against us, the state that had arrested Behan, the trade union bureaucracy who denounced the strike by refusing to make it official, and the employers and their powerful association. If this typically cataclysmic Healy analysis goes much too far, there is no doubt that it was a serious strike aggressively fought on both sides, which could have been a useful springboard to greater involvement in the struggles that were beginning to develop. As part of that strategy the Newsletter Industrial Conference was held on a programme of democratic rank and file control of the unions and an end to bureaucratic privileges. It was quite a good conference: there were certainly a number of genuine delegates who were enthusiastic about the programme. Peter Fryer was in the chair and Brian Behan and Harry Constable, a leading London docker and Club member, spoke from the platform. Gerry Healy lurked, not too anonymously, at the back of the hall sending written instructions to the chairman with such annoying frequency that Fryer threatened to vacate the chair if he did not stop.

This was really the high point in the fortunes of the Club. According to those who knew Healy much better than I did, he had been the soul of tact and discretion, a model of patience in recruiting and assimilating two or three hundred ex-members of the Communist Party. For these, his familiars, this was an unprecedented display of tolerance and good temper that could not, and did not, last. A series of pressures and events conspired to send him off the rails. First, he was under some pressure from Brian Behan, who took a distinctly jaundiced view of Labour Party entry work. Next, the press, alerted by the South Bank Strike and the *Newsletter* Conference, began to look into the affairs of the Club.

A badly researched and inaccurate feature appeared in the *News Chronicle*, but a much more accurate article or two appeared in the *South London Press*. Much encouraged by Behan, Healy decided that this would be a good time to make a dash for freedom and the Socialist Labour League (SLL) was born. In tune with his gallows humour, Healy wrote to the Labour Party requesting affiliation for the SLL. It was not forthcoming.

For many of us who had joined from the Communist Party, the policy of entrism was one that required some swallowing but, having done so, it seemed a bit light minded to chuck out ten years of work because of a couple of press stories. Having come to this conclusion we argued in that way in the branch and at aggregates. The storm of vituperation this called down on our unsuspecting heads seemed out of all proportion. As editor of the *Newsletter*, Peter Fryer was in the eye of the storm and found the atmosphere in the office unbearable and Healy's conduct totally impermissible. He left, never to return. Healy really did a number on this one. He claimed that he was having the ports and airports watched for sightings of Peter. He contemplated a special issue of the *Newsletter* with the headline: 'Has the GPU Got Peter Fryer?' Unfortunately he did not print it, because it would have afforded Peter a bit of a laugh in Nottingham, where he was staying with his old friend John Daniels.

Although Healy did not choose to look for Peter in Nottingham, he did pay a visit to Len and Freda Knight on the same errand. This was a visit of the intimidatory kind that takes place on the wrong side of midnight. A peremptory knock at the door brought Freda from her kitchen, where she and Len were imbibing their pre-bedtime cocoa. As she opened the door, Bob Pennington, at that time London Organiser of the SLL, started to push his way in saying, *"We want a discussion with you, comrade"*. This message was delivered in the accents of a B-movie gangster, so beloved of Healy and his satraps. Freda was a spirited person and shoved back, replying, *"Then come back at a reasonable time"*. Inevitably, Freda, who was quite small, was gradually pushed back into her hall, when out of the kitchen came Len. Unlike Freda, Len was big, about six foot two and chunky with it, and he started swinging when he was level with the kitchen door. He stopped swinging when his fist connected with Pennington's head by the front door.

Less a tooth or two, Pennington landed in a rose bed and, when the dust had settled and Len had calmed down a bit, Healy and Cliff Slaughter appeared out of the gloom for their discussion. It was not a meeting of minds.

A faction was formed to air our discontent: it had about twenty members and was called the Stamford Faction, after the grounds of the stately home where it was formed.[1] A document was written, *The 1959 Situation in the SLL*, which was distributed by Peter Cadogan. Peter's idea of distributing an internal factional document was to put an advertisement in *Tribune*. This resulted in the signatories all getting a letter from Healy's tame solicitor claiming damages for libel. Cadogan rather airily replied that he would, *"Try the case in the court of working class opinion"*, wherever that is, while Len Knight went to the Labour MP Sidney Silverman who was a pretty nifty lawyer. We heard no more of the libel action but Len was expelled for punching the London Organiser and Freda and I were expelled for intervening noisily at an SLL public meeting: The National Assembly of Labour.

In the course of the struggle in the SLL, I met Tony Cliff and Michael Kidron at Peter Cadogan's home in Cambridge, and Cliff extended an invitation to the Socialist Review Group's next aggregate. Being at a loose end on the day in question I turned up. It was a very open meeting, as were all the Socialist Review Group meetings in those days. I recall Sam Levy was in attendance as was Ted Grant, who was selling copies of *Socialist Fight* that were so badly duplicated as to be unreadable. There were maybe 40 or 50 people in the room. It was the early days of CND and there was a great deal of talk at the time about the four minute warning we would get before extinction. Cliff put forward his own slogan: *"In the event of nuclear attack put a piece of brown paper on top of your head"*. For some reason I was much amused by this, and also by his injunction: *"The comrades have got to start pulling their socks"*. However, I did feel he should improve his articulation if he was to avoid giving offence with this catch line. A few days later I joined

---

1. Among the members of the Stamford Faction were: Ken Coates, John Daniels, Dorothy Tildsley, Marion Cook, Peter Fryer, Pat McGowan, Len Knight, Freda Knight, Ellis Hillman, Peter Cadogan and Jim Higgins.

the Socialist Review Group and the rest, as they say, is history, or at least the subject of this book.

It may be that some will find the title of this work confusing, or obscure, or both. It is quite simple really. The first article I ever wrote for *International Socialism* was in issue No 14, a history of British Trotskyism from 1938 to 1948, entitled *Ten Years for the Locust*. Its point was that a promising organisation, the Revolutionary Communist Party (RCP), with some very talented people had, through faulty politics and perspective, come to grief. They were, with one or two exceptions, not bad people and had all the very best intentions, but they foundered because they were irrelevant to the British working class movement. The members could run harder, stretch further and make even greater sacrifices, but all to no avail: the locust had eaten the RCP's years. Nevertheless, it was not all wasted; for ten years they kept alive the revolutionary tradition that, to a greater or lesser degree, informs most of the left today. That these new groups have found it impossible to transcend the differences of the past, and continue to live vicariously through the *Collected Works* of the heroes, is the reason why the locust can still find ample sustenance. To those who find that the story is too critical for their taste I can only apologise, and restate my conviction that the criticism is well merited, because the International Socialists (IS), successors to the Socialist Review Group and precursors to the Socialist Workers Party, was the very best chance we have had since the 1920s to build a serious revolutionary socialist organisation. It was a chance that was not taken and those who were responsible for that error have much to answer for and should be called to account if only in the pages of this book.

Life goes on, however, and we must keep trying. When the Good Soldier Svejk, after all his travails and adventures, is at last reunited with his regiment, the long suffering Lieutenant Lukacs tells him to hop up on the troop train. Svejke smiles seraphically and says: *"Beg to report sir, I am hopping up"*. I hope that when I eventually find my way back to the revolutionary train, that is going somewhere other than the Eastern front, I will be able to report that I too *"am hopping up"*.

Finally, I would like to thank everyone who has helped me in preparing this book and especially: Bill Ainsworth, Peter D. Morgan, Geoff Carlsson, John Palmer, Roger Protz, Richard Kuper, Cyril Smith, Ruth Nelson, Al Richardson, Ted Crawford, Stan Newens, Richard Kirkwood, Granville Williams, Alice Murray, Andy Wilson, Ian Land, Sarah Washington, Jules Alford and Phil Evans, whose cartoons will surely be the reason why anyone will keep this book. And to my friend and companion Jane Allen – who has suffered the re-enactment of several vicious faction fights over her dining table with little more than a whimper of protest and retained sufficient patience to go on and sub-edit the entire manuscript – my gratitude and loving admiration. Finally, to Marion Higgins, whose unfailing support – in every way – during some of the hardest times, was always appreciated if never adequately acknowledged, belated but heartfelt thanks. Any faults or errors are, of course, all my own work.

Jim Higgins
Norfolk, September 1996

The Young Cliff

If I were to tell you what I believe to be my family history it would take a very long time... It would be a story that I, the individual... believe to be true although, in my role as a sceptical anthropologist, I feel that very little of it can possibly be true. It is a fabrication which has the form and the function that justifies my personal masquerade, the way I present myself to the world.
Edmund Leach, Lecture, Kings College Cambridge, 1989

I'm not able to tell myself lies.
Tony Cliff, *Socialist Worker Review*, July 1987

History is a record of that combination of the significant and the insignificant and we are all in some way connected to its processes and must live with its consequences. For most revolutionaries of the last 80-odd years the *annus mirabilis* was 1917. On November 7th of that year, in Petrograd and Moscow, the Russian workers and peasants took power under the leadership of the Bolshevik party. The day before, in London, A.J. Balfour, Britain's anti-semitic foreign secretary, with the typical generosity of someone giving away that which belonged to somebody else, declared Arab Palestine to be a Jewish National Home. In Palestine itself, a few months before either of these seminal events, on May 20th in fact, Tony Cliff (né Ygael Gluckstein) was born into a middle class Jewish family. Depending on whether you are a keen member of the Socialist Workers Party (SWP) or not, this gives 1917 a two thirds, or a one third approval rating.

Life in Palestine under the British Mandate was repressive for all sections of the population but bore particularly harshly on the Arab majority. The Arabs, a largely agrarian community, had little or no tradition of working class organisation, whereas the Jewish population, overwhelmingly Zionist in their sympathies, carried with them a trade union consciousness and virtually every kind of socialism. Social Revolutionaries of the right or left persuasion, Mensheviks and Menshevik Internationalists, Stalinists and various shades of social democracy were all represented in greater or lesser numbers in the 1920s and 1930s.

Zionism had fewer gradations, with the mainstream being of a social democratic persuasion. Reflecting its origins in 19th century European rationalism, it expressed a nonreligious commitment to the national home. Indeed, in the 1920s the Mapam Youth section caused some scandal in Jerusalem by marching to the Wailing Wall demonstratively eating ham sandwiches. The problem in logic involved in the Zionist notion of a 'chosen people', without a divine being to do the choosing, does not seem to have caused them much difficulty. In the same way the idea of socialist equality for all, professed by those who demanded their homeland in a place that was already home to a lot of Arabs, was encompassed with ease, but then logical contradiction has never been a bar to social democratic thought.

Revisionist Zionism, the brain child of Ze'ev Jabotinsky, was both anti-socialist and accepted all the myths and legends of Jewish folk history. The attitude was much like that of the dictator in Genet's play, *The Balcony*, when he speaks of "*This truly national nation*". Genet's phrase encompasses all the low grade mysticism and the accompanying nonsense of petty bourgeois nationalism. Whereas orthodox Zionism sought to build on the Balfour Declaration and negotiate more and bigger settlements, the revisionists wanted it all, on both banks of the Jordan, and they wanted it now. The limits of the new homeland were only circumscribed by the boundary of an over-active imagination steeped in dubious history. Thus the slogan, 'From the river to the sea', set the bounds from the Euphrates to the Mediterranean, neatly including Syria and the Lebanon. On the wider shores of the cloud-cuckoo homeland was the suggestion that the borders be set by reference to Abraham. Whatever he could see from the highest point should be Eretz Israel. As this turned out to range from Saudi Arabia in the south to Turkey in the north, one can only assume Abraham was incredibly long sighted and that there was perfect visibility in Biblical times.

The revisionists, of course, were not just mystical buffoons; among them were right wing activists of a particularly virulent stripe. The Stern Gang sported black shirts, took their salute and their inspiration from, and had their cadres trained in, Mussolini's Italy. Yitzhak Shamir, the last Likud prime minister before Neten-yahu, was a leading figure in this band of cutthroats. Another leading revisionist was Menachem Begin, who played a prominent role in the Irgun Zvai Leumi, the armed wing of revisionism. It was the Irgun, with the Stern Gang, under Begin's leadership, that

CLIFF
AS A CHILD

was responsi-ble for the Deir Yassin massacre and it was the Israeli govern-ment under Be-gin's premier-ship that was responsible for the massacres of Sabra and Chatila. These were true be-lievers, tough and always ready for extreme measures in pursuit of that 'truly national nation'.

None of this is to say that mainstream Zionism was the soft face of Jewish nationalism. Cliff used to tell the story of a Mapam meeting, addressed by Ben Gurion, that he attended at the age of 16. At the end of Ben Gurion's speech, Cliff gave it as his opin-ion that, "*What Ben Gurion said is contrary to dialectical materialism*". This, almost certainly an accurate description of Ben Gurion's speech, gave sufficient offense that a couple of heavies escorted the adolescent Cliff from the hall and proceeded to break one of his fingers.[1]

---

1. This story was told to me by Cliff, circa 1960. I am informed by

Rather later, when Chanie Rosenburg, who subsequently was to marry Cliff, arrived from South Africa – full of starry eyed enthusiasm for the 'socialism' of the kibbutz – the first job she and her fellow immigrants were given was to load a truck with rocks and then drive to a nearby Arab village to throw them at the inhabitants. Nowadays, of course, settlers carry Uzis rather than rocks, but the principle is much the same – to keep the natives in their place.

This was the place where Cliff came to political maturity. The miserable lives of the Arab masses turned him to socialism. Reading the *Communist Manifesto*, together with an abridged edition of *Capital*, convinced him he was a Marxist. Like most leftists of that time, his Marxism found expression in the Stalinist mode. There is nothing surprising, or reprehensible, in that. Nowadays anyone coming to Marxist politics is most likely to find them dressed in some style of Trotskyist apparel. In the mid 1930s there were only a few hundred Trotskyists in the whole world, and the forces that were visible, formidable and ranged against fascism were all organised in the Communist International. That the Nazis came to power as a direct result of the disastrous policies of the Communist International is a fact that was not immediately apparent at the time, and the feeble voice of the Trotskyists was difficult to hear in out of the way places like mandatory Palestine.

"CLIFF IS A PEASANT.
A VERY TALENTED PEASANT,
BUT A PEASANT."

Inevitably, around 1935, the critical works of Trotsky began to filter through to Palestine, not least the writings on Germany which, to this day, Cliff believes to be Trotsky's finest work. At about this time he met a German Trotskyist, who said that when Hitler took power, in 1933, there were about 100 Trotskyists in

Granville Williams that at a meeting in Walsall in the early 1970s, Cliff related that his finger was broken by British soldiers in Palestine when he was arrested. Perhaps they were different fingers.

Germany. From Joe Stalin's big battalions to the undermanned awkward squad of Trotskyism, was a considerable reduction not only in hope, but also in the possibility of action. But as Martin Luther said, *"Here stand I. I can do no other"*. So Cliff took on board Trotsky's admonition for, *"the primitive accumulation of cadres"*. It was one lesson learned from Trotsky he has never abandoned. Over the years, Cliff's enthusiasm for the thought of Leon Trotsky has waxed and waned quite a bit, and his ideas on organisation have gone from the wider shores of libertarianism to the bathyscopic depths of centralism; but they have an unfinished feel to them, an air of impermanence, for above all else they must serve to enhance the primitive accumulation of cadres. For the onlooker, this ability to simulate a well lubricated weather-vane might seem, on occasion, unprincipled. At other times, it might remind you of the truth of Marx's phrase, *"There is nothing more disgusting than the petty bourgeois in the process of primitive accumulation"*. The peasant may dream of being Emperor, but for now he will make do with his neighbours' few measly acres. As one of Cliff's collaborators said, *"Cliff is a peasant, a very talented peasant, but a peasant"*.

At an early stage in his career, Cliff also learned another practical lesson in making recruits: keep at them – you never know when they might weaken. The first recorded success of this cunning ploy was with Jabra Nicola, the Arab editor of the Palestine Communist Party's legal paper. Nicola worked nights and so Cliff *"discussed with him for hours every day and for weeks on end"*. After two months, Jabra Nicola succumbed to the power of Cliff's dialectic and, one assumes, lack of sleep. This, what might be called The *Darkness at Noon* school of conversion, was also effective in recruiting Chanie Rosenburg after her arrival from South Africa. He appeared at Chanie's kibbutz and immediately launched into a 48 hour nonstop lecture. One enquired of Chanie if, over the two days, he repeated himself. She was unable to answer, because his Hebrew was delivered in an accent and at such speed that she could not understand a word of his discourse. Perhaps the power of the dialectic is less significant than deprivation of sleep.

Mike Kidron, who arrived in Palestine from South Africa in 1946, held out against a nonstop rant for a fortnight before surrendering. In the early 1950s, Stan Newens, later a Labour MP and now a Labour MEP, describes being seated in Cliff's tiny front room and subjected to a high speed monologue as Cliff paced up and down gesturing wildly, at considerable risk to Stan's feet and features. Cyril Smith relates how, at about this time, he was introduced to Cliff by Anil Munesinghe. He too received the short – approximately four breathless hours – discourse on state capitalism. At the end of all this, dazed and somewhat overawed, Cyril nevertheless opined, "*I still think Trotsky was right in* The Revolution Betrayed". To which Cliff replied, "*Never mind that, why don't you join the group?*" This particular type of argument effectively says, "*You should join my group for all of these powerful political reasons. If, however, you do not accept them, join anyway*". Cyril was unimpressed and did not speak to him ever again.

At the beginning of my membership of the Socialist Review Group I was unaware that Cliff would go to quite extraordinary lengths in pursuit of a recruit, no matter how unlikely the venue or the prospect. On one occasion I was unwise enough to allow myself to be talked into accompanying him to Leeds, to attend a peace conference organised by Harry McShane. Economy being the watchword, which means neither of us had any money, we borrowed Mike Kidron's car to make the trip. This machine, a fine example of the early half-timbered Morris Minor, had a few drawbacks: defective brakes, worn tyres and a tendency to steer to the right. Otherwise it was a pleasure to drive, so long as you kept it off wet roads, when its little steering foibles became lethal vices. Cliff, John Phillips, my wife Marion and myself set off for Leeds. The day was sunny and the road bone dry, conditions in which the Morris's modest performance, antique appearance and eccentric steering showed to best advantage.

The conference, attended by about twelve people, did not have much to commend it, although Harry McShane's opening statement in which he said: "*This conference may not be as significant as Kienthal and Zimmerwald...*" was absolutely truthful. Laurence Otter, also in attendance, claimed to represent three anarchist organisations and five Internationals, but this aroused so little interest that nobody asked him to specify which ones.

Suffice it to say, at the end of the conference our membership figures were unchanged and we faced a 180 mile journey on dark and, would you believe it, rain-swept roads. The car threw off its mild demeanour and behaved abominably, drifting into bends with the rear end trying to catch up with the front. Poor visibility was made worse by the fact that the headlight beam just managed to get past the glass, where it limply subsided to lie dead on the tarmac. Despite being semi-paralysed with fear and suffering the extremes of eye strain, I managed to steer all the way to the outskirts of Bedford before disaster struck. A small hump-back bridge leading to a vicious left hand bend, and the additional misfortune of an oncoming car with real headlights, proved a disastrous combination. With wheels locked and its driver completely dazzled, the Morris skated with some grace, like Torvil on a bad day, to meet the other vehicle. With a characteristically sickening clang, the two cars met and embraced, while various bits fell off their respective front ends. Happily, nobody was hurt but the lady in the other car would insist on reminding me that I could have killed her, until my wife explained that while killing her had not been my intention, it could become the next urgent task.

CLIFF'S FATHER WRITES TO TROTSKY.

Legal formalities completed and the badly wounded Morris Minor taken off to a nearby garage, we slowly and despondently made our way to Bedford station to catch a train to London. Between us we had just enough money for the fare. Fortunately we did have lots of time because there was a 90 minute wait for the next train. Damp, tired and, despite the conference, not feeling very pacific, we went to the waiting room. In what I can only presume to be an attempt to cheer us all up, Cliff decided put on a bit of Jewish folk dancing. This, apparently, could only be performed on the waiting room table and so we helped him up on to this impromptu stage. Think of the Riverdance ensemble and then banish it completely from your mind; it was nothing like that. Think more of Anastas Mikoyan dancing the gopak at Joe Stalin's cruel command. Next, imagine that Anastas was on Speed rather than Georgian brandy and wearing his truss upside down and you have got some idea of the steps. Then, add on some bloodcurdling – and possibly grossly obscene – Hebrew cries and no whispers and you have just a partial understanding of the full horror of the performance. By clapping loudly and laughing hysterically we managed to convince him that our happiness could not be increased by further folk dancing and eventually the train came to take us to London. On the journey Cliff unwisely broached the idea of a trip to Birmingham, where two members of the Socialist Party of Great Britain (SPGB) were reported to be disaffected from their party. My response indicated that the cheering effects of Jewish folk-dance are quite limited. For some weeks, until his car was repaired, Kidron had to go everywhere in taxis, he could not afford to go by bus, because the bus drivers would not wait for him to borrow the fare off somebody at his destination.

Cliff is aided in his self-appointed task by a single minded attention to immediate goals and an ability to ignore the fact that yesterday's goal was quite different and its supporting argument diametrically opposed to today's. This ability to be totally dedicated to the argument of the day and oblivious to everything else does, though, have its negative side. On one occasion he visited my home to engage me in a discussion, so important that its subject completely eludes me. At the time I had two Chow dogs, one of them a puppy. Cliff launched into his dissertation while George, the puppy, lay doggo, in faithful hound mode, at his feet. At some point in the discussion I became aware that George was eating Cliff's shoelaces. Before I could wrench the dog from the shoes, or Cliff from his discourse, the laces were completely consumed. Readers will be pleased to hear that George suffered no ill effects from this distressing incident, although Cliff was fairly pissed-off.

Having heard how effective the recorded cases of Cliff's attritional recruitment technique were, one is surprised to learn that when he left Palestine, in September 1946, there were only 30 members in the Palestine section of the Fourth International. The work, of course, was illegal under the British regime and, even were it practical politics, mass agitation would have been heavily circumscribed. More importantly, in Palestine as in the rest of the Middle East, the key to revolutionary politics was in the Arab masses: the attitude of the Arabs to Jewish workers was conditioned by the reactionary attitudes of their own ruling class, reinforced to a considerable degree by the Zionist campaigns for a boycott of Arab workers and Arab products. Even assuming it was possible to overcome these prejudices, to carry out work of this sort, the Jewish agitator had to learn another language and learn about a quite different way of life before any sort of dialogue could occur. It was dark lonely work, but somebody had to do it.

At one point, as if to prove they were not anarchists, the Palestine Trotskyists showed their preference for the propaganda of the word over the propaganda of the deed. The four or five members of the group went out one night, after dark, with their brushes and paint. In a number of prominent places, they painted something like the following stirring call to action: 'General Strike Tuesday – All Out'. Such was the industry of the comrades that few workers could have missed the message. Came Tuesday and the workers to a man ignored the call – as did all the members of the Trotskyist group.

Another interesting sidelight is in the story that Cliff's father, on his son joining the Fourth International, wrote to Leon Trotsky, one Jewish father to another, as if commending young Ygael to the boss of his new firm. Similarly, when Cliff came to Britain in 1946, his father wrote to Salmon and Gluckstein, then a big retail company, suggesting some possible family connection that might be suitably favoured. Neither of these efforts seem to have borne any fruit; he was not offered a seat on the International Secretariat of the Fourth International, or the board of Salmon and Gluckstein. It's enough to give nepotism a bad name.

The first time that Cliff broke into print in English was in 1938, in the pages of *New International*. That year, in the October and November issues of the magazine he wrote about the Jewish-Arab Conflict, under the nom de plume 'L Rock'. At first sight, this pseudonym might suggest the conceit of a Djugashvilli choosing Stalin, man of steel, for his party name. I am told, however, that a Gluckstein is some kind of semi-precious stone, so Rock (or Cliff come to that) is a reasonable sort of name to assume in order to fool any Palestine Policeman who happened to be browsing through the latest issue of *New International*.

The articles themselves are interesting and informative; in particular they show an opposition to the feudal, semi bourgeois leadership of the Arab national movement, together with a thoroughgoing anti-Zionism and anti-imperialism. They are long on analysis and short on prescription, which is how it should be if you have some experience and knowledge of the subject but no way of doing anything about it. The prose style gives all the satisfaction of chewing chopped bristle but over the years, if only in this, Cliff has been consistent, never once sliding into easy readability.

Like all the other dedicated members of the Fourth International, Cliff believed implicitly in Trotsky's prediction that, under the tremendous pressures engendered by war, the workers would not only put an end to a terminally sick capitalism, but also the Stalinist bureaucracy. Small the Fourth International might be, but its few adherents were convinced that they were riding the wave of history. The trick was to position the cadre in such a way that it would be able, at short notice, to adopt a leadership posture. This inevitably resulted in what later turned out to be some fairly bizarre predictions.

In Britain, for example, the Workers International League (WIL), forerunner of the Revolutionary Communist Party (RCP) put out a pamphlet in 1942 entitled *Preparing for Power*. This document, written by Ted Grant[1], contained many priceless little hostages to fortune, such as: *"A split in the Labour Party is inevitable… The left will be driven to break the coalition and form an open opposition in Parliament, and what is more, they will almost certainly get a majority"*. Or, *"Britain is entering a prerevolutionary situation"*. Or, yet again: *"A failure of the coming revolutionary wave would provoke outbursts of despair among the petty bourgeoisie and the backward strata of the working class. Basing itself on this mood, the bourgeoisie would within the shortest space of time create a fascist party"*. Finally: *"Our untrained and untested cadre will within a few years at most be hurled into the turmoil of the revolution"*.

---

1. Ted Grant is a leading figure in the history of British Trotskyism. He was the theoretician of the Workers' Interrnational League, the Revolutionary Communist Party, the Revolutionary Socialist League and Militant. After the split in Militant in he has led a small entrist group in the Labour Party.

If this seems to be a little over-excited, rest assured that it is no more so than anyone else in the Fourth International. The WIL's conviction was that the radicalisation would be so fast and so deep that it would rapidly exceed the reformist bounds of the Labour Party and quickly move on to the Independent Labour Party (ILP), which in its turn, would be unable to contain this revolutionary fervour. The masses would then inevitably turn to the Fourth International to lead them to Soviet power. The future often makes fools of those who venture into the prediction business and, it has to be said, Ted Grant was no exception to this rule.

Later on, in the Revolutionary Communist Party, the argument as to positioning was about whether you should enter the Labour Party to encourage and then lead the leftward hurtling masses, or stand independently displaying the revolutionary standard around which the workers would rally. Pablo and the leadership of the Fourth International favoured the former course, supported by Gerry Healy[1], while Jock Haston[2] and Grant were for the open party tactic.

For Cliff, who was in general agreement with the imminent upheaval theory, it was clear that Palestine was an unlikely place for the first wave of the coming revolutionary storm. For any serious Marxist the place to be was in Europe, where the hammer blows of war had been most destructive, where the expected social pressures would be greatest and where there was a significant working class movement with a long standing socialist tradition. During the war it was difficult almost anywhere, but especially in Palestine, to obtain uncensored news of the workers' movement abroad and almost impossible to hear anything of the revolutionary movement. A member of Cliff's group, Dan Tait, did go to the UK just before the war and was instructed to send back reports in his letters home. For revolutionaries, usually without access to

---

1. Gerry Healey: recruited to Trotskyism by Jock Haston in the late 1930s, he was always noted for his predilection for factionalism and the vigorous – some would say, unprincipled – way he was prepared to fight.

2. Jock Haston: an attractive human being and one of the most talented of British Trotskyists. Secretary of the RCP, later a National Council of Labour Colleges (NCLC) lecturer, then Education Officer for the ETU. Despite his right-wing Labour posture in his later years, he was always a pleasant and sociable companion.

complicated ciphers and codes, this is normally effected by arranging one's correspondence to have a decent space between the lines of chit chat and then, with a clean nib, writing in the spaces with lemon juice. When allowed to dry naturally this is invisible, until it is subjected to heat with a candle flame, when the secret message is revealed in pale brown characters. Dan was instructed that, on his arrival in Britain, he should get in a good supply of lemons and send back regular reports. That such reports were not forthcoming was not because Dan was dilatory or lacking in revolutionary spirit, it was solely due to the fact that from 1939 to 1945 lemons were unobtainable in Britain, a shortage completely beyond the comprehension of anyone living anywhere near Jaffa. Bananas too were absent from wartime fruit bowls but, as these were useless for secret writing, their loss was less keenly felt.

By the end of the war, it was time for Cliff to move to a larger stage. The shortage of first hand reports from the UK may have engendered the illusion that one might be doing more than exchanging a handful of cothinkers in Palestine for a not much bigger handful in Europe, but hope springs eternal in the revolutionary breast. At least the RCP had an almost overwhelmingly working class membership, although by 1946 it was beginning to decline. Cliff was manifestly a man of ability, with a good knowledge of Marxism and economics, and the RCP leadership, where they were not over-embarrassed with such talents, invited him to attend the meetings of the Political Bureau.

The picture begins to emerge of the man and his background, years of semi-legal activity in a country ruled by foreign imperialism, with a tiny working class split on grounds of race and religion. Despite the difficulty, hope is maintained by adherence to the Samuel Smiles school of political thought that promises: *"this Marxism can move mountains if only you try very, very hard"*. The working class are seen, correctly, as the centre of Marxist analysis but, from lack of acquaintance with the genuine article, the workers seem to acquire an undifferentiated character. In this 'Marxist' science they appear as one dimensional factors in the revolutionary equation. All the professed passion for the workers cannot mask the fact that the other elements in the equation, for all practical purposes, loom larger: the revolutionary party and its organisational form and the vanguard of the vanguard, the leadership. In this scheme the politicised worker becomes a fetish, a powerful juju with infallible instincts, providing he/she agrees with the leader's preoccupations.

Because the real life worker, in his nature as a human being, is far more complex a creature than the theoretical abstraction, then an ideal, and idealised, worker is constructed whose thoughts, as part of a collective and as an individual, are elucidated from theory rather than observation. In this schema, the goal has been set, and can thus be largely ignored; all that is left is to build some imaginary yellow brick road, with the 'Wizard' directing every step in the construction. Such an idealist way of looking at things is perhaps understandable, a human reaction to hope too long deferred; a consequence of working in Palestine for years to reach a membership of 30, a number that would be hard pressed to command a majority in the Jewish Bakers Union: then to come to Britain and spend the next fourteen years building a group of less than a 100. This despite a willingness to make concessions in the interest of 'primitive socialist accumulation'.

Much of this, of course, does not require a background in the Middle East. All of the first generation of Trotskyist leaders (and most of those of the second generation) spent all their formative years and most of the rest, in small and ineffective organisations, watching history pass them by despite their dedication to its materialist interpretation. By sheer will-power they managed to impose their personalities on the group, aided by the fact that there were not too many people to impose it upon. It is, for example, not an accident that Gerry Healy's groups were thuggish, that Ted Grant's were intensely boring and that Cliff's were characterised by wild swings of emphasis, unsanctioned by supporting argument or democratic vote. All of these leaders still have their partisans, but then so do some of Jim Jones' or David Koresh's followers – at least that is the ones who missed the bus to Jonestown or Waco.

It is in this light that the liberal regime of the International Socialists, up to 1968, should be viewed. First, the chance of large scale recruitment was nonexistent and the tempo of events was mostly set by the glacier-like dynamism of the Labour Party. Whatever Cliff conceived to be the important questions were certain of getting a run in the group press, and the inclusion of contrary material was, at the lowest level, a useful recruitment device for the wary and less committed. For Cliff, the group is like something he owns and, in the final analysis, can dispose of as he wishes, even on a whim; for he has a whim of iron. It is as if his investment of more time and more sacrifice gives him extra shares in the concern. If others feel they have an equal right to contribute in a way that he may think is mistaken, then he will defend his own revelation with all the ferocity of a lioness defending her cubs. By hook or by crook (in practice both) the transgressor will be cast into the outer darkness, cast out of the movement and no longer allowed to participate in the socialist emancipation of mankind.

If one were to attempt to place Cliff in the order of merit in the Trotskyist movement, leaving aside Trotsky, who positively towers over all of his followers, he would surely get an honourable mention. If he is not in the Premiership, along with Shachtman and C.L.R. James, he is certainly in the top quartile of the Endsleigh League, along with such luminaries as Ernest Mandel and James P. Cannon, which is a great deal more than the Beezer Home Freezer League where Healy laboured so long and where his successors remain, looking for someone worthy of a bit of quality leadership.

As a person Cliff is pleasant enough, with a sense of humour that sits squarely in the self-deprecatory Jewish school and is often very funny. He is personally generous and kind hearted and, if one has more than a passing interest in revolutionary socialism, can be an entertaining if obsessed companion. With those who are prepared to listen and to work at his appointed tasks, he becomes positively affectionate. Woe betide the chosen one if he or she falls short of the mark or develops contrary ideas. From flavour of the month he is transformed into last night's dodgy vindaloo. One after another, young comrades are taken up and made much of, their every word treasured as a pearl of great price; then, in a few months, they are rejected for a newer, shinier model of revolutionary enthusiasm. Such partings have the appearance of the sad, bad end of a love affair, accompanied by all the bitterness of such occasions.

In this way quite a few promising comrades have been lost to the movement, a movement that has never been endowed with an over-abundance of cadres. This is criminally wasteful, especially as he who is the devil incarnate today worked well only yesterday and might provide some service tomorrow. To deny ourselves this possibility is dis-accumulation of a particularly primitive kind that is not, and should not be, easily forgiven.

All of these faults are, of course, the indications of human failing, from which most of us suffer, for none of us can levitate above our own space and time. Fortunately, most people are afflicted less grievously but it is for this reason that we should be on our guard against the arrogance of certainty and blind faith in our own intuition. It is the reason why democracy is not an optional extra for revolutionaries; it is an essential principle that is the sole defence against capricious and egotistical leadership. A moment's thought will surely tell us that no matter how infallible we would like our leading figures to be they have all so far proved pretty fallible in making the revolution. Democracy, in purely practical terms, is essential because genuine synthesis results from the exchange of ideas and few people can address their own brain like opposed lawyers addressing a jury and anyone who claims they can should almost certainly find themselves guilty of perjury. Revolutionaries should expect to make sacrifices for the movement, but the sacrifice that should never be made is that of conscience. In a revolutionary organisation, no guru's certainty should carry more weight than your democratic conscience.

All too often the escape from our own fallibility is the party, an immaculate repository of all wisdom, a fault free beacon for mankind in a darkling world. It is a matter of some concern that a party, built by materialists and atheists based on their own ideas and aspirations, should then be endowed with supernatural powers. Like the idealised picture of the working class, the party becomes an icon for deflected reverence. That the party is more than the individuals who make it up is only to say it can be more effective for its purposes than a lot of disconnected people pursuing similar goals in isolation from one another. The party can never be more than the people who control it and, in the case of the Socialist Workers Party (SWP), that is Cliff, armed with his well honed, razor sharp facility for opportunism and a prophetic nose. Even were these attributes as infallible as their owner believes them to be – and they are not – they are no substitute for the direction of an experienced and educated membership, with a leadership willing to learn as well as lead.

A Foreign Country

Tell it not in Gath, publish it not in the streets of Askelon;
...lest the daughters of the uncircumcised triumph.
The Bible, Samuel Two, 1:19

In September, 1946, Cliff arrived in Britain. That Britain of fifty years ago was, in L.P. Hartley's phrase, *"a foreign country, they did things differently then"*. For Cliff, of course, it was quite literally, a foreign country. It had suffered severely during six years of war, it was a place of rationing, shortages and queues for practically everything. For a socialist, though, what was more interesting was the existence of a large, organised and distinctive working class. Almost a million members of the Mineworkers' union laboured in the pits, hundreds of thousands of engineering workers followed their trades in Scotland, the North East, North West and the Midlands, while the massive general unions organised their members the length and breadth of the country. The Communist Party, having shed the Stalingrad levy, claimed 40,000 members.

The most significant political fact, however, was the existence of a Labour government with an overwhelming majority. The year before Cliff's arrival on these shores, the Labour Party was elected on a wave of popular enthusiasm, to its own astonishment and contrary to the advice from the Communist Party, which advised a maintenance of the wartime coalition of Labour, Liberals and Communists, together with, *"progressive Tories, like Winston Churchill and Anthony Eden"*. It was a time when spontaneous political discussions took place in bus queues, in British restaurants and on street corners. In cinemas, for some time after the election, newsreel pictures of leading Labour ministers were cheered as they entered 10 Downing Street, or climbed into a ministerial Humber. According to the newsreels of those days, ministers did little else. Maybe the most significant political fact was the radicalism of the massive and still mobilised conscript armed forces. There had been soldiers' strikes in the Far East and the Middle East and there was a rebellious spirit among the troops. Unfortunately, the party in which they put their trust, as the instrument of social change, was the Labour Party, an error of judgement both understandable and regrettable. The Communist Party, as already noted, clung to the warm familiarity of coalition politics, a comradeship of the Anderson shelter. Here, in a very real sense, was that crisis of the working class as the crisis of leadership so often alluded to by Trotsky. The only party offering that kind of leadership, however, was the Revolutionary Communist Party (RCP), the British Section of the Fourth International and, sad to say, very few soldiers and not many more civilians heard the message.

Cliff's destination, however, was the RCP, a party that directed some 400 members from its headquarters in the Harrow Road, Paddington. Here was an organisation that had survived the rigours of the war and emerged, for the first time, as a united section of the Fourth International. The party had some industrial experience, especially in the Royal Ordinance Factories and in the mines and had been the subject of a government initiated prosecution for aiding the Tyne Apprentices' Strike.[1]

The RCP was almost entirely working class in its composition and was led by a group of extremely talented people: Jock Haston, the General Secretary, Roy Tearse, the Industrial Organiser and a group of South Africans – Millie Lee, Heaton Lee and Ted Grant. These were the ones (together with Ralph Lee) who, in 1938, had refused James P. Cannon's advice to unite with the other British Trotskyist groups and help found the Fourth International. The reasons for this refusal are complicated and concern an earlier ac-

---

1. For a full treatment of British Trotskyism in the war and post-war period see Al Richardson and Sam Bornstein's *War and the International*. The same author's book *Against the Stream* is an excellent history of British Trotskyism in the 1930s.

cusation that the Lees, in South Africa, had been involved in some kind of defalcation of black workers' strike funds. There was no substance in the allegation because, quite apart from the transparent honesty of Heaton, Ralph and Millie Lee, African workers just did not have any money for anyone to do away with, but the slander had been a useful weapon in an obscure faction fight.

In 1938, relations over the accusation were bitter enough for Haston, Grant, and the Lees to sever relations with their accusers and to go so far as to refuse inclusion in the new International.

Whether or not Haston and Co. were justified in their refusal, they were roundly castigated in the founding congress report as reactionary and nationalist. In addition, they seem to have incurred James P Cannon's displeasure, a condition that carried a lifetime guarantee. In 1943, the first instalment of Cannon's revenge arrived in the shape of Stewart (Sam Gordon), a member of Cannon's faction in the US-SWP of some years standing. It was his task to assist in the unification of the British Trotskyists.

The Fourth International's official section in Britain was the Revolutionary Socialist League (RSL), the result of the 1938 fusions. Immured in the Labour Party and riven by factionalism, it had about 75 members divided into three factions: a majority Militant faction, led by Denzil Harber; the Trotskyist Opposition, led by John Lawrence and Hilda Lane; and a Left Fraction, led by Robinson and Mercer and including Harry Selby – who was much later Labour MP for the Gorbals. Harry was a barber and, it is said, on Saturdays after having taken a drink or two, he would cut the comrades hair for nothing. As a result, you could always tell a Glaswegian left winger by the rough hewn character of his hairstyle and the signs of long term scarring of the scalp. Haston's group the Workers International League (WIL) had some 250 members, with an occasional faction led by Gerry Healy whenever he could think up enough grounds to mount one.

It was to these signs of internal unpleasantness that Sam Gordon applied himself with vigour. He was instrumental in bringing together Healy and Lawrence in a factional alliance that was to last into the 1950s. It was also Healy's first association with Cannon, one that was to last into the 1960s. In 1944, the RCP was formed of all these contending elements. Despite the manoeuvring, Haston was elected General Secretary and the leadership of the new party was virtually the same as it had been for the Workers International League.

At much the same time, Cannon was also in the process of returning the International Secretariat (IS) of the Fourth International to Europe (it had been moved to New York during the war). It was, however, to be a Fourth International created in Cannon's own image. With his special brand of bluff arrogance, Cannon handed the reins of the International to, *"Our young men in Europe"*. The 'young men' in question were Pablo (Michel Raptis) a Greek who had attended the founding Congress of the Fourth International under the pseudonym of Spero, and the genuinely young, Belgian, E Germain (Ernest Mandel).

The young men in Europe, naturally enough, joined hands with Cannon's other protégés, Healy and Lawrence. In the light of Healy's subsequent root and branch denunciation of Pablo and all things Pabloite, it is interesting to recall that for years Healy took his politics straight from Pablo and Mandel. It was possible to say that Healy's faction was truly internationalist; it was formed in America, nurtured in Europe and offensive everywhere and in all circumstances.

This then was the party that Cliff had travelled so far to join, an organisation grossly undermanned for the revolutionary tasks it set itself and, in addition, riddled with internationally nurtured factionalism. It did have the advantage that it maintained a relatively liberal regime, protecting the rights of minorities and observing the provisions of its constitution, and it was bigger and better than the Palestine section. Unfortunately, that is not saying very much. If these handicaps were not enough, it also suffered, along with the rest of the International, from serious political problems.

Much of the difficulty experienced by the Trotskyist movement rested on the pronouncements of Trotsky himself. In the

1930s he was convinced capitalism was incapable of developing the productive forces. Without the socialist revolution there was only a perspective of unemployment, hunger, misery and war. The renewed revolutionary wave, however, would surely come as a result of the massive social and political dislocation of the war. In Russia, the Stalinist bureaucracy, as a shallow rooted caste, would be unable to withstand the trauma of world war and the working class would retake power and rebuild the soviets.

All of us have a tendency to whistle in the dark to keep our spirits up and, in the encroaching blackness of the late 1930s, Trotsky gave expression to several such spirit enhancing whistles as in:

> *Ten years were necessary for the Kremlin clique to strangle the Bolshevik Party and to transform the first workers' state into a sinister caricature. Ten years were necessary for the Third International in order to stamp into the mire their own programme and transform themselves into a stinking cadaver. Ten years, only ten years.*

REORGANISING THE IRISH SECTION
OF THE FOURTH INTERNATIONAL

> *Permit me to finish with a prediction. During the next ten years the programme of the Fourth International will become the guide of millions and these revolutionary millions will know how to storm earth and heaven.*[1]

Trotsky clearly believed this analysis, but the strident style of his message may

---

1. Recorded address to the US-SWP conference, 1938, reproduced in the British *Socialist Appeal*, June 1942.

well have been designed to enthuse his tiny cadre to Herculean labours. Unfortunately, for all too many of his followers, anything he said was revealed truth crossed with the eternal verities and, after his death, there was nobody able to evaluate the new reality. The speech of 1938 was seen as a promissory note ready to be cashed not later than 1948. Cannon, whatever his own views, encouraged this iconography while, at the same time, preparing the alibi. Just after the end of the war in Europe and the Pacific, a report of a Cannon speech appeared in the *Militant*:

> *Trotsky predicted that the fate of the Soviet Union would be decided in the war. That remains our firm conviction. Only we disagree with some people who carelessly think that the war is over. The war has only passed through one stage and is now in the process of regroupment and reorganisation for the second. The war is not over and the revolution which we said would issue from the war in Europe is not taken off the agenda. It has only been delayed and postponed for lack of leadership, for lack of a sufficiently strong revolutionary party.[1]*

Not everybody was quite as besotted as this. Felix Morrow and Albert Goldman in the US-SWP, relying more on the evidence of their senses, rather than ten year old exhortations, saw the signs of capitalist recovery. In Britain, Haston and the RCP majority agreed with Morrow and Goldman.

Newly arrived, Cliff supported this particular majority line. Indeed, he produced his *All that Glitters*,[2] proving that capitalism was not completely finished. Where he diverged from Haston, Grant and the rest of the majority, was in the evaluation of the class nature of the Soviet Union. Jock Haston had, before joining the Communist Party and later the Trotskyist movement, been close to, although apparently not a member of, the Socialist Party of Great Britain (SPGB). Since 1917, the SPGB had characterised the Soviet Union as state capitalist and whatever the theory lacked in sophistication, it made up for in consistency and longevity. The question arose in the Trotskyist movement because the

---

1. Quoted in *War and the International*, op cit, p. 1`73.
2. This is a quote from Gray's, unpublished, *Ode on a Distant Prospect of Eton College*, which actually reads "*Not all, that glisters, gold*". In this case the misquotation is neither deliberate nor harmful.

post-war reality cast doubt on their traditional characterisation of Russia as a 'workers state'. It became necessary to explain the existence of Russia's satellites in Eastern Europe. What was their class nature? Trotsky, the normal fountainhead on these matters, presented certain difficulties. In essence, Trotsky said Russia was a workers' state because:

1. The working class took power in 1917,
2. Nationalisation,
3. The monopoly of foreign trade,
4. Planning.

In Eastern Europe conditions two to four were all satisfied, but the working class had nothing to do with setting up these regimes. The Fourth International answered the question by proclaiming that Russia was a workers' state and Eastern Europe was state capitalist.

Jock Haston, in the cold uncertainty of 1946, basing himself, perhaps, on the proposed Labour nationalisations in Britain, or the drive to state control of industry in Eastern Europe or, because he had reverted, briefly, to the cosy warmth of the SPGB's line, declared Russia state capitalist. Ted Grant, as was his custom, agreed wholeheartedly with Jock Haston, although always ready for a quick reversal if Jock should change his mind. Cliff, however, with the encouragement of the Fourth International's secretariat, vigorously opposed the notion that Russia was state capitalist. Briefly the debate raged and then, in a strange reversal, which if more widely applied to our faction fights would add immeasurably to their entertainment value, the opponents convinced one another of the justice of the other's view. Cliff, with the enthusiasm with which he always lards his latest wheeze, proceeded to set out his new state capitalist ideas in a 200 odd page document. The RCP majority, presumably grateful that Cliff had set them straight by adopting their erroneous position, duplicated and circulated this monster *Internal Bulletin*.

No doubt Cliff would have gone on to form a faction on the basis of his new theory. Unfortunately fate, in the unprepossessing shape of Chuter Ede, the Labour Home Secretary, intervened with a letter requiring Cliff to leave the country with the minimum of delay. It is interesting to note that in those days the Home Office retained certain of the social amenities from a more polite age. The letter, having delivered its terse message concluded, *"I remain sir your humble and obedient servant, Chuter Ede, His Majesty's Secretary of State for the Home Office"*. Rather than be sent back to the Middle East, Cliff applied to the Republic of Ireland for residence. The Irish, on the mistaken assumption that the British government were kicking Cliff out because he was a Zionist and thus acceptable to their nationalist sentiments, were prepared to allow him into the Republic. The International Secretariat sent out the word from Paris that, *"Comrade Cliff has been directed to reorganise the work of the Irish section of the Fourth International"*. This is fairly rich, considering that Cliff's only contact with Irish Trotskyism was to go to the pictures once a week with Johnny Byrne who, at the time, was a Shachtmanite.

Back in Britain, post-war realities were pressing hard on the RCP. Whatever Trotsky had promised, 1948 saw the revolution receding further and further away. The organisation was not growing, in fact it was contracting. Healy's aggressive minority were happily firing the bullets prepared in Paris and New York. The politics of this minority were of imminent capitalist crisis closely followed by the struggle for power. If the RCP majority had the better of the argument, their policy of maintaining the open party condemned them to fritter away whatever strength they had in a world where Labour reformism held sway and industrial militancy was controlled by the Communist Party.

Healy fantasised that there would be such massive and rapid radicalisation that there would be no time to build the revolutionary party. The place to be was in the Labour Party, to lead the masses as they flocked in their millions into that party. The analysis was rubbish, but the entry tactic made sense. It would have allowed the declining revolutionary forces a field of political activity that was being increasingly denied them outside. At this point the International intervened decisively, allowing Healy's minority to exist as an entry faction in the Labour Party, in no way subject to the disciplines of the RCP which was, after all, the British section of the Fourth International.

This piece of gerrymandering was, until then, unprecedented, contrary to the letter and spirit of the Fourth International statutes, and it revealed a contempt for the rights of members and the responsibility of leaders. The Fourth International was an organisation whose prospects had been suspended for the duration and turned out to have no past, a present that combined empty vapouring with sordid manoeuvring, and a future that offered more of the same. Until 1948 most sections of the Fourth International might have been forgiven for thinking that, while revolution at home was remote, the International was at the leading edge abroad, where revolutionary hopes were high. After the Second World Congress of the Fourth International, only the most besotted could maintain this illusion. Trotsky's high-flown rhetoric of 1938 was exchanged for the flyblown vainglory of Michel Pablo in 1948. Ten years the mountains were in labour and gave birth to a pipsqueak. Max Shachtman, who had been the driving force behind the Founding Congress in 1938, abandoned all hope in the Fourth International. Here is Shachtman on Pablo's report of ten years of the Fourth International:

> *The only claim to distinction the report could make is that it was one of the most lamentable performances in the history of the movement. For carefully scraped out emptiness, it remained unexcelled by any of its rivals at other sessions. To be sure, the reporter took care to refer to the reactionary character of the Stalinist and reformist parties; he noted with pride that the centrist organisations had not become mass movements, whereas the Fourth International, in the face of great difficulties, had not disappeared; he did not fail to dwell loudly on his unshattered faith in the working class, his confidence in Socialism, and his conviction that the Fourth International would overcome all obstacles – including, presumably, such reports as he was delivering.*
>
> *It is debatable if the speech sodden with cheerless commonplaces, would have been appropriate even at some anniversary celebration in a mountain village. Its suitability as a report of the Executive Committee to a congress was not debatable. Consequently it was not debated – not at all, not by anyone and not for a single moment...*

Jock Haston together with most of the older RCP leaders began, in his phrase, 'to walk away'. It was not an isolated phenomenon.

This same old RCP majority leadership now suggested that the organisation should enter the Labour Party. Despite the fact that the RCP majority had considerably more members than Healy's entry group, the International Secretariat of the Fourth International decreed, with Haston concurring, that Healy should retain the leadership. On Haston's part this was less a sign of self denial and more an indication of his intention to remove himself from the fray with the utmost despatch. This he did and, in the same way that some heroes are awarded posthumous VCs, Healy expelled him retrospectively. Gerry always wanted his pound of flesh.

For the second time, the British Trotskyists were united in one organisation, if smaller and with much diminished hopes this time. Healy, however, was about to ensure that this unusual state of affairs did not last much longer.

Pandora's Box

If you open that Pandora's box you never know what Trojan 'orses will jump out.
Ernest Bevin

Life in a Healy group when there are political differences is not much fun. In 1950, the differences involved the few who subscribed to Cliff's state capitalist analysis; Ted Grant and the remnants of Haston's followers; the ex-RCP Open Party faction and, finally, those who were united only in their contempt for the old Revolutionary Communist Party (RCP) leadership who had abandoned them and in their dislike for Healy, his politics and methods. As Ken Tarbuck, then a young member of the group, wrote much later:

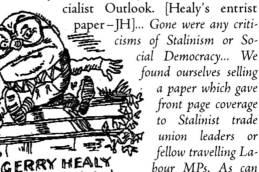

We found it difficult to adjust to the new regime and above all we found it extremely hard to stomach Socialist Outlook. [Healy's entrist paper—JH]... Gone were any criticisms of Stalinism or Social Democracy... We found ourselves selling a paper which gave front page coverage to Stalinist trade union leaders or fellow travelling Labour MPs. As can be imagined this did not

do much for our morale. On top of this we found as ex-majority supporters we were treated like second class citizens... we began to hear rumours of expulsions or departure from activity of people who had been members of the movement for years... our secret faction invited Tony Cliff to meet us, which he did and we had a long discussion about the Group and the International. He had a very plausible line that went something like this:

> If one continues to see Stalinist Russia as a workers' state and admit that the Stalinists can carry through a revolution (Eastern Europe and China) then you end up adopting Stalinist policies (eg, *Socialist Outlook*, the IS line on Yugoslavia, etc., and Stalinist organisational methods are used, eg., Healy's group.) The only way out of the dilemma was to adopt the state capitalist line.'...

We were quite impressed with this line of argument, but at that point we refused to throw in our lot with his faction.[1]

The youthful Tarbuck was elected as a delegate from Birmingham to the 1950 Group Conference, mandated to move a resolution critical of *Socialist Outlook*. It was a conference where Healy had assured himself of a majority by dissolving and amalgamating branches and rigging the delegacies. Opponents were routinely abused. At one point Healy shouted out to Ted Grant, "*Get back to the dung heap*". All of this behaviour was quite alien to party life in the RCP and, when Ken reported back to the Birmingham comrades, they decided that Cliff was right. Most of the other 'state caps' had already been expelled, on one pretext or another, and so they resolved to go out with a bang.

It was then decided that Percy Downey (an ex-RCP member who, funnily enough, also happened to be a barber) would submit a resolution to the Birmingham Trades Council putting a third camp position on the Korean War. The upshot of this was an immediately summoned meeting of the 'Club' at which Healy was present. He laid a resolution for the expulsion of Percy and refused to allow any discussion of the political issues, he insisted that the only issue was, "did he, or did he not, break discipline by putting the

---

1. John Walters (pen name of Ken Tarbuck), 'Origins of the SWP', in *Workers News*, April 19991.

resolution to the Trades Council." *However, when the vote was taken there was a tie. Healy then called a halt to the meeting, declaring the branch was suspended until further notice.*[1]

A little later Healy imported a 'loyalist' to break the tie and carried the expulsion. Not only that, all those who voted with Percy Downey were also expelled.

> *Healy had fallen into our trap since we went on to help found the Cliff Group... Had there been anything like a democratic regime such as had existed in the RCP we would not have wanted to leave the organisation. And of this I am sure, had there been a credible alternative to Healy around that maintained a workers' statist position Cliff would not have made so many recruits. Despite being hampered by the immigration laws at that time Cliff was very active contacting people, meeting them and discussing for as long as it took to recruit them. This entailed some personal risk for Cliff, since he faced being deported back to Palestine and a very uncertain future...*[2]

With the accession of the comrades from the Birmingham branch the way was clear for the formation of a state capitalist group in Britain. Altogether, there were 33 members, almost all of them young and ex-RCP. (Although this is a very small number it should be compared with the 70 members of the 'Club' which, despite taking some 150 odd from the RCP, had managed to expel or repel most of them). Beside Ken Tarbuck – who, incidentally, remained an active Marxist until his death in 1995 – and Percy Downey, there were a number of very talented people in the new group: Jean Tait, Peter Morgan, Bill Ainsworth, Geoff Carlsson, Ray Challinor, Duncan Hallas and Anil Munesinghe.[3]

The founding conference of the Socialist Review Group took place on 30th September and 1st October, 1950, in Camden Town. Of the 33 claimed members, 21 were in attendance, from six branches (London, Thames Valley, Crewe, Birmingham, Sheffield and Manchester). The immediate area of recruitment was to

---

1. *Ibid.*
2. *Ibid.*
3. Munesinghe subsequently returned to Ceylon, where he joined the Trotskyist Lanka Sama Samaj Party and was later a minister in Mrs Bandarinaike's government.

be among ex-RCP members and the emphasis for Labour Party activity was to be the Socialist Fellowship (the organisational expression of the *Socialist Outlook*). Subscriptions were set at a minimum of 1/6d per week, with a likely income of £3 10s 0d.

The Socialist Review Group secretariat was to be in Birmingham, with a youth secretariat in London. The youth work would be around a duplicated journal that would hope to involve other groups (the most likely being the Grant/Dean group). The theoretical journal, also duplicated, was to be called *Socialist Review* and priced at 6d. The paper was seen as a vehicle for the education of the members and would emphasise Eastern Europe and Russia, with articles by Cliff, the Ukrainian group, Shachtman and Grant.

On relations with the Fourth International, the founding delegates were anxious to display their loyalty:

> *Being a Trotskyist tendency and believing that our position on Russia rounds off Trotskyism to the needs of our epoch, we shall fight for the building of the Fourth International as a genuine Trotskyist organisation. We shall apply for membership of the Fourth International. If we are denied admission, we shall propagate our ideas in the Fourth International and in the organisations close to it. Open letter on these lines to be sent to the International Secretariat claiming recognition.*[1]

The conference adopted three documents by Cliff as the essential theoretical basis of the new group: *The Nature of Stalin's Russia* (the RCP internal bulletin), *The Class Nature of the People's Democracies* (a fifty page duplicated pamphlet dated July 1950) and *Marxism and the Theory of Bureaucratic Collectivism*. At that time, when the worldwide Trotskyist movement was struggling to reinvent its theory in the light of the post-war reality, Cliff was setting out his marker against Trotsky on Russia, the Fourth International on Eastern Europe and the alternative theory associated with Max Shachtman and his co-thinkers. If, like so much of Cliff's work, it was of uneven quality, it is still among the best he has produced.

As a closing grace note to the proceedings the assembled comrades resolved: *"To send greetings to Natalia and inform her of the formation of state capitalist group"*.[2]

----

1. Minutes of the Founding Conference of the Socialist Review Group.
2. Trotsky's widow, Natalia Sedova Trotsky in Coyoacan, Mexico. Along

The Socialist Review Group saw itself as Trotskyist like the RCP except that it had a better theory about Stalinism. The constitution set out the rights and duties of membership in the standard democratic centralist format:

> *All decisions of the governing bodies are binding on all members. Any member violating a decision shall be subject to disciplinary action... all minorities have the right to express dissenting opinions within the group, the National Committee shall maintain an Internal Bulletin as a medium for discussion of these dissenting opinions... censure, reduction to probationary status, suspension and expulsion may be taken against any member committing a breach of discipline... Charges against any member must be made in writing and the accused furnished with a copy, such charges are considered by the body in which they originate... at which the accused can attend and vote... Any member has the right to appeal against a decision to the National Committee...*[1]

Although a majority of the members lived in London the secretariat was based in Birmingham, which was handily placed midway between London and Sheffield. The secretary was Bill Ainsworth, a senior shop steward at the Rover factory and an experienced and talented ex-RCPer. Letters were sent out to dissident Trotskyists abroad: Lenz and Jungclas in Germany, Chaulieu in France, Mangano in Italy and Raya Dunayevskaya in the USA.

The members clearly saw themselves, with similar groups internationally, as the basis for a revitalised Fourth International. Like so many people to whom a blinding revelation has been vouchsafed, they found it difficult to understand that anyone could fail to succumb to the power of the new theory. In pursuit of this objective, Bill Ainsworth wrote to the secretariat of the Fourth International detailing the political and organisational bankruptcy of the Healy Group (the existing British section) and requesting that the Socialist Review Group be recognised as the British

---

with the veteran Spanish Trotskyist Grandizo Munis, Natalia was extremely critical of the Fourth International and had also adopted a state capitalist position.

1. Article 8, Socialist Review Group Constitution. As one can see, the 1950 constitution fairly evenly balanced the demands of centralism with the requirements of democracy, which is more than can be said for later constitutional novelties.

section; and, failing that, that it should, *"at least be recognised as a sympathetic organisation of the Fourth International"*.[1] Pablo and Germain were strangely immune to the persuasive powers of state capitalism, and neither of these requests was granted.

The group was now formed and its puny size dictated that it should work in the Labour Party. Contrary to some opinions, entrism is not the easiest way to spend one's political life. A tactic that derives from weakness is always hard to apply for those who have so recently enjoyed the luxury of unfettered freedom of revolutionary expression. On first entry, the revolutionary must practice a modest stillness (it would be asking too much to ask for humility as well) while acquiring some familiarity with the personal and political differences between the existing members. Such reconnaissance work is vital if one is ever to have any influence in the future. The political agenda will inevitably be set by others; the preoccupations of *Tribune* supporters may be the closest approximation to your own politics there is on offer. A resolution calling for free treatment of pensioners' bunions might well be preferred to one on nationalisation under workers' control. The practical revolutionary entrist will, on most occasions, have to be satisfied with increasing the tempo a little and enhancing the radicalism of resolutions. Recruitment in this kind of milieu is on a one to one basis and extremely infrequent.

If political fulfilment is in short supply in the Labour Party, there is no shortage of meetings: from ward to constituency party to borough party, each one of these tiers with its appropriate executive committee and a full complement of secretaries, chairmen, etc. It was possible to spend all one's spare time at meetings and in the process acquire the trappings of any number of petty offices. During his entrist phase Gerry Healy used to be introduced at public meetings as chairman of some obscure ward of Streatham Labour Party.

One place where the Socialist Review Group made some serious attempts to operate as entrists was in Birmingham. The Borough Labour Party held an annual municipal policy conference where the party's manifesto for the elections could be discussed and suggestions made for improvement. The Socialist Review

---

1. Letter to the Secretariat of the Fourth International, October 30th 1950, handwritten by Bill Ainsworth.

Group comrades decided to put forward a document that not only suggested new policy but also explained the failures of the Labour Council and the drawbacks in local government finances. The pamphlet was entitled 'Twenty Questions', after a popular radio programme of the day. It was written as a cooperative exercise, with each member of the group taking responsibility for researching and writing a section. In twenty small pages the pamphlet made a very good job of putting a socialist case for education, housing, direct labour, wages, de-rating, leisure and the ruinous effects of local government finance where practically all the income goes to pay off the moneylenders. The pamphlet appeared over the names of just two of its authors: Peter Morgan and David Mumford. This turned out to be a wise precaution. The right wing on the council, led by Denis Howell (then a councillor but later an MP and a Minister of Sport, and now a member of the House of Lords), were most offended by the pamphlet and were demanding expulsions. Eventually the two miscreants were brought up on charges before a packed Borough Party meeting of more than 200 (they used to get meetings like that in those days). By 108 votes to 96 they were expelled. The headline over the report in the *Daily Mail* read: 'Twenty Questions: One Answer'. Two years later both were readmitted to full membership. It was an instructive episode and one that indicated that there was, at the time, some life worth saving in the Labour Party.

The broad sweep of revolutionary politics had to be reserved for Socialist Review Group meetings. In 1951, the Socialist Review Group, as a newly formed state capitalist group, was particularly exercised about the Korean War and the fact that the British section of the Fourth International was giving uncritical support to the North Koreans. With these thoughts very much in mind, the Secretariat met Ted Grant in July of that year. The discussion was on the possibility of unity between the two groups. The *Socialist Review* people argued that fusion could take place on the basis of the old RCP programme, plus the formulation, 'Against both Moscow and Washington'. Grant, on the other hand, was already leaning heavily on the notion that nationalisation was the only necessary condition to define a workers' state. His group was discussing the possibility that Labour might introduce socialism peacefully and took the view that if Labour nationalised industry then it would be a workers' state. This obsession with nationalisation subsequently led Grant to bestow his favours in some very strange locations – Burma, Algeria and Egypt, to name but a few. Naturally enough, Grant and his followers were for unconditional defence of Russia in the event of war. For the Socialist Review Group comrades this was a capitulation to both Stalinism and Social Democracy, and the idea that unity would result in anything constructive foundered on the rocks of Grant's predilection for state 'socialism'.

In the five years since Cliff's arrival in the UK, British Trotskyism had foundered, not because of world shattering forces but from sheer miscalculation and irrelevance. The RCP had been founded in 1944 on the illusion that the party was on the threshold of a new October Revolution. The years of hard work and sacrifice came to nothing and the Haston leadership resigned, with a sigh of relief, from the unequal struggle, leaving the withered stalks that remained to the locusts. The movement lost not only a gifted leadership, but most of the cadre as well. By late 1951, there were probably not many more than 100 organised Trotskyists in Britain. Healy ran his group of zealots with a set of principles deriving from Nechaev rather than Trotsky. Grant sailed his small and rudderless craft along the unfamiliar coastline of social democracy, rather like some early mariner before the invention of the compass; while the Socialist Review Group considered itself the proper successor, albeit writ small, of the RCP, with an added entry tactic and a better theory on Russia. Just to prove that a better theory is no guarantee against vainglory, in September 1951, the National Committee passed the following resolution unanimously:

> We believe that the world Trotskyist movement is divided into defensism and anti-defensism. The defensists capitulate to Stalinism; the anti-defensists are the only real Bolsheviks, headed by Natalia Trotsky. We declare that we will not make any fusion with any group that stands for the defence of either Russian or American Imperialism.

The strange usage here suggests that this resolution was probably written by Cliff.

Leaving aside the idea of dynastic succession implicit in the reference to Natalia, the resolution is a classic example of the minor sectarian bird as it fluffs up its drab plumage in a vain attempt to appear big and rather beautiful. As usual, Marx has a word or two on the subject:

> *The sect sees the justification for its existence and its point of honour not in what it has in common with the class movement but in the particular shibboleth which distinguished it from the movement.*[1]

---

1. Marx & Engels, *Selected Correspondence*, p. 258.

Accidents of Character

World history would indeed be very easy to make if the struggle were taken up only on condition of infallibly favourable chances. It would on the other hand be of a very mystical nature if 'accidents' played no part. These accidents naturally form part of the general course of development and are compensated by other accidents. But acceleration and delay are very much dependent on such 'accidents', including the 'accident' of the character of the people who first head the movement.

Marx

Moving from an open party to Labour Party entry is rather akin to a gregarious claustrophobic applying for long term solitary confinement. You have to learn a whole new mode of expression (Labour Party jargon is no worse than Trotsko-jargon, just different). It is also necessary to mitigate your undiluted politics in the cause of winning friends and not being expelled. Thus, in the 1950s and for some years to come, your immediate allies were Tribuneites and semi-Stalinists, who abounded in the Labour Party. At the same time it was necessary not to allow your politics to be suborned by the wiles of left social democracy. For example, the Healy group virtually adopted the Stalinist sympathies of their allies in the *Socialist Outlook* and later on, during the German rearmament debate, it was necessary to deter Socialist Review Group members from seconding resolutions with such preambles as: "*The Germans who have already started two world wars…*"

The first issue of *Socialist Review* appeared in November 1950. It was sub-titled 'Live Writing on World Politics' and sold for sixpence. Content aside, this was quite good value for 36 duplicated pages, each one of which had justified right hand margins, a time consuming and tedious job with conventional typewriter and stencils but Bill Ainsworth insisted that it appear as professional as possible. In line with the founding meeting's policy of seeking recruits amongst ex-RCP members and the Socialist Fellowship, the lead article, 'The Struggle of the Powers', was by Roger Tennant, another of Cliff's pseudonyms used during his period of Irish exile. In internal documents he was referred to as Roger to fool the Special Branch. The article outlined the Korean war as the outcome of the rival imperialisms'–America's and Russia's–bids for world domination, while V.S. Felix wrote 'In the Mirror of Stalin's Parliament' an analysis of the newly elected Supreme Council of the USSR. A reprint from the POUM's *La Batailla* detailed the 'Class Struggle in Hungary' and Bill Ainsworth wrote a detailed critique of the pro-Stalinist content of *Socialist Outlook*, showing the magazine's uncritical support of both North Korea and Yugoslavia.

The programme of the new journal was cunningly outlined in a piece by Peter Morgan: 'Amended Draft of Policy Submitted for Socialist Fellowship Conference'. This document had a certain root and branch quality to it that might have caused some unease at Labour Party headquarters had they been aware of it. The Labour Party's policy document 'Labour and the New Society' was castigated as *"one more milestone on the road away from socialism"*; Russia and the Western powers were characterised as equally obnoxious imperialisms. Nationalisation of the land, all large financial institutions, industrial and distributive enterprises, without compensation and under workers' control, socialist planning and the monopoly of foreign trade were also called for. In addition to a state financed national building plan, all luxury hotels and mansions were to be requisitioned and all existing housing to be controlled and allocated by tenants' committees. Prices and any necessary rations were to be controlled by the Cooperative Societies and distribution workers. A rising scale of wages and a declining scale of hours was also thought to

be, and probably was, a popular demand. The call for the abolition of the monarchy, the House of Lords, the standing army and the officer caste was balanced by the demand for a militia with the election of officers and full trade union rights for all ranks. The document was nicely rounded out with a call for an end to secret diplomacy, an end to annexations or reparations, for freedom of the colonial peoples and the United Socialist States of Europe. After all this it is rather sad to read the plaintive footnote at the end which says: *"This draft was not accepted for the Socialist Fellowship Conference"*.

The next few issues of *Socialist Review* were little different from the first. Articles on the Stalinist states predominated, outweighing by some margin highly critical articles on the Labour Party. For a few months in 1951, the magazine had a line drawing on the cover, a combined portrait of Marx, Engels, Lenin and Trotsky as if to prove the paper's revolutionary credentials. Today, nearly 50 years later, the magazine does not read at all badly, with substantial pieces by, among others, Duncan Hallas, Ray Challinor, Geoff Carlsson, Peter Morgan and Tony Cliff. What it does not read like, of course, is an entrist magazine.

By April 1952, however, *Socialist Review* acquired for the first time a printed format and the approximation of an entrist paper. The additional capacity of the typeset page was utilised to examine at length the Bevanite controversy. While placing no faith in Bevan himself the magazine called for the construction of an *"ideologically rearmed"* left against the *"unholy alliance of the neo-Tory right wing Labour leadership and the Tories proper"*.[1] In the next issue, P Mansell (Jean Tait) reviewed Cliff's 'Stalin's Satellites in Europe', published under the name Ygael Glückstein. It will come as no surprise that the reviewer warmly supported, *"… the author's thesis that the 'People's Democracies', like Russia are bureaucratic state capitalist regimes…"*[2]

The very next issue saw the adoption of the strap-line, above the title, 'Neither Washington nor Moscow, but International Socialism'. This splendid formulation – which has the merit of being simple to understand at the same time as it indicates, with some precision, the political essence of the magazine – was originally

1. *Socialist Review*, vol. 2, no. 1, p. 12.
2. *Socialist Review*, vol. 2, no. 2.

coined by the Independent Socialist League, the American group led by Max Shachtman, one of the leading expositors of the theory of bureaucratic collectivism.[1]

Despite the advances made in the journal, the first few years of the Socialist Review Group's existence were not easy. The comrades were, in the main, young and inexperienced, and however far reaching their ambitions their ability to act was extremely circumscribed. The original intention to recruit from ex-RCP members and the Socialist Fellowship came to nothing. Apart from a few fragments, of which *Socialist Review* was one, the Trotskyist movement had virtually ceased to exist. A movement that had organised a few hundreds was now down to tens, and those widely separated, so that the possibilities for debate of disputed questions was fairly remote. Revolutionaries worked in their Constituency Labour Parties (CLPs) selling a few hundred copies of their journals and stagnated.

For the most part, work in CLPs is non-political, involving fund raising, canvassing, socials and, it seemed to me, endless coach trips to Southend. Whatever their attractions, these are not fertile places for a usually solitary revolutionary to put down roots and grow. An aggregate of the entire Socialist Review Group would not have commanded a majority in the average Constituency Labour Parties. In the adult party recruits were very hard to come by. As is often the case, lack of progress led on to membership losses. Bill Ainsworth left, it is said, to devote himself to the possibility of inter-planetary travel; Duncan Hallas, who had become a National Council of Labour Colleges Organiser (so too were Jock Haston and Sid Bidwell among others), was posted to Scotland and drifted away for the next fourteen years. Ken Tarbuck left, returning for a time to orthodox Trotskyism. These losses, given the grave shortage of experience and talent, were hard to replace.

In the Labour Party League of Youth (LLOY) there was a more sympathetic audience for the revolutionary message and, in this field of potential recruits, some actually joined. Stan Newens, who subsequently became a Labour MP, and is currently an MEP, was one of these, joining in 1952. Stan was one of the first of a long line of people on whom Cliff bestowed his most favoured comrade status. He was courted and made much of, attention that

1. See Appendix: 'Origins of the Theory of State Capitalism', p. 201.

he, and his wife, repaid in a great deal of loyal group work in the Labour Party League of Youth, the Labour Party and in writing for *Socialist Review*. In addition, Stan was also UK business manager of *Labor Action*, which, along with *New International*, was distributed here through the Socialist Review Group. As the owner of a motorcycle he was regularly pressed into service carting Cliff round the country on his pillion on recruiting forays. Throughout his stay, the group was pursuing an entry tactic in the Labour Party, which Stan had joined in 1949.

It is probably true that Stan Newens was, and certainly is, most happy working in a Labour Party environment and it is also true that in any revolutionary group he would be closer to the right of it than the left. His political stance was not something that Cliff was unaware of – after all he was a group member for eight years – but somebody with a temporary inside track to Cliff must have objected to Stan's politics. Two young busmen from the Hendon branch wrote in denouncing Stan and others, with much play being made of Eduard Bernstein and revisionism. Perhaps not unreasonably, taking the view that the fine Italian hand of Tony Cliff lay behind these recondite references to the man that Lenin and Luxemburg loved to hate, Stan decided to get on his bike. Today, he sums it all up: *"In my opinion Cliff never really understood the British labour movement... Cliff was always concerned with the internal organisation, rather than the broader work, which was for other people".*[1]

Joining at the same time as Stan Newens was Bernard Dix (he actually **was** a Shachtmanite) who wrote both in *Socialist Review* and in the ISL press under the name Owen Roberts. Later he became an Assistant General Secretary of NUPE, but resigned when he failed to become General Secretary, retiring to Wales where he took up left nationalism. He died in January 1996.

In September 1951, the first expulsion took place when Ellis Hillman managed to get himself on the wrong side of Cliff. For the light it may throw on later exercises in disciplining the cadre, it may be worth detailing this at length. Hillman had, apparently, been asked by the Secretariat to prepare an internal discussion document and with all the self confidence of the bright, but very young, decided on a major revision of the group's theory of state

---

1. *Workers Liberty*, No 18, Feb 1995.

capitalism. In seventeen, single spaced, foolscap pages he developed the notion that the Stalinist parties were the state capitalist societies in embryo. This attempt to marry state capitalism with bureaucratic collectivism did not go down well. The Secretariat rejected the document on the grounds that Stalinist state capitalism grows out of the need for capital accumulation as set out by Cliff in his RCP Internal Bulletin. Duncan Hallas also wrote a lengthy reply, published later as part of *Documents of the International Socialists*, a somewhat one-sided exercise as Hillman's original document is not published.

What must have been especially galling to Cliff was that Hillman had been thoroughly enchanted by the works of the Johnson-Forest tendency[1] and, with an air of breathless awe, as if he had just met the Messiah on the Road to Damascus, he wrote:

> It is no exaggeration to say that Comrades Johnson-Forest's latest *work* State Capitalism and the World Revolution *is at a level at least the equal of Trotsky's last works and a logical and fruitful development of them. The works on the state capitalism thesis that have been written so far have become obsolete and superfluous with the publication of Comrades Johnson-Forest's masterpiece...*

Having set to nought large chunks of Cliff's magnum opus, Hillman than went on to produce another document (internal bulletin writing can become addictive and damages your membership prospects), *Organic Unity*. This proposed a closer working, with a view to unity, with Grant's group. We have already seen that the Group was refusing all unity with defencist groups and few were more defencist than Grant's.

Hillman's days were numbered. First he was the subject of a few stray, in fact mutually inconsistent, accusations of alien loyalty. On the basis of his piece on *The Nature of the Stalinist Parties* he was accused of being a Shachtmanite, on the basis of *Organic Unity* he was a Grantite and, on general principle, because they were unpopular at the time, he was also accused of being an IKDer.[2] Quite a lot of heresy for one so young.

---

1. A group in America led by J.R. Johnson (C.L.R. James) and Freddy Forrest (Raya Dunayevskaya).
2. The IKD were a German Trotskyist group who produced a theory of retrogression which suggested that the decline of capitalism was

At a London meeting, Hillman was manoeuvred into refusing to retreat from the proposition, *"That if the general interests of the revolutionary socialist movement came into conflict with the particular interests of our Group, the larger discipline of those general interests would have to prevail"*.[1] In fact, the statement is really unexceptional: the interests of the revolutionary socialist movement would be paramount for all serious people, you might think. Not if you are Cliff (or, incidentally, Gerry Healy). For them the general interests of the revolutionary socialist movement are synonymous with the particular interests of the group, especially as the basic line is enunciated by themselves. This effectively means that Cliff's immediate preoccupations are the stuff of which socialist revolutions are made. Hillman obviously did not understand this eternal verity and complained to the Secretariat:

> *Recently it has become clear that bureaucratic clique methods have been used by Comrade Roger to: 1. Prevent views on unity being heard in Birmingham.. 2. Remove the Y[outh] C[ommittee] editorial board to Manchester. These manoevres (sic) constitute a violation of healthy democracy... Those who have protested most loudly about democratic centralism and group discipline have not even bothered to carry out the decisions of their own group. For instance, Comrade Roger was instructed by the London Group to write regularly for the SR and not dish up old Information Digest articles. I must say that these* **instructions have been violated, have not been carried out** *[emphasis in the original]. Where is the democratic centralism here? Comrade Roger is repeating all the same mistakes he made last year. We now have half the Fourth International with us, he said that last year. We also had 60 comrades last year. Such moonshine stories are based on absolutely no evidence... The Tito parties are Comrade Roger's latest fad. These groups, he said, may go over to* **our** *position...*[2]

---

such that socialism was impossible, with barbarism a distinct possibility. Funnily enough, though the IKD believed Russia to be state capitalist they were initially supported by Shachtman, but were vigourously opposed by the Johnson-Forerst Tendency.

1. Ellis Hillman, 'The Nature of the Stalinist Parties', Socialist Review Group Internal Document.
2. Ellis Hillman, 'Letter to the Secretariat', Sept 1951

This refers to the time, after his break with the Cominform, when Tito established sympathetic groups in Western Europe. Of course, none of them came anywhere near a Trotskyist group, despite the fact that Tito was assiduously courted by the Fourth International. Pablo wrote an open letter to the Yugoslav Party starting, *"Dear Comrades, We who have always supported the Yugoslav revolution…"*, and Healy kept a big picture of Tito on his office wall. Given Cliff's position on the East European states, it is odd that he thought that state capitalism would prove an attractive theory to Tito's followers, but then he was never one to let a theory stand in the way of a new recruit. Tito's International lasted no longer than it took to establish favourable terms with the Western governments.

For all the spirited manner of his response, Ellis Hillman's expulsion was confirmed. Some years later, but before I read the documents, I asked Cliff why Ellis had been expelled. *"For telling lies"*, he replied, with all the ring of truth in his voice. Fortunately for Cliff, nobody else thought that was not necessarily an expellable offense.

First, the good news, great leader - there's been a revolution against the authorities in the West!

The bad news is - it's in Hungary.

In 1952, Cliff was allowed back into Britain, Labour MP John McGovern having intervened on his behalf.[1] This gave a considerable boost to the organisation. Not only was he older and vastly more experienced in revolutionary politics than his comrades, but he also displayed that firm assurance and air of certainty that is so characteristic of sect leaders from Clapham High Street to Waco, Texas. About this time the traditional democratic centralist or-

---

1. John McGovern was for some years one of the Clydeside group of ILP MPs, in the 1930s he visited Palestine and met Cliff there. He subsequently rejoined the Labour Party. His last progressive act was organising Cliff's readmission to these shores. He later worked tirelessly for Moral Rearmament.

ganisational forms began to disappear, flaking off like the rust on an unused car. This, however, was not as a result of one of Cliff's infamous 'stick bending' exercises, just a different form for a different audience. If this gave rise to a certain laissez-faire attitude in organisational matters that is not necessarily to the bad, so long as it is not presented later as proof of a cunningly worked out plan.

For many of the groups, the maintenance of 'Leninist' forms of organisation are a kind of play acting. It does not help in their activity in the working class, because there usually is none, but its elaborate system of committees does fill their time nicely and affords them an opportunity to abuse one another with names from the rogues gallery of Bolshevik history. Top of the hit parade in this context is the accusation that an opponent is performing the strike-breaking role of Kamenev and Zinoviev in 1917. I have heard this accusation several times. Indeed, it has been applied to myself on two occasions; once by Gerry Healy and later by Chris Harman. I intend no amalgam here; Healy was funnier but Harman had a lot more hair – I always thought he had a passing resemblance to Zinoviev. Healy did not look a bit like Kamenev, though, more like Babe's much older brother.

For the Socialist Review Group, organised Trotskyism, nationally and internationally, was basically irrelevant to their experience. What had once seemed to be so important and attractive, like affiliation to the Fourth International, was almost forgotten – rather like the snapshots of one's youth; ridiculous clothes, weird haircut, definitely callow and a fit subject for ribald jokes. That organisational and political separation was the prelude to the Socialist Review Group relinquishing the forms of organisation that the orthodox still cling to so tenaciously and call 'democratic centralism'. That a small group of socialists operating in conditions of legality requires all the paraphernalia of Central Committees, Political Bureaux, Control Commissions, etc., is that species of substitutionism which imagines that if you have Lenin's forms you are able to give them Lenin's content. Not true, as any objective observer of the Socialist Workers Party will tell you.

In September 1953, Mike Kidron arrived from Israel. Prior to this he had no history in the Trotskyist movement. His only organised political life, up to 1953, was membership in the Johannesburg branch of Hashomer Hatzair. This, he says, was largely for social reasons, but he became anti-Stalinist when he was ill in 1946, unable to move or read. Some Communist Party members visited him to read lengthy extracts from the *History of the CPSU(B) Short Course*. This, the spiritual equivalent of a fortnight in the basement of the Lubyanka with Comrade Yagoda, turned him irrevocably against Stalinism. He arrived in Israel in 1946, a couple of weeks before Cliff, who was married to Kidron's sister Chanie Rosenburg, left for Britain. In that time Cliff gave him his own short course introductory lecture, delivered in one lump and lasting two weeks, with only brief interludes for food and ablutions and even less time for sleep.

For the next ten years, Kidron set a great deal of the style and a measure of the political agenda for the Socialist Review Group. His lack of a Trotskyist background turned out to be an advantage, in that he had little inclination to take anything as holy writ, even the work of Tony Cliff, and he fitted well into the looser organisation that the Socialist Review Group had become. Beside his membership of the Socialist Review Group, Kidron was also, as Chanie's brother, a fully paid up member of the family. To many this gave the not entirely mistaken impression that to be in on the decision making you had to be a relation. Despite the low membership, this still excluded the overwhelming majority of the group and was deeply offensive to some.[1] For all that the intellectual input had been considerably increased by the arrival of Kidron, the advance of the group was very slow. In the first five or six years of its existence, the Socialist Review Group barely maintained the membership it had started with in 1950.

The turning point, although it did not seem so at the time, was the events of 1956, the Anglo French-Israeli Suez adventure and, more importantly, Kruschev's secret speech to the 20th Congress of the CPSU(B), followed by the Russian invasion of Hungary. These were world shattering events. The burden of Kruschev's speech, with its partial denunciation of the crimes of Stalin and not much about Stalinism, had sufficient of the appearance of a liberal turn for the Hungarian Communist Party reformers, led by Imre Nagy, to remove the more obnoxious Stalinists, such as

---

1. See James D. Young, in *A Taste of Honey*, published by the IS Group, 1995.

Rákosi and Gero, and slacken the most burdensome aspects of the regime. For a brief time it seemed that they would get away with it, but the criminal adventures of Eden and his chums at Suez provided just the smokescreen the Russians needed to invade Hungary, put down the rebellion, execute Nagy and install their own puppets.

The repercussions of the Kruschev speech and the Hungarian revolution hit the Western Communist Parties like a well aimed brick to the vitals. Not least of those in pain was the Communist Party of Great Britain. For years the British party had been able to stifle all critical voices in its ranks but this discussion was quite beyond their power to control. Peter Fryer, who had been the *Daily Worker* correspondent in Hungary, gave full, eloquent and angry evidence. His criticisms were more sympathetically received when it was learned that his reports on Hungary, written from that country, were being spiked and replaced by 'reports' by the *Daily Worker* editor, J.R. Campbell, from Moscow.

The furore in the Communist Party was unprecedented. Aggregate meetings up and down the country were highly critical. Leaders such as Pollitt and Dutt, who were accustomed to uncritical adulation at party gatherings, were roundly condemned. Dissident members attended meetings in their hundreds to be addressed by Isaac Deutscher, who expatiated at length on the crimes of Stalin and the value of Marxism in general and Trotsky in particular. E.P. Thompson and John Saville produced a highly critical theoretical magazine, called the *Reasoner*, within the party (the *New Reasoner* after they were expelled) and while it was anti-Trotskyist it was located within a Marxist-humanist framework.

At this remove, it is difficult to realise the trauma experienced by Communist Party members when they came to realise that Stalin's feet of clay extended up to his hairline. From omniscience to putrescence in the time (several hours) that it took Kruschev to delineate the ex-'father of socialism's' less attractive traits, is just a little too quick for those weaned on the importance of loving Stalin. For the best of the Communist Party members, the most pressing question was: are the crimes of Stalin inherent in Marxism and its application?

This was the sort of question that the Trotskyist movement was uniquely well qualified to answer. Its whole propaganda phase, it had never got beyond it, was an attempt to revalidate Marxism in the face of Stalinist barbarity. Each of the groups, in their own way, attempted to capitalise on the concerns of Communist Party members. Cliff produced his pamphlet, *Russia From Stalin to Kruschev*. It has to be said that it is not a very good pamphlet, spending too much space on Kruschev's intention to take on both the form and the content of Stalin's rule which, in any case, did not happen. It failed to explain Stalin or Stalinism and gives the appearance of hasty preparation, together with uncertainty about how to influence Communist Party members. The pamphlet's high point comes very early, on what would normally be the dedication page. Cliff reproduces a stanza by one Znamya, published in 1946, in honour of Stalin:

> I would have compared him to a white mountain
>   but the mountain has a summit
> I would have compared him to the depths of the sea
>   but the sea has a bottom

One hopes, for Znamya's sake, that Stalin never realised this was just another bum joke in English.

Healy, with his own printing press and access to the American SWP's Trotsky opus, *The Revolution Betrayed*, was rather better prepared and more sure-footed. He produced a lengthy pamphlet by Peter Fryer, *My Case Against Expulsion*, and another reproducing the full text of Kruschev's speech with a commentary. Concentrating on history and leaning heavily on Trotsky's detailed critique, he was far better able to convince Communist Party members that there was a Marxist life after the party.

In 1955, there were fewer than 100 members of the Club. By 1956 there were 150 and by 1957 there were more than 400, the increase coming almost exclusively from the Communist Party. This is no great number, it is true, but among them were some very talented people – John Daniels, Brian Behan, Tom Kemp, Brian Pearce, Alasdair MacIntyre, Cliff Slaughter, Frank Girling, Peter Fryer and quite a few others.

Against this the Socialist Review Group could count just the one recruit. Dudley Edwards was an engineering worker who retained a powerful affection for *The British Road to Socialism*, the CPGB's programme, first produced in 1952, with the personal

Peter Fryer in Hungary

endorsement of Stalin. It was not much but I suppose it was something.

The Luxemburg Years

Cliff found that Luxemburgism was convenient. It was something he could hold up to those being expelled elsewhere, which promised a comfortable home.
Ken Coates, *Workers' Liberty*

The ferment on the left in the mid-1950s, as we have seen, brought forth renewed effort from a revolutionary movement that had grown virtually moribund in the stultifying atmosphere of the Labour Party. For all that the immediate rewards were not much, the Socialist Review Group put a significant investment into improving their propaganda image. From December 1956, *Socialist Review* appeared in tabloid form. This not only gave much more space for articles, but also looked infinitely more attractive than the dull and rather mean looking A4 magazine. With Kidron as the editor, the catchment area for writers expanded and the quality of the writing improved. In the period of a couple of years, the essential basis of the Group's politics were brought forth, polished and made accessible in the pages of *Socialist Review*.

Cliff wrote on the permanent arms economy and state capitalism, Kidron on the changing nature of reformism and the growing importance of rank and file working class organisation. Another South African, Seymour Papert – a man of considerable talent and an early computer wizard, he invented the computer language Logo – was recruited by Kidron and, for a few years, he added considerably to the impact of *Socialist Review*. His review of John Strachey's, at that time very influential book, *Contemporary Capitalism*, for example, is an excellent attack on Strachey and, incidentally, one of the better statements on the permanent arms economy.[1] Eric Heffer (who with Harry McShane and I.P. Hughes formed the membership of the Socialist Workers Federation – it is not clear at this remove what they were actually federating) wrote regularly in the magazine on industrial topics. Interestingly enough, given his subsequent career as a Labour MP and a sometime junior minister, he refused to join the Socialist Review Group because they were members of the reactionary Labour Party. In his defence, he was never heard to say, *"Watch my lips, no Labour Party"*.

One of the big issues of the day was the Algerian war of independence. The subject was covered in *Socialist Review* by the International Socialist League member Andre Giacometti (Dan Gallin, later a leading figure in one of the International Trade Union Federations that was kept rigorously clean of CIA influence). Unfortunately, the Socialist Review Group and Giacometti together with the Club, supported the MNA (Algerian National Movement) against the FLN (National Liberation Front). For the Socialist Review Group, this would seem to be because the MNA was led by Messali Hadj, who had been a Communist in the 1920s. For Healy it was almost certainly because Michel Pablo and his International Secretariat of the Fourth International (ISFI) supported Ben Bella and the FLN. In the event, both Healy and Cliff's groups looked a little silly when Messali Hadj was found to have been a long standing French agent. (In both Algeria and metropolitan France, the struggle between the MNA and the FLN gave rise to considerable bloodshed. The bitterness between the International Committee of the Fourth International (ICFI)[2],

1. *Socialist Review*, vol. 6, #6, March 1957.
2. 1. The saga of the ISFI and the ICFI is a complicated one and not for those with weak stomachs, but in brief; Pablo and Germain (the leading spirits of the ISFI) stood for deep, long term, entry into the Communist and Social Democratic Parties and sustained factions in those sections opposing this strategy – essentially the French and American sections. When the dispute came to a split in 1953, Healy went with the Americans, and the majority of the French section, and became secretary of the new ICFI. By 1963 the Americans found themselves agreeing with the ISFI on their enthusiasm for the Cuban revolution and they united with them to form the United Secretariat of the Fourth International (USFI). Healy and the French group led by

of which Healy was the secretary and the ISFI as a result of this fighting reached unprecedented heights of vituperation with the Banda brothers, especially, uttering some pretty blood curdling threats. The ISFI, in the persons of Pablo and the Dutch Trotskyist Sal Santen, were engaged in the production of false identity documents—some said counterfeit banknotes too—for the FLN and both of them actually served a prison sentence on the documents charge. Pablo, after the FLN took power in Algeria, became Minister for Abandoned Properties in Ben Bella's government, an appropriately named office, which led Gus Macdonald to suggest he was, *"still Secretary of the Fourth International"*.)

In the new, enlarged format the paper was able to deal more comprehensively with the day to day issues of politics. Its style was distinctive and was potentially a good vehicle for building influence in the Labour Party, the trade unions and the workplace. It was clearly a Marxist journal that took itself and politics seriously, but it eschewed the hectoring tone and sectarianism that informed so many of its contemporaries.

Ted Grant's group, the Revolutionary Socialist League, (at the time the British section of the USFI) published a truly dire journal called *Socialist Fight*. It was, fortunately, so badly duplicated that most of its pages were unreadable; for this relief much thanks.

The Club, by drawing heavily on Healy's very limited stock of restraint and self control, produced astonishingly non-sectarian propaganda. *The Newsletter* was a professionally produced magazine, edited by Peter Fryer, which, while paying lip service to Labour Party work, was far more concerned with industrial matters and catering to the influx of ex-Communist Party recruits and their milieu. Of particular value to the Club was their theoretical magazine, *Labour Review*, edited by John Daniels (an educationalist and previously a candidate member of the Executive of the CPGB) and Bob Shaw (a man noted for his total dedication to Gerry Healy and his equally total lack of a sense of humour). This was, briefly, an exceptionally good read and certainly one of the reasons why the Club recruited comparatively well among disaffected CP'ers.

Lambert denounced this fusion and refused to join, continuing with the ICFI.

While these improve-
ments to the Socialist Review Group and Club jour-
nals were as the direct result of people taking thought,
they also arose from a new
atmosphere and an attempt
to meet the challenge of the
times. After a long period
of quiescence there were
significant stirrings. The
crisis in the Communist
Party gave rise to a re-
examination of Marxism
and a revalidation of non-Stalinist va-
rieties. Suez and the Hungarian revolution awakened the enthusiasm for single issue campaigns and mass demonstrations. The
old structures – the Communist Party on the left and the Labour
Party on the right – were unable any longer to contain and con-
strain a movement that had acquired a certain spontaneity, both
in its activity and its leadership. Most significant of these new
movements was the Campaign for Nuclear Disarmament (CND)
and its even more spontaneist wing, the Committee of 100. These
were movements that could organise mass demonstrations and
actions, that were quite beyond the control of conventional politics. CND was too large and unstructured for organisations as
small and inexperienced as the revolutionary groups to even attempt to control but, just by turning up and talking reasonably coherent sense, revolutionaries could have an influence far beyond
mere numbers.

The slogan 'Black the bomb, black the bases' found a wide appeal in the ranks of CND and, especially, the Committee of 100.
The movement had at its head a number of leftist Labour figures,
Michael Foot, Canon Collins, J.B. Priestley, etc., and it looked to
the election of a Labour government to bring its plans to fruition. However, the very real perception of a nuclear Armageddon
ensured that there was a small, but not insignificant, minority in
CND who were attracted to the revolutionary idea of organised
working class action against the bomb, a conclusion that is not too

far from the socialist idea of the centrality of working class action to solve all of society's ills.

At the beginning of CND, the Communist Party refused to participate on the grounds that it would detract from the work of the British Peace Committee which – unlike CND – the Communist Party controlled. This was not only of benefit to CND, but also to revolutionaries working in the new movement. The Aldermaston Marches in 1958 and 1959 had to get by without the presence of the Communist Party, a loss they bore with admirable fortitude. When it became evident that the British Peace Committee was totally moribund and that *the* mass movement was CND, the CP'ers switched to CND, like small furry creatures deserting a sinking peace movement. As latecomers their influence was never that great, although in local groups they had a tendency to propose activities that would not offend the local Anglican clergy – there were quite a lot of vicars in CND.

Within CND, the overwhelming political colouration was Labour; if not members, very hopeful voters. Another strong part of the spectrum was a sort of middle class liberal anarchism and then, a narrower band, the revolutionary left. Effectively this meant the Socialist Review Group and the Club – Grant's Revolutionary Socialist League was not at all in evidence. Of these the Club, with its new recruits from the fallout of the 20th Congress, was far and away the biggest. The Club's internal regime had been much softened, both to recruit and retain these new members, and there were those in the Socialist Review Group who felt that the leopard might have changed his spots – the puma of course is a leopard without any spots at all, but is nevertheless a very dangerous animal.

As befits revolutionaries, the emphasis in the campaign within CND was to point to the working class as the only force capable of ending the nuclear threat to mankind. Both the Socialist Review Group and the Club supported blacking the bases as well as the bomb and, after a period of reasonably harmonious appearances at the same demonstrations and marches, the Socialist Review Group proposed to the Club that the editorial boards of the *Newsletter* and *Socialist Review* should hold joint meetings to coordinate and increase the effectiveness of their work.

It was, therefore, not too surprising when a letter arrived, dated 10th May 1958, from the British Section of the Fourth International and signed by Burns (Healy's party pseudonym). The letter outlined the agreement that the two organisations had on CND work and their agreement on the Algerian revolution and stated that, "*despite important differences on the class nature of the Soviet Union, we are coming closer together*". It proposed:

> a. *The immediate exchange of documents outlining the prospects of our respective groups for building the revolutionary party in Britain.*
> b. *A joint committee... of six members from each organisation... to work out ways and means to arrange a fusion.*
> c. *This committee would arrange joint editorial meetings, coordination of trade union, youth and Labour Party work, exchange of lecturers and joint discussion groups...*
> d. *The committee will draft the conditions for unification which would be mutually agreeable to the members of both organisations.*

According to Cliff, the initial response to this unity proposal was favourable in the Socialist Review Group. Only Chanie Rosenburg, Jean Tait and Cliff himself were opposed to unity with the Club. The reasons for this are not clear but one can, perhaps, assume that the comparative success of Healy in attracting dissident Communist Party members was a considerable factor in this enthusiasm for unity. Cliff did not remain in a minority for long. In conversation with me he claimed that the change in the majority's attitudes came from Healy's refusal to publish an article by Cliff, on state capitalism, in the Club's theoretical magazine, *Labour Review*.

Whatever the reason, a reply was sent to the Club on 26th of June 1958, signed for the executive committee of the Socialist Review Group by Robin Fior. Fior is an extremely talented designer, if a mildly eccentric one. He it was, I believe, who invented the 1960s typographical foible for rejecting upper case type for the universal application of lower case.[1] As one might expect, the

---

1. One of Fior's more enthusiastic campaigns in Islington Labour Party was to have the logo on the side of the corporation's dust-carts all in lower case. On another occasion he was contracted to design and produce the programme for a Brendan Behan play at the Theatre

letter is beautifully laid out, with varying indents for different points. In deference to the innate typographical conservatism of revolutionaries, both upper and lower case type is employed. That is, however, the only concession to Healy's sensibilities. In paragraph one, the letter condemns the Club's workers' state theory, their softness on Stalinism, their previous support for Pablo and his thesis of 'Centuries of Deformed Workers' States', together with policy flip flops on Tito's Yugoslavia, before and after his break with the Cominform.

Paragraph two criticises the lack of democracy in the Club. It contrasted the open discussions in Lenin's time against the practice of Stalinism. It pointed out that in the Socialist Review Group, if there were differences they were aired in the paper. It went on to say that known disputes in the Club had yet to see the light of day in the *Newsletter*. In a final and ringing phrase that could, with some benefit, be embroidered on a sampler and hung on the SWP office wall, it said: *"Until we can agree that* **all** *[emphasis in original – JH] general political differences should be discussed openly, honestly, and democratically, we cannot feel that the ground is ready for fusion of our two organisations"*.

That, of course, was the end of all talk of unity and there can be little doubt that had the union actually been effected, the Socialist Review Group comrades would have fared no better than they had done in 1950. The episode is of nothing more than passing interest except in so far as it sheds some light on the nature of the Socialist Review Group. For example, Fior's letter is correct when it speaks about differences being expressed in the pages of *Socialist Review*. In the course of the 1950s, the Group had come quite a way from its origins in the Fourth International. During that decade, the Socialist Review Group had attempted to come to terms with the problems raised by the fact that capitalism had, contrary to all expectations, survived the war and was clearly expanding and that the predictions of its early collapse looked sillier with every year that passed.

Royal, Stratford East. In the event he failed to produce the finished programme. Nevertheless, he turned up to the opening night, on a complimentary ticket, cheering the production noisily. I am told he now lives in Portugal.

The revolutionary movement had not grown in any way to match the enormity of the tasks it faced, or even its own pretensions. Social Democracy, after the first flush of enthusiasm in 1945, was gradually eroding its own support. The underlying reason for the long boom was, according to the Socialist Review Group, to be found in the Permanent Arms Economy. The slow decline of social democracy as a distinctive political force was seen against the background of a trade union bureaucracy that was increasingly divorced from the members and their aspirations, at the same time as it was involved with both government, of all stripes, and employers, in a corporatism designed to engender social peace at the expense of the working class. The arena where working class living standards were effectively decided was the shop-floor and the day to day leadership were the shop stewards and other rank and file representatives.

This growing coherence in revolutionary politics was accompanied by a growing away from the organisational forms of the past. Much of this – the emphasis on democratic norms, the preoccupation with the rank and file and the errors of reformism – found theoretical validation in the work of Rosa Luxemburg. The full flowering of this came with the production of the 96 page pamphlet, *Rosa Luxemburg: A Study by Tony Cliff*. (The use of cross-heads in lower case and the wide left hand margin is a dead give away for the Fior design. The third edition of the same work manages to have a tendentious, not to say tedious, introduction by a Lindsey German and still be six pages shorter.) This pamphlet was written in January 1959, but did not actually appear until January of the following year. As the advertising proclaimed: *"41 years after her murder, one year behind schedule, eleven months after the original announcement and four months after reviewing it, we are happy to announce* Rosa Luxemburg". In that four month early review, Michael Kidron, despite some rather over-excited hyperbole, made several valid points that indicate the Socialist Review Group's attitude to the revolutionary tradition. Luxemburg was:

> probably the greatest tribune the western proletariat has produced since Marx and Engels... incapable of being accommodated in the turgid streams of social democracy or Stalinism. Even the minuscule groups of misnamed Trotskyists have found her too turbulent a spirit to commit to their gallery of deities... the greatest teacher

of our time, a never ending source of inspiration to the isolated so-
cialist minorities of today... Nothing could stem her tirades against
the machine and the machine men, the lifeless multi-limbed bu-
reaucracy that grew on the movement in her day and is still there.
Nothing could trim her infinite belief in working class initiative, in
consciously conceived self directed working class action... Her deep
understanding of the role of leadership,...led her into battle not
only against the Gaitskells of the German labour movement of her
time, but also against the Lenin of the early, hunted Bolsheviks.[1]

From this you will probably have gathered that if Luxemburg was
not on the top step of the pantheon, this could only be because
Marx and Engels were occupying that space.

The only slight criticism Kidron felt moved to make was the
following: *"Sometimes the logic of ideas leads the author [Cliff – JH] to*
ignore his subject, completely imputing to her a train of thought more his
than hers". The objective observer may feel that the condition here
described is one that has gone from acute to chronic in the long
journey from Luxemburg to Trotsky, taking in Lenin on the way.

Whatever we might think about the emphasis of this Luxemburg worship, it was certainly a breath of fresh air amid the stale
orthodoxy of 1950s Trotskyism. Alone among the revolutionary
groups, the Socialist Review Group had used the time fruitfully.
It was actually attempting an overall analysis of capitalism, reformism and Stalinism together with a credible strategy of working class advance, cast within the framework that encouraged self
activity and openness within a genuinely democratic framework.
This was a real advance on the Group's origins in the RCP and
one that made it a potentially strong pole of attraction. If the first
ten years had been a disappointment, with all the high hopes of a
theoretically renewed Fourth International dashed, the next ten
were, at least in part, to be the justification of all the seemingly
wasted years.

---

1. *Socialist Review*, vol. 9, #12, September 1959.

In That Dawn

Bliss it was in that dawn to be alive,
But to be young was very heaven...
William Wordsworth, on the French Revolution

If the Socialist Review Group's first decade saw little or no increase in membership, it had seen a notable increase in political clarity. The messianic pretensions of orthodox Trotskyism were almost entirely absent. The emphasis was on working class self-activity and initiative, as the precondition for socialist advance, rather than seeing *the* revolutionary group as the centre of the universe and, wherever necessary, rewriting cosmology to accommodate this astronomical presumption.

At each stage in the Group's theoretical journey the ideas were developed to explain the new reality. State Capitalism was a response to the increasingly untenable notion of a 'workers state'; the Permanent Arms Economy was an attempt to explain the post-war long boom; and the changing locus of reformism called attention to the fact that most improvements in working class conditions came not from social democracy or the trade union machine but from rank and file pressure. While these theories are not necessarily inter-connected (it is, for example, quite possible to believe in any one of them, without having to accept the other two) in the life of the Socialist Review Group they had a certain natural progression. The result was a group that still bore some of the marks of its Trotskyist origins, but also showed a refreshing willingness to accept the reality of the post-war world and a modesty in accepting that any revolution relying on the Socialist

Review Group for its success would have to exercise considerable patience.

Armed with its theory, the Socialist Review Group was rather like the young man who was all dressed up but with nowhere to go. Then the Labour Party obliged by re-establishing its youth movement. Over the years the Labour Party had had an extremely troubled relationship with the young. The first League of Youth was founded in 1923. The Labour Party, from the beginning, was suspicious of the young and their tendency to adopt radical policies. Thus the League of Youth was permitted no national organisation or National Committee. After a troubled few years of existence, the real battles took place in the 1930s. The Communist Party saw the League as a rich pasture for their united front policy. Their main agent in the League of Youth was Ted Willis. (Subsequently Willis was the author of the Dixon of Dock Green television series, for which services to 'art' he was ennobled, to end his days as a Labour peer.) After some battles with Transport House, he decamped, taking a large chunk of the League into the Young Communist League and, in 1938, the League of Youth was disbanded. The Trotskyist movement did have people working in the League: Jock Haston, Ted Grant, and Gerry Healy, together with their comrades, operated around their paper *Youth For Socialism*, but their forces were small and their influence negligible.

Immediately after the war, a youth movement began to develop spontaneously, without any prompting from Transport House. This revived Labour League of Youth (LLOY) suffered the same restrictions as before – no national organisation or national focus in a conference, no elected leadership and no rights or function within the main body of the Labour Party. Its history was a muted repeat of the prewar model. Left wing branches were dissolved and any spark of initiative was firmly suppressed. The Trotskyist movement, slightly (but not much) larger, now committed to Labour Party entry, worked in the League and made some recruits, but lack of resources and the lack of a national focus, allied to the draconian regime imposed by the Labour Party, ensured that neither the movement itself nor the entrists got rich.

By 1955, the LLOY was so depleted by suppression and declining membership that the Labour Party closed it down before it fell down. In an attempt to keep a more docile youth movement, the Labour Party set up Youth Sections. These were integral parts of the local adult party with virtually no independence and an upper age limit of 21. In East Islington Constituency Labour Party, for example, it was not possible to join the Youth Section unless you were actually related to an adult member of the constituency party. This is even more restrictive than it might seem, because there were only a few tens of adult members in East Islington CLP, many of whom were some years beyond child-bearing age.

For the Labour Party, a youth appendage, despite its distressing tendency to be left wing and lacking in respect for its elders, had certain advantages. Quite apart from the fact that it promised a renewal of party members, it contained those who were, at least in theory, most able to carry out the onerous tasks of electoral politics. The Tories had been in power for nearly ten years (in fact, they lasted another four) and as recently as 1959 had, yet again, been re-elected. New blood was clearly the order of the day. The success of CND as an organisation was an earnest of the possibilities if only the youth could be persuaded to behave.

That the timing of the launch, in 1960, was good is proved by the fact that after just a few months of existence the Young Socialists had over 700 branches. The constitution of the Young Socialists was comparatively liberal and good behaviour was to be ensured by having Bessie Braddock, a very large and formidably right wing ex-Communist who sat on the Labour Party's NEC, and George Brinham, a trade union official with a seat on the Labour Party National Executive, to supervise the new movement's activities. Stern disciplinarians Brinham and Braddock may have been, but they had no chance of controlling a youth movement that was, in large part, a response to the growth of unilateralism in a Labour Party whose official policy was solidly, even enthusiastically, for the bomb. If the Labour Party leaders had actually intended the Young Socialists to be an ideological arena and recruiting station for the revolutionary left, they could not have done a better design job. With little yelps of glee, the revolutionary groups nipped smartly in to enjoy the pickings so generously provided by Transport House.

The first vehicle to carry the Socialist Review Group's message into the Young Socialists, was *Rebel*, a four page A5 publication. It was produced, in Cliff's back room, on a pocket size Adana press, by John Philips, Michael Heym, Chris Harman and John Palmer, among others. Truth to tell, it was a fairly nasty little product but it did have a certain power of attraction. In 1961, the supporters of *Rebel* and those of *Rally*, the youth paper of the Revolutionary Socialist League, came together to produce *Young Guard*. It was, in many ways, an uneasy alliance and the monthly support meetings could become rather fraught, especially because the *Rally* contingent, like Healy's Socialist Labour League, took the view that Britain should unilaterally disarm, while Russia, because theirs was a 'workers' bomb', should not. One was reminded of the old Communist Party ditty, 'The Song of the Red Airmen', whose refrain contains the immortal words, "*We'll drop the workers leaflets, while we bomb their bosses*". For all these disputes at readers' meetings, the pages of the paper were, for the most part, pleasingly free from sectarian disputation, with art and religion getting a measure of attention as well as politics.

THE SCOTS INVADE
ENGLAND AGAIN (1961)

The early 1960s were a time of demonstrations, especially against the bomb, and there was invariably some activity to organise within the Young Socialists, ensuring that it was more than just a discussion group with responsibilities for canvassing. The Aldermaston Marches of Easter 1960 and 1961 were each attended by more than 100,000 people and the movement looked to the Labour Party, that was in any case about due for a period in office after so many years of Toryism to adopt the unilateralist cause. It was a measure of the growing radicalisation of the time that, at the 1961 Labour Party conference, unilateralism was adopted as party policy. The following year, of course, after much arm-twisting and help from the trade union bureaucracy, multi-lateralist policy was reinstated, thus ensuring that Aneurin Bevan, had he lived long enough to become Foreign Secretary, would have been able to go fully clothed, in nuclear finery, to the conference table.

An early benefit of the work in the Young Socialists was the recruitment of a number of young Glaswegians, several of whom had been active in the engineering apprentices' strike in 1960. In 1961, an advance guard of them arrived in London including Bill Thompson, Ross Pritchard and Gus Macdonald. Frank Camp-bell and Bill Kane arrived a bit later. Others, like Peter Bain and Ian Mooney, stayed behind in Glasgow. They were a particularly talented and personally attractive group of people, with an early dedication to that relaxed 1960s lifestyle, which is nowadays the object of considerable nostalgia. Before leaving Glasgow, they convinced Paul Foot that socialism was more about the working class than wine and cheese parties.

Gus Macdonald did not stay long but he briefly worked full time for the Socialist Review Group, edited *Young Guard* and was a useful publicist for the organisation.[1] Bill Thompson was an ac-complished folk-singer and song writer. One of Bill's songs, a cel-ebration of the qualities of beer, had a chorus that went:

> *Dialectic, schmialectic, Oedipus schmoedipus too!*
> *Give me a bevvy, give me a brew!*

Bill accompanied himself on the guitar although his preferred instrument was the trombone. Unfortunately this was not much heard in folk circles, especially if the performer wanted to sing at the same time. The talent for folk-singing was shared by others and this, together with a truly Glaswegian facility for consum-ing massive quantities of ale, made for some memorable social

---

1. From the Group he went to *Tribune*, then the *Scotsman* and later Granada TV where he was a moving force in starting *World in Action* – known at the time as the 'Trot slot' – and thence to become chairman of Scottish Television [update: he went on to become Baron Macdonald of Tradeston, CBE, a member of the House of Lords, taking the Labour Party Whip – Andy Wilson].

and political evenings, weekend
schools and Young Socialists
conferences. Bill also organised the Group's first press, in
a small shop off the Holloway
Road. When we bought it the
machine, a clapped out British
Salmson Ranger, seemed to be
a bargain at £300. This was an
illusion as was proved a year or
so later when we managed to
unload it for £3. It displayed
a number of inherent design
vices, plus some crippling additions acquired over too many

ABOVE: REG UNDERHILL'S
IMAGINATION, ACCORDING TO
HIGGINS.

years. Despite the fact that Bill had no training as a printer, although helped by Ross Pritchard when in serious difficulty, he
managed to produce *Labour Worker* and the third edition of Cliff's
book on Russia. A triumph of willpower and dedication over the
dumb insolence and pure sabotage of a piece of dead machinery.

In the Young Socialists there was a ready-made audience eager
to discuss left politics in an open ended fashion. To meet this
demand Cliff produced a syllabus for a course of twelve weekly
lectures in socialist theory. The opening lecture was on dialectical
materialism, and the whole course took in all the main features of
Marxist study including economics, state and revolution, permanent revolution and the permanent war economy. The notes for
the lecture on the permanent war economy had its lighter side
containing, as it does, reference to the 'Olive Oyl dilemma'. At
first sight this could be mistaken for some arcane economic phenomenon, derived perhaps from the Italian vegetable oil industry,
and elucidated by someone who could not spell oil. Not a bit of
it, this refers to Popeye's girl friend who, like the capitalist who
faced the contradiction of having to devote greater and greater
resources to arms expenditure at the expense of investment to
meet international economic competition, often found herself
pulled in two directions. Like many full time revolutionaries,
Cliff was much addicted to afternoon children's television, and
the Popeye cartoons were a particular favourite. His mistaken as-

sumption that people over ten, who actually worked for a living, would catch these obscure cultural references was one of his more attractive foibles.

It may be of interest to note that the twelfth and last lecture in the series, 'Tasks of Marxists in the Labour Movement', contains inter-alia:

> *Marxists should not set themselves up as a party of their own. They should remember that the working class looks to the Labour Party as the political organisation of the class (and no doubt when a new wave of political activity spreads among the working class, millions of new voters will flock to its banner and hundreds of thousands will join it actively)... Marxists should strive to unite with the Centrist Left in activity in defence of the traditional working class content of the Party...*

Entrism was firmly entrenched at the time, but not for too long.

The success of the work in the Young Socialists could be accurately measured and, by 1962, the Socialist Review Group had a membership of around 200. Many of these members had been schooled, one might even say over-schooled, in the faction fights in the Young Socialists. As was to be expected, the main opposition was not the right wing, who were a tiny minority, nor the Tribunite left who were not much bigger, but the Healyites. Healy's greatest, some would say his only, talent was the ability to produce a cadre of single minded clones well practiced in the extremes of vituperation that carried with it an underlying note of menace. In the pages of *Keep Left*, the SLL's youth paper, and at countless meetings up and down the country, *"Mr Cliff's state caps"* were accused of a list of crimes from collusion with the right wing, to anti-sovietism, syndicalism and being generally beastly to the SLL. *Keep Left* had been in existence for some years as the paper of the Healyite youth. For most of that time it had been a rather tatty duplicated product but now it flowered into a printed journal.

The official paper of the movement, financed by Transport House, was *New Advance*. Contrary to the over-optimistic expectations of the Young Socialists, the Young Socialists' paper would not be controlled by them, nor would they appoint the paper's editor. The line and direction of *New Advance* would be set by the

Labour Party bureaucrats. As if to confirm their peerless judgement the National Executive Committee appointed Roger Protz to edit the new paper. Roger's tenure of office was short lived. At the 1961 Young Socialists conference he issued a leaflet saying that the paper was undemocratic: *"A paper for the Young Socialists, not a paper of the Young Socialists."* As if to prove his point, the Labour Party then sacked him. His replacement was the 47 year old Reg Underhill, an archetypal bureaucrat with all the flair and imagination of a brick privy. Having made the break Protz decided to go the whole hog and became the editor of *Keep Left.*

While the Young Guard supporters were most likely to take their pleasures in pubs and folk clubs, the focus for *Keep Left* was the mods and rockers phenomenon. Mods affected a rather smooth appearance, with well trimmed locks and neat attire and spent a lot of time customising their Vespa and Lambretta scooters. Mods drank lager. Rockers, on the other hand, favoured long greasy locks and the motor cyclist's well-worn leather look, giving the appearance of having been marinaded in sump oil. Rockers drank bitter. At Bank Holidays the two groups would meet at a selected seaside resort, to chase and hit one another. The national press loved all of this theatrical, and in truth rather low level, mayhem. *Keep Left*, of course, supported and attracted the rockers. Presumably they thought the rockers were more authentically working class, especially if you think the workers are scruffy and rather thick. While it lasted, some Young Socialists meetings acquired a certain frisson of impending Bank Holiday violence.

On May Day 1962, the official Trade Union-Labour Party rally, which was organised by the London Trades Council, was to be addressed by George Brown. In opposition to this the SLL plumped for its own march, which *Keep Left* supporters were issued with a four line whip to attend. Came the day and the Trades Council rally was not all that well attended, but there was a fair contingent from Young Guard. George Brown, nowadays a forgotten figure but then a leading Labour Party right-winger of some talent, marred perhaps by ill temper that was in its turn exacerbated by his weakness for strong drink, addressed the crowd over the loud speaker system and expressed himself in provocative right wing terms. The response was immediate and noisy and a scuffle developed directly in front of the flatbed truck on which

George was speaking. "*You won't silence me,*" said Brown, "*I have the microphone*". At that very moment the microphone was dragged from his grasp and busted.[1] George was reduced to a spluttering but enraged silence. It was very funny to watch. In Glasgow, at much the same time as Brown was being silenced, Hugh Gaitskell provoked a large scale walk out from his May Day meeting. More fortunate than Brown with his microphone, Gaitskell was able to abuse his departing audience as, 'peanuts'.

George Brown was aware that the perpetrators of this outrage were lefties of some kind and probably Trotskyist and, anyway, they were young and that was crime enough. Keeping his rage warm overnight, he stormed in to Transport House the next day and set in motion the procedure necessary to have this heresy extirpated. The Glasgow Young Socialists Federation was disbanded and an enquiry set up to look into *Young Guard*. In June 1962, *New Advance* appeared with the less than startling news that *Keep Left* was connected to the SLL, which had been proscribed by the Labour Party in 1959. In not very much time *Keep Left* was added to the proscribed list, its three supporters on the Young Socialists National Committee were expelled, as was Roger Protz by his constituency Labour Party. The unfortunate Healyite youth, who were innocently engaged elsewhere in sectarian exclusiveness at the time when the original offence was committed, suffered for the transgressions of others. As Oscar Wilde said about the death of Little Nell, "*It would take a man with a heart of stone not to laugh*".

Proscription did not do much to kerb the *Keep Left* supporters, nor did the promise, extracted by the NEC from *Young Guard* that they would not be factional, hamper either group of supporters from carrying on much as before. Some of the joy was going out of it, however, and by the 1963 conference, *Young Guard* Editor Chris Davison reported: "*Gone was the tremendous enthusiasm and excitement of the first conference. In its place was an air of suspicion, tension, even foreboding.*" The elections to the Young Socialists Na-

---

1. The cover picture of *International Socialism*, no 10, Autumn 1962, depicts the actual smashing of the microphone. I recognise one member of the Revolutionary Socialist League and some six Group members in close proximity and at least one, Pat Sutherland, actually manhandling the microphone.

tional Committee resulted in a clear majority of supporters of the proscribed *Keep Left* with no seats at all for *Young Guard*. This was the result of an electoral pact between *Keep Left* and the right wing which, given their past accusations, was a bit rich. In September 1963, the RSL supporters on *Young Guard* split to start their own youth paper, *Militant*.

Far from the proscriptions mitigating the faction fighting, it became worse and the atmosphere in the Young Socialists branches almost uninhabitable for those of a delicate disposition or a distaste for sectarian irrelevance. At the 1964 Young Socialists conference, held in Brighton, the extra curricular *Keep Left* meeting was addressed by Roger Protz who, in a low key speech, called for left unity.[1] The other speaker was Young Socialists National Committee member for Scotland, John Robertson. He was having nothing to do with anything sissy like left unity. "*Young Guard*," said Robertson, "*is an amalgam of political tendencies… formed to lead a witch hunt to smash* Keep Left… *If you are not 100 per cent with us, you are 100 per cent against us. Get out of our way or we will go over your bodies*". This was an almost perfect piece of Healyism, combining lies, slander, bombast, hypocrisy, sectarianism and the threat of physical violence. Robertson may well have earned extra brownie points for his performance. Shortly afterwards he was expelled from the Young Socialists for selling *Keep Left*. For a short time after the conference Roger Protz helped to produce *Militant*. He found the experience somewhat dispiriting and accepted a request from Gus Macdonald to help with *Young Guard*. For the next ten years he edited IS papers and later took *Socialist Worker* to its highest recorded circulation

The Young Socialists was now on its last legs: a Save the Young Socialists campaign supported by *Tribune*, *Militant* and *Young Guard* was really the last hurrah. In January 1965, *Keep Left* supporters announced that they were the Young Socialists. In consequence the movement now had two distinct organisations – an SLL controlled Young Socialists and a Labour Party Young Socialists (LPYS). At the time it was estimated that the LPYS had fewer than 5,000 members and the Young Socialists about 1,000. The experience had about run its course: all three revolutionary

---

1. It was not known at the time, but Roger had already resigned from the editorship of *Keep Left*.

groups had benefited from the Young Socialists and Reg Underhill felt a lot older, even if he was no wiser.

Coinciding with the beginning of the Young Socialists, the Socialist Review Group made its first serious attempt at producing
a theoretical magazine and *International Socialism* appeared with
Mike Kidron as editor.[1] The new magazine was conceived in an
ecumenical spirit, with a readiness to engage in discussion with
left reformists and social democrats. The editorial board reflected this policy and, in the first few issues, such elements as Ken
Coates, Michael Segal and Henry Collins filled the role of left
reformists – typecasting really. Peter Cadogan, who also served at
this time, is more difficult to place as he represented only himself and expressed no coherent, let alone identifiable, political
position. Alasdair MacIntyre, having rejected Christianity and
then Gerry Healy, presumably as another god that failed, joined
the editorial board and then the Socialist Review Group. Here
was a philosopher who, if he had not yet changed the world, had
changed himself – several times. During his brief stay he made a
contribution of some value, as speaker and writer and, for a time,
he edited *Socialist Review* – and then he went back to Christianity.

John Fairhead was another peripatetic eccentric who came to the
editorial board and membership of the Group. What was unusual
about him was that he had been a full timer for the Revolutionary
Socialist League, serving on the leading body of the Fourth International (United Secretariat). John had a great respect for Trotsky,
although he disapproved of his elegant prose style because he felt
it deflected the reader from the gritty reality of the message. On
one occasion he reviewed a new edition of Trotsky's *Where is Britain Going?* in *International Socialism Journal* (ISJ), and gave it as his
considered opinion that so great were Trotsky's prophetic powers
that even now some of them had yet to come to pass. Now that is
what I call a true believer.

---

1. There had been one issue of an earlier *International Socialism*
journal – a duplicated production with articles by Cliff, Kidron and
Giacometti. The 1959 edition of Cliff's Rosa Luxemburg pamphlet
was labelled 'International Socialism, issue 2 and 3'. For a brief period
after the restart there was confusion in the numbering of issues, but
it was eventually agreed that the first of the 1960 issues was number
one.

Fairhead's political life was extremely strange. He had been a member of the RCP before the RSL was formed. After he left IS, he joined up with the British section of the Latin American Bureau of the Fourth International. This was the brain child of Juan Posadas, a Latin American Trotskyist, who took the view that the nuclear holocaust should be welcomed as the necessary precursor to the triumph of communism. It may be that this was an early and unrecognised example of the species shift of BSE to humans. Readers will probably be surprised to hear that Posadas' British group had as many as five members. They published a paper called *Red Flag* which was much addicted to the five deck headline, such as: 'The Downing Street Strike Opens the Road to the General Strike and the Conquest of Power by the Masses'. The strike in question concerned a handful of building workers who were refurbishing 10 Downing Street at a leisurely pace. Tiring of all this excitement, Fairhead then became a Labour councillor in Paddington. Attending the Labour Party conference he made a contribution attacking the left and, on his return to Paddington, joined the Tory Party. Shortly after this he joined the Monday Club, where he served on its executive committee. Whether in this capacity he advocated pre-emptive nuclear strike to ensure the victory of capitalism is not known. He died a few years ago.

The new magazine was well thought of and added a degree of intellectual respectability to the Group. It gave an arena in which the immediate political concerns could be given a theoretical underpinning and it afforded the editor, Michael Kidron, at the time the outstanding intellectual figure in the group, a suitable vehicle for his talents. Editorial meetings were often enlivened by impromptu discussions that were at least as informative as the printed copy. On other occasions, when the discussion of the appropriate cover picture became protracted, Cliff would suggest there be no picture, just a list of contents. This was guaranteed to drive Robin Fior, the designer, into paroxysms of rage at Cliff's philistinism.

By the beginning of the 1960s, several of the people who had played a part in the 1950s had left the group. Stan Newens and Bernard Dix, having been denounced, resigned in 1959. The following year, James D. Young, Seymour Papert and David Prynn left. However, this was offset by the influx of new members. Peter Sedgwick, who had been a member of the Communist Party until 1956, joined in the late 1950s. Sedgwick was a man of deep socialist conviction, a highly developed sense of humour, an enviable writing style and an eccentricity to match the scale of his talents. His politics were of a libertarian character but not, as some have suggested, anarchist. At that time unorthodoxy was no bar to membership. Ex-Communist Party members Tony and Nessie Young joined, having passed through Healy's Club on the way.

In these days of harsh 'Leninist' orthodoxy, it is hard to recall the atmosphere at the cusp of the Socialist Review Group and the International Socialism Group. The regime was relaxed and activity was directed by persuasion and moral pressure rather than the threat of sanctions. The leading committee was, for most of the time, called the Working Committee because it dealt with correspondence, finance, future activity, branch reports and development plans – all the boring housekeeping that has to be done if the Group was to survive. Politics came up and were developed at meetings of editorial boards and at aggregates. It was also the case that changes in line would, as it were, spring fully fledged from Cliff's left ear. This was less serious than it might seem because there was no insistence on a monolithic line before which the comrades must genuflect in a suitably humble fashion. If Cliff had an advantage, it was that his articles had a better than even chance of appearing once he had written them. On the other hand, almost anyone else had a pretty good chance of saying the contrary and also of having it published.

It was this that was stimulating in the Group; it was open and open minded, there was virtually no need for an internal bulletin because there was nothing to be said, worth saying, that could not be said in the open press. Here was a Marxist organisation that seemed to have learned the lessons of the past. It did not require the mindless uniformity that characterises both Stalinism and graveyards, nor did it suffer from the delusions of grandeur that afflicted orthodox Trotskyism and Baron Munchausen. Unlike these two, it had noticed that the real world gave rise to problems for which received wisdom had no answer, and it attempted to provide a Marxist response to these difficulties. If some of the politics fitted only where they touched, this was of less consequence than that the gaps in them were not hidden and their originators were as likely to point out this fact as anyone else. Most significant of all was the insistence on the central role of the working class as the only agent for social change. For Cliff, at this time, the Group was a 'post Bolshevik' formation, not one that was lurking in a telephone kiosk only waiting to spring out, resplendent in Leninist underpants worn bravely over the trousers. For the young who were coming into politics for the first time it gave intellectual coherence to their spirit of rebellion and its libertarian style gave some feel of what a new life might be like under socialism.

With the 1960s, the quietism of the post-war years started to fade. The long night of Tory power at Westminster was drawing to a close. The working class was beginning to stir again and the chance to test the Groups' theories would be not long delayed.

Important People

*[trade union leaders]... had overnight become important people.
They were visited by MPs by Lords and other well born rabble,
and sympathetic inquiry was suddenly made into the wishes and
needs of the working class.*
Engels

Membership figures are not the be all and end all of revolutionary politics and it is a fact that to increase from 30 to 200, while a useful step and a necessary one on the way to the first million, means no more than that the propaganda can be spread just a little wider. Even so, there was an improvement in the social composition. We have already noted the development of the Group in Glasgow, where an overwhelmingly young and working class base was leavened, if that is the word, by Paul Foot, then carrying out his stint of provincial journalism before qualifying for the big time in Fleet Street. Another recruit of that time was Stuart Christie, who subsequently left IS to become an anarchist. In this new role, he went off to Spain with a suitcase full of anarchist literature and, according to Nicholas Walter, a plan to assassinate Franco. Almost immediately apprehended, he was sentenced to 30 years in gaol. In Glasgow, the IS comrades organised a

protest at his sentence outside the Spanish consulate. Ian Mooney prevailed on his mother to run up a fair replica of a Spanish flag that could be symbolically burned outside the consulate. As the man who provided the flag, Ian insisted on being allowed to set it alight. To ensure a merry blaze he first soaked it with lighter fuel. Unfortunately he was extremely shortsighted and, while he successfully soaked and lit the flag, he also soaked and lit his own boots. Thus what might have been an easily forgotten protest has danced – along with Ian Mooney's flaming boots – into the annals of Glasgow socialist folklore. (Stuart Christie was freed a few years later and was associated with the Angry Brigade, who were responsible for blowing some bits off the Post Office Tower. However, he was found not guilty of this offense.)

Harry McShane was close to the Glasgow IS members. He had been a member of the Social Democratic Federation (SDF) before the First World War, a close comrade of John Maclean and a leading figure in the Communist Party and the National Unemployed Workers Movement before the Second World War and, after he left the Communist Party in 1953 in the wake of the Berlin uprising, a follower of Raya Dunayevskaya. If, in most places, the results were not as promising as Glasgow, there was a heartening trickle of, mostly young, workers joining mainly from the Young Socialists. In the nature of youth, they were inexperienced and had little or no position in their union or place of work. It was, however, a basis with which to work and, for a group that took the long view, an earnest for future developments.

In 1961, *Industrial Worker* was launched as an agitational industrial paper, with the overly-ambitious aim of involving workers in the writing and selling of the paper. The first editor was Karl Dunbar, assisted by the members of the Kilburn branch of the Group, and a few ETU members. The paper could not be described as a runaway success, although it contained some good articles and involved a few non-group people in the writing.

Karl certainly had ambitious plans for the paper with a programme of special supplements on particular industries and unions, none of which came to fruition. As part of his plan to brighten the newspaper he acquired, for a few pounds, the letter press half tone blocks from *Tribune*, who were going over to litho presses. This was a novel departure for the Group because, until then, *Socialist Review* had managed to get by without pictures at all.

Karl Dunbar, quite rightly, took the view that the right picture was worth a thousand words. As if to prove this contention he produced a well used block that, he claimed, showed a black worker and a white worker carrying a trade union banner. Without doubt this picture, suitably captioned, would enhance our article about racism. This, together with the rest of the copy, was sent off to our printer, a Pilsudskist Pole who atoned for his antique equipment, his awful print and execrable politics by being incredibly cheap. In the fullness of time the edition hit the streets. There over our caption, 'Black and white workers unite to fight racism', was a picture of a small black child and a small white child doing a bit of finger painting on a piece of paper pinned to an easel. Our shame at this blunder was only partially mitigated by convincing ourselves that both of these infants were probably resolutely antiracist.

Socialist Review at about this time became something of a poor relation, nurtured only with such energy as was left after *International Socialism*, *Young Guard* and *Industrial Worker* had been produced. The format was reduced to A4, and the articles were inevitably shorter, with the natural consequence that it became less authoritative and less interesting. By 1962, it ceased to exist, unable to find living room in the small space left for it by the other three journals. Having outgrown the actual magazine, the Group had to find another name, and 'International Socialism' was chosen as the replacement.[1]

In line with the junking of *Socialist Review*, there came a revamp of *Industrial Worker*. The title was changed to *Labour Worker* and in line with this it became the main agitational paper of IS, covering all the themes of the group's politics. By 1964 the circulation was in excess of 2,000 and the first *Labour Worker* conference, that same year, attracted about 140 people.

As the newly named IS Group grew, albeit slowly, the more experienced members were actively involved in servicing the work in the Young Socialists. For example, most Young Socialists branches met once a week and part of that meeting was devoted to political

---

1. The next change of name to the International Socialists seems to have occurred in the late 1960s, for what reason I have no idea.

education: anyone with a smattering of knowledge and some ability to impart it, was involved in Young Socialists education. At the same time there were papers to write and to produce, trade union and Labour Party meetings to attend and, on top of all that, IS Group meetings. It was a busy and exhilarating time.

In 1964, for the first time for 13 years, there was a Labour government, born in the white heat of Harold Wilson's rhetoric about 'the white heat of technology'. At the time the Labour slogan was, 'Thirteen wasted years'. Twelve months later, Gus Macdonald coined a new one: 'Fourteen wasted years'. For all that, it is true that many socialists were extremely hopeful of the Wilson administration. Distance had lent a certain roseate enchantment to the post-war Attlee government and Wilson was thought to have been on the left of that administration. Certainly, in the beginning, Wilson had a talent for the rolling phrase and the telling sound bite that suggested, without actually promising anything, that great things were in the offing. In practice it had far fewer ideas and was significantly less radical than Labour in 1945.

Along with every other post-war government it planned to solve British capitalism's problems at the expense of the working class, this time through the medium of incomes policy. No matter how you dress it up as 'socialist planning', incomes policy is not intended to even out incomes – indeed, it invariably hits those on the lowest incomes hardest – but to give British capital the edge by giving it a bigger slice of the cake. It is a policy that puts the emphasis on national discussions, with the TUC General Council wearing threadbare the carpets in the corridors of power. The powerful magnates of labour, together with captains of industry and Labour ministers, were negotiating how big the cake should be and how small could they make the workers' slice. For industries where national bargaining was the norm the effect was almost immediate; for those industries where local bargaining by rank and file representatives set a large chunk of pay above the national wage, the employers' hands were strengthened. It was a recipe for disillusion, at least amongst those who started off with any illusions. IS had none.

In January 1966, the stewards at ENV took the initiative in calling a meeting to set up a Shop Stewards' Defence Committee (SSDC) to defend shop floor organisation and develop the struggle against incomes policy through rank and file committees around the country. The meeting, of about 200 people from various factories and committees, was addressed by Reg Birch, a leading, but dissident, CPer, Jim Hiles, a building worker, and three IS members (Geoff Carlsson, Geoff Mitchell, both stewards at ENV, and Jim Higgins). The plan was an ambitious one and, in the event, it turned out to be over-ambitious.

A number of meetings were held in different parts of the country but, at the time, there was insufficient base to support a continuing organisation. The SSDC did issue, under its imprint, the pamphlet *Incomes Policy, Legislation and Shop Stewards* by Tony Cliff and Colin Barker. It was an excellent pamphlet, far better than anything else on the subject produced either before or since. It explained why British capitalism needed incomes policy, how it worked and how to fight it. The introduction was written by Reg Birch. It was, if not a mass sale item, extremely popular and sold in thousands, most importantly to shop stewards' committees and to trade union branches.

The growing disenchantment with Labour meant that there was a small but growing audience for IS politics. Here were some promising areas in industry which represented, in IS terms, a considerable advance. There were members in ASTMS, the POEU, TGWU, the ETU and the AEU.

Jewel in the crown was the ENV factory in Acton, North London, an engineering works making pre-selector gearboxes. (The name derived from the French, 'En V', a reference to the cylinder layout of the aero engines it made during World War I.) The story of ENV is both interesting and instructive, it shows the importance of day to day leadership at rank and file level; it also indicates how serious political militants can, through patient and sensitive work, develop policies that increase the solidarity and consciousness of the workers. It also indicates with brutal clarity that, in the final analysis, there are definite and well defined limits to trade union struggles.

It is worthwhile, perhaps, to detail some of the history of what was certainly influential in forming SR/IS politics; an experience that informed much of the industrial strategy.[1]

---

1. This account is taken from 'The ENV Strike', *Socialist Review*, Jan/Feb 1952 and 'The Lessons of the ENV Strike', *Socialist Review*, April/May

In the 1930s, the factory had been badly organised and wages and conditions were poor, comparing unfavourably with other local factories. In the aftermath of the war, however, the shortage of skilled labour, allied to the organising ability of the stewards, meant that rates were as good as, if not better than, those generally paid in North London. It was a factory where the day to day issues of work and the rank and file response were the currency of conversation. From the most militant to the most moderate there was a feeling that the price of good conditions was eternal vigilance; each section policed its agreements rigorously. Naturally enough, the employers were not enchanted by this state of affairs and were continuously attempting to steal a march by the introduction of new machines and practices.

An employer's cost-cutting strategy often has the effect of over-exciting the ambitious, but cerebrally challenged, line supervision, and at ENV they had just such a foreman. Taking his lead from the disastrous course pursued by Charles I, he enunciated a doctrine of the divine right of foremen. If anyone on his section had a grievance his decision, so far as he was concerned, was final, despite the fact that procedures were in place to take matters further up the management tree. Inevitably, this behaviour formed the subject of a meeting between the convenor and the management. During the course of this meeting the offending foreman physically menaced, swore at and threatened the convenor Bill McLoughlin. All of this was reported to a mass meeting of the workers and a decision was taken to strike until the foreman was sacked.

The strike lasted for thirteen weeks and was hard fought, with the stewards organising financial support all over Britain – they collected a total of £14,000 which was a considerable sum at the time. The Transport and General never made the strike official and attempted to sow discord between T&G and AEU members. Eventually, the AEU executive agreed to a Court of Inquiry, whose findings would be binding on both parties. It was to be under the chairmanship of Professor Jack, an academic and a well known chairman of allegedly impartial inquiries. His findings,

---

1952, both by Geoff Carlsson, and 'A Working Class Defeat: The ENV Story', in *International Socialism* #31, by Joyce Rosser and Colin Barker. This text has also been checked by Geoff Carlsson.

which were meant to appear Solomon-like, were in fact about as partial as you could get. The foreman was to be moved to less sensitive work but McLoughlin was to be removed from his convenorship. The AEU Executive member Scott – like McLoughlin a Communist Party member – urged the acceptance of Jack's ruling and, with only Geoff Carlsson's lone opposition, the stewards' committee reluctantly accepted.

Here was a dispute that challenged the employer's traditional prerogatives of hire and fire and fought for three months for this principle. In the process the TGWU had been opposed and the AEU, despite the fact that the North London District was firmly under the control of the Communist Party, shuffled off the dispute to a quasi judicial tribunal. Interestingly enough the greatest financial support did not come from Communist Party strongholds, such as Ford Dagenham (£25) or Austin Longbridge (£50) where, in those days, there were literally tens of thousands of workers. It was a strike with a result that would normally be expected to break the union organisation at the factory. That it did not was a function of the way that the workers were involved regularly in discussions and decisions about the way forward.

It was also due, in large measure, to some excellent work by two young revolutionaries: Sid Wise and Geoff Carlsson. Both of them had been members of the Revolutionary Communist Party, Wise subsequently joining Healy's organisation and Geoff Carlsson to help found the Socialist Review Group. Neither of them were radical birds of passage, serving a little industrial time that would spice up their reminiscences in the Senior Common Room. Nor were they intent on a career as full time union bureaucrats. Starting in the mid-1950s, first Wise and then Carlsson was the convener. As a matter of principle they insisted on a full meeting of the workers once a week at which they discussed matters of immediate and of long term interest. They worked out a programme of demands to combat redundancy.

The levee *en masse*, far from proving a cumbersome device, actually defined and refined significant areas of policy. With informed discussion a spirit of support for the programme was powerfully engendered. As a result of this conspicuous solidarity, ENV had a number of trailblazing agreements, ones that could only be raised, never mind achieved, by workers convinced of their case. Thus they had a policy of no overtime and if only one individual worker just one hour's overtime then the entire factory was guaranteed three months without redundancy. Time and motion study was banned by the workers and nobody anxious to maintain production was seen with a stop watch.

Just before Christmas 1957, the management informed the convenor, Geoff Carlsson, that there would have to be a ten per cent redundancy. At the mass meeting, the workers were adamant that the programme for redundancies should be followed. When Carlsson informed the manager that they would not accept redundancy, the managers handed over the running of production to the shop stewards, mistakenly assuming that they would cave in at this daunting prospect.

Having accepted the responsibility, the workers had to organise a four and a half day week, transferring men to different sections where necessary. The process was not without problems and a deal of seat of the pants fine tuning was required, but for nine months the factory stayed united. At the end of 1958 an upturn in trade made the continuation of the policy unnecessary. For nearly a year the workers organised the disposition of labour within the factory and, effectively, the production process. Obviously, there is no such thing as socialism in one factory, but this has all the hallmarks of workers' control. Even when it was finished, the self confidence acquired during that time made possible further advances. Long before it became at all common in engineering, women workers had equal pay at ENV, wages were the highest in the district and turnover of labour was minimal.

Not only were conditions good at ENV, but they had a highly commendable record of solidarity with other workers on strike. In 1963, for example a strike of mainly black workers started in the Southall factory, Marriott's. A levy of one shilling a head was collected at ENV for 30 weeks collecting £1,717, or 18 per cent of the total collected nationally.

In 1962 the American firm of Eaton, Yale and Towne bought ENV. This was a tough management who intended to break the power of the workers and were prepared to run through any number of managers in pursuit of this objective. Emerson's, a large work study company, were introduced to the factory, but nobody would cooperate with them, so they sat around for some months and then went away. Productivity bargaining was introduced on the promise of no redundancy. The packers, for example, agreed to a reduction from 16 to 12 men and to help with loading the lorries, in return for increased pay. In fact, there were only 12 packers in the first place and they had always helped load the trucks. Similarly the fork-lift truck drivers accepted one shilling an hour to 'become mobile'. That is, to actually carry pallets into, as well as from, their own section. With a management like that, who needed a compass to find their own backside, it really would have been sensible for Eaton, Yale and Towne to permanently hand over the organisation of the factory to the workers.

Sadly, it is in the nature of industrial life that, eventually, all good things come to an end and ENV was no exception. The management decided that, despite ever more far fetched stratagems, there was no way of establishing a rift between the stewards and the workforce, and it was necessary to push things to the limit. In August 1966 they announced a phased shutdown of the factory. For the first time there was uncertainty amongst the workers, an uncertainty that also existed in the shop stewards' committee. Were the management serious, or was it yet another stratagem to obtain concessions? The convener, Geoff Mitchell and the chairman, Geoff Carlsson, believed that the management was bluffing and that it should be challenged by strike action. Unfortunately, a majority of the stewards' committee and the workforce did not agree with them. Management's well established, but untruthful, rumour was that any strikers would be guilty of industrial misconduct and thus lose redundancy pay, which for a stable and long standing workforce such as ENV's was substantial. Carlsson and Mitchell and several hundred workers were sacked over the next few months. ENV stayed open a little longer but the company never managed to assert full management prerogatives and not long after it closed its gates for the last time.

Over his years in the factory, Geoff Carlsson, like any sensible revolutionary worker, found allies where he could. He worked with Communist Party members, with the Club member Sid Wise and with anyone else who agreed on the need to strengthen the organisation and defend and extend the workers' interests, but he did not spend his time castigating 'Stalinists' or attacking Sid Wise for thinking Russia a 'workers' state'. He sold *Socialist Review* and, when appropriate, argued his politics and in 1959 he ran for President of the AEU. Although he had no chance of election, the AEU rules allowed that each candidate was entitled to an election address circulated at the Union's expense. In his address he condemned wage freeze, class collaboration and sell out by right wing Labour and trade union leaders. While commending some Communist Party militants, he pointed to their antics in Eastern Europe and their anti-working class measures at home. When the votes were counted, the right-winger, Carron, had 57,127 votes, Reg Birch, the Communist Party candidate, had 19,799 and Geoff had 5,615. A very creditable performance for someone with no electoral machine.

At ENV recruitment to the IS Group was slow. For some years the only recruit was Les Bennett, but when the breakthrough did come in the mid 1960s it was, superficially, spectacular. Over a number of months a series of discussion classes were held in the Harlesden Labour Club, generally led by Cliff but also by Jim Higgins and Geoff Carlsson, on and around the main themes of IS politics and contemporary issues. After some time, an ENV IS branch was formed with 12 members. Some were young and of no previous affiliation but several were ex-CP members of some years standing – Geoff Mitchell, John Hogan and Danny Flynn among them. This resulted in an increase in *Labour Worker* sales in the factory and to a certain hostility from Communist Party members in the district, although this was mitigated by the fact that Reg Birch, a long time leading Communist Party member in the AEU, was conducting a struggle against the party that would lead to him founding one of the short lived Maoist groups. In the fight against the management the existence of the IS branch in the factory was not noticeably more effective than its members were as individual militants. It was too recent an entity to have raised any general consciousness in the factory and its real strength would have been as an integral part of a nationwide network of IS factory branches. There were no other factory branches and, paraphrasing the old saw about socialism, there is no such thing as a branch network in one factory.

The cliche runs that even the defeats and failures experienced in the struggle are valuable if they are analysed properly. And, funnily enough, it is true. The experience of one of the most advanced and militant factories in the car industry could not help but provide valuable lessons. Even the inability to develop the Shop Stewards' Defence Committee was of value, in that it indicated very clearly that the transfer of experience takes time, continuing effort, patience and resources. Revolutionaries are very good at working hard, some put in heroic stints at the agitation-face. On time, they seldom have enough of it, are invariably racing against it and are frequently tempted to take a short cut, a temptation they are often unable to resist. So far as resources are concerned, they never, ever have enough of them. We can, however, as Trotsky enjoined us, 'Learn to Think', and that is what IS set out to do. To try and learn from the experience of the small but encouraging growth of the Group in general and its ability to attract a few experienced militants.

Without bending any sticks to the point of wood fatigue, it was necessary to attempt to provide the sort of analysis and activity that would attract and involve advanced workers. It had to be a policy that offered the perspective of working to build in the workshop and the unions at rank and file level, work that would generalise the struggle and the experience of the most advanced factories and workshops and spread it into less developed areas. In a word, it was a perspective, no matter how long term, of developing trade union demands into class demands. It was building the bridge to the revolutionary party.

The Outdated Cosmetics of Youth

Rise like lions after slumber
In unvanquishable number-
Shake your chains to earth like dew
Which in sleep had fallen on you-
Ye are many – they are few
Percy Bysshe Shelley, *The Mask of Anarchy*

For Marxists, as for any other kind of optimist, current in-ability to perform a task does not imply that one will always be unable to perform, nor that one should not look into how things might be done if circumstances became more favourable.

Whatever the value of Cliff's state capitalist theory, what it did do was to focus on the question of workers' control over the abstraction of property forms, the thesis on the 'changing locus of reformism', again set the working class into the centre of analysis. The questions that were raised by the Labour government's dedi-cation to incomes policy and strike breaking at home (and grovel-ling support for America's war in Vietnam), were more and more concerned with the value of an entry tactic that did nothing for recruitment and obscured the perspectives for socialism.

An entry tactic can find its justification in a perspective that sees future mass radicalisation that will find first expression in a great influx of workers to the Labour Party. This was effectively the thesis of all the Trotskyist groups in the early 1950s. It was predicated on general capitalist crisis sooner or later (in Healy's case almost immediately and for the others a bit later). In this sce-nario the revolutionary forces in the Labour Party would be able to place themselves at the head of this new revolutionary force. This was the view held most consistently by Ted Grant and the Militant Tendency, for some 40 years, then, with a piece of stick bending that must have made Cliff sick with envy, Peter Taafe, Grant's right hand man, took the overwhelming majority of the Tendency out of the Labour Party, leaving poor Ted with a small entrist rump.[1]

For the Group, in the first years of its existence, the Labour Party was the milieu in which a tiny group could just about survive. The Young Socialists provided an invaluable young cadre, but by 1965 it was virtually moribund. As a life support system for ailing revolutionary groups, the Labour Party began to lose its charms when it became possible to exist outside. Not that the Labour Party ever did more than keep the patient alive and it always had the air of Mother Theresa's hospice for the terminally sick, rather than the plush lined care of the London Clinic. With a few hundred members it was possible to live and grow, albeit modestly, in the fragments of the movement that existed in the mid 1960s.

There was no specific decision to leave the Labour Party, rather a gradual realisation that there was more important work to be done elsewhere. For IS, at least, it was a practical rather than a principled question and one day we were no longer in the Labour Party. No one gave thanks, or a sigh of relief, because it really did not matter that much. The Group worked on the fringes of the growing militancy in the factories and workshops: in the Roberts Arundel strike, in Stockport, at Myton's building site in the Barbican, where an IS member, the late Frank Campbell, was one of the stewards; at Pilkingtons and many more isolated but important strikes. The work was difficult and unglamorous, often no more than manning a picket line but the comrades were becoming known in their localities and were also learning something about working class action. The strikes were reported in *Labour Worker*, which grew, in size and professionalism under the editorship of Roger Protz.

The idea of working in the fragments meant that one felt that despite small resources we could have some positive effect on the day to day struggles, if only a small one. I can recall driving along a road near Harrow and noticing some Asian workers setting up a picket line outside a small factory called Injection Mouldings. There were about 50 workers and, despite the fact that they were paid a pittance, after sending money home and keeping them-

---

1. NB, this is not intended as a sexist remark.

selves, they had saved enough to finance a short strike. Although they had joined the AEU, they had not been in long enough to qualify for strike pay. A majority of them spoke little or no English, but their steward, a tough and very bright young chap, (who was, incidentally, rather a good cricketer) was eloquent in English and Urdu. I stopped and introduced myself and we discussed how to organise the picket and to avoid trouble with the police. We organised several support meetings, at one of which Nigel Harris spoke well, and John Deason spent a fair amount of time in discussion with them and helping both on and off the picket line. The strike, which went on for several weeks, was eventually successful in securing a significant increase in the hourly rate. Several of the strikers joined the group for a short while, but that was more from gratitude for solidarity than political agreement and IS did not have the resources in people or organisation to secure their integration into revolutionary politics.

The experiences throughout this period confirmed that IS's theoretical appreciation of the key nature of the rank and file was turning out to be a good guide to revolutionary practice. It also confirmed that trade unionism, even of the most militant kind, cannot, of itself, represent a mortal threat to the system. No matter how long drawn out or bitter a strike might be at the end of it, win lose or draw, both sides have got to get up, dust themselves down and coexist, until the next time. Trade unions may recruit capitalism's gravediggers, but capitalism also provides the raison d'etre for the trade union's existence and, almost as important, an enhanced lifestyle for officials. In this contradiction is the reason for the bureaucracy's betrayals and the key to the way rank and file bodies can adapt and transcend the limitations of trade unions.

It was obvious that any strategy the revolutionary left developed in the 1960s and 1970s would have to come to terms with the need for rank and file organisation and how to aid its construction. The obvious course was to examine the history of this movement in Britain.

Very little seems to be known, today, about the movement before the First World War. The bare bones of the shop stewards' movement was created in the craft unions' need to collect subscriptions and to ensure that there was no dilution of craft status, but quite soon developed to carry out the members' needs where the union machine could not or would not oblige. The upsurge of general unionism from the 1880s, showed the potential strength but more febrile character of mass trade unionism. The Labour Representation Committee was in the first instance a form of trade union lobby, from the inside, prepared to support any candidate willing to pursue the unions' parliamentary programme.

In the first decade of the 20th century, British capitalism developed and became infinitely more wealthy than ever before. Working class living standards had not kept pace and parliamentary reform was grudging and inadequate, despite the fact that British trade unions had existed longer and organised more workers, both in numbers and as a proportion of the whole, than anywhere else in the world. The time was ripe for the introduction of a new idea for working class advance. French syndicalism and American industrial unionism found a ready response among militant British trade unionists. Tom Mann and Guy Bowman formed the Industrial Syndicalist Education League in 1910. The year before a strike occurred at Ruskin College involving students fed up with the sterile orthodoxy of official policy, which led to the founding of the Plebs League – National Council of Labour Colleges (this last was the organisation that, in the 1950s, provided a kind of outdoor relief to tired Trotskyists). James Connolly came back from America, enthused by the ideas of Daniel DeLeon on industrial unionism and Marxism, if not by DeLeon's atheism, and helped form the Socialist Labour Party. A new generation of militants was influenced by the movement that was forcefully asserting the central role of the rank and file and the need for workers' control. A.J. Cook, Richard Coppock, A.A. Purcell and Noah Ablett were future trade union leaders whose ideas were formed in this period. Men, such as J.T. Murphy, Willie Gallagher, Tom Bell and Arthur McManus rallied to the De Leonite message and were later to form an important part of the leadership of the Communist Party of Great Britain.

For all the seeming spontaneity of syndicalism, it displayed a rather formal character in practice. Mass action was built into the theory but without tactical flexibility. The general strike, or 'great national holiday' in anarchist parlance, was a possible outcome from each and every limited action. The mass strike then transcends its limited trade union character and challenges directly for power. This ability to see the mighty ocean in a drop of water may be a useful insight, but you should not try to float anything with a serious displacement in a glass of water. In practice, of course, while the wider reaches of syndicalist theory kept the devotees' enthusiasm warm, the practical demands for union amalgamation into industrial unions achieved a wider response. Indeed, a number of trade unions that were formed in the early 1920s, the UPW, the TGWU and the AEU, adopted constitutions that were based on industrial union principles and enshrined the goal of workers' control. Another demand for union alliances across industries met its response in the Triple Alliance of miners, railwaymen and transport workers. In 1921, it was called 'the Cripple Alliance' after the NUR and Transport Federation sold out the miners.

All of this was given much greater impetus by the development of the Shop Stewards and Workers' Committee Movement (SS-WCM) in the First World War. Despite arrests, deportations and conscription, a frequently successful series of struggles were conducted on rents, dilution, conditions and pay. Inevitably they were local actions, that would spread no further than the range of the cry of pain that set them in motion. The organisational forms of that time, despite defeats and retreats, closures and downsizing, still exist to this day and the inability of the trade union machine to fully incorporate them means that even in the worst periods of reaction the movement has been saved from the excesses of trade union experience abroad. Not only that, it is also the earnest of hope for the future.

The yawning gap in syndicalist theory seemed to be decisively closed by the Russian Revolution. For the first time in history the workers had actually taken and kept power. The enthusiasm for this event conferred immense prestige on the Bolsheviks and imbued their every suggestion with significance and conviction. In 1919 the Communist International was formed as a world party

How d'you spell "Incomes Policy," Mum?

"W, A, G, E, F, R,......"

of socialist revolution and, in September 1920, the Red International of Labour Unions (Profintern) was announced to direct union struggles into a revolutionary direction. Its *Programme of Action* called for: strikes, demonstrations, factory occupations, street actions, armed manifestations and insurrection. The trade union policy for amalgamation and industrial unions, allied to the implicit aim to turn every action into offensive class action, was an indication that RILU was almost as influenced by syndicalism as Tom Mann had been. This time, however, the policy came with all the prestige of the Russian Revolution behind it.

In Britain the SSWCM agreed to the need for an unofficial industrial movement under the leadership of the Communist Party of Great Britain. Unfortunately, the *Programme of Action*, with its implicit assumption of imminent revolutionary struggle, appeared just at the time when the militant wave was ebbing. In 1921 the miners, abandoned by their partners in the Triple Alliance, fought for 13 weeks and were virtually starved back to work, suffering a 34 per cent wage cut. Building workers, engineering workers and dockers were separately taken on and separately defeated. By the end of 1922 more than six million workers had suffered a cut of at least eight shillings a week, this at a time when £2.10s was a good wage. In such circumstances, there was less chance of building a rank and file movement than an unemployed workers' movement and that is what they did. It was thus not until 1924 that the inaugural conference of the Minority Movement was held, although there already existed Minority Movements in several industries most powerfully in mining. At the first conference, about a quarter of a million workers were represented; a year later the total was almost a million. In factories and unions up and down the country, bulletins and news sheets publicised the Minority Movement and its programme of militant demands. At the 1925 TUC, Harry Pollitt, secretary of the National Minority Movement, seconded a Garment Workers resolution that called for shop floor organisation, opposition to capitalist co-partnership schemes and for the overthrow of capitalism. It was carried by a two to one majority.

That was the high point of the movement and the story of the General Strike, the Anglo Russian Committee, the Communist Party and the TUC lefts is too long for this book. Suffice it to say that the Minority Movement's eventual decline into dual unionism and third period idiocy was a direct result of the policies of 1926. The Minority Movement was a failure but it nevertheless had some useful lessons – lessons that are at the heart of the discussions about the nature of the party and the class and their relationship one to another.

The workers, under capitalism, spontaneously form trade unions; this we know from Karl Kautsky – ably seconded by Lenin in *What is to be Done?*. Actually you do not need either of these authorities, it is demonstrably the case. It is also the case that workers, given their trade union proves ineffective, will develop their own democratic forms of organisation to aid their struggles. It is furthermore the case that many workers, given the experience of both conventional and rank and file organisation, may find that neither form meets their needs. They will attempt to achieve these reforms through parliament with a Labour Party or some political action committee.

All of these forms of struggle are, by definition, conducted within a capitalist system. Obviously these are not exclusive categories, they interact all the time, but in the final analysis there is no resolution to the workers' struggles so long as capitalism continues to exist. The reforms last as long as the workers have the strength to make them stick. Let the relation of forces turn to the bosses' advantage and they will be back making the most of their chances. In addition, the best reward invariably comes from mass involvement under democratic control. Conventional trade union negotiations, with or without strike action, provides less and is additionally subjected to the caste interest of the bureaucracy.

So far as parliamentary reformism is concerned, that which makes trade union forms of struggle unproductive ensures that there is nothing much doing from legislation. No more than a cursory glance at what New Labour has in store for us in the way of goodies will indicate the truth of this point. Under these circumstances a small but growing layer of militants look for and become receptive to, especially when engaged in a struggle, a thoroughgoing socialist analysis. Through a socialist organisation it becomes possible to connect up militants who would otherwise remain isolated. It is possible to build up a vast store of information from discussion with these militants to develop with them a programme of advance that is both militant trade unionism and transitional politics. There are few things more rewarding on which a group's meagre resources, in money and manpower, can be expended than work with rank and file militants. If a revolutionary organisation professes to have no interest separate from that of the advanced workers, it is a good idea for it to behave as if it believes what it professes.

The popular pamphlet, *Incomes Policy, Shop Stewards and Legislation*, was an attempt to emphasise the class interest that was fundamentally different from the 'national interest' displayed in Labour policy and the plethora of government, trade union and employer committees that presumed to regulate the workers' rights. The next pamphlet on productivity bargaining, *The Employers' Offensive*, was based on more actual discussion with workers than the earlier pamphlet. It attempted to develop an aggressive strategy for opposition to the employers' latest stratagem through a programme with a sliding scale of demands that would prove useful whatever the situation faced by the workers. In its immediacy it went a step further than the *Incomes Policy* pamphlet because it contained transitional demands that put pressure on both the employers and the unions within the framework of existing struggles. It was an exercise in agitation rather than generalised propaganda and marked a modest but significant advance for IS. For all that it broke new ground, the productivity pamphlet was published under a cloud that arose from Cliff's inability to learn from, or acknowledge the contributions of others he considered to be political competitors. This fault, grievous enough in itself, began to look chronic when it seemed to descend to plagiarism. In this case it was Ken Coates and the Institute of Workers Control. According to Ken Coates, large bits of it were taken complete and unacknowledged from an internal publication of the Institute of Workers' Control written by Coates and Tony Topham. As if to add insult to plagiarism, at the same time Coates was being denounced for 'left reformism' and other heinous crimes. Coates continues the story:

> I wrote what I thought was quite an amusing letter to Cliff. It certainly seemed to get under his skin and brought an abject Cliff up to Nottingham, grovelling, begging that we should not print it. He said that the plagiarism was not his fault, and that a committee

had written the book, and that the copying out had been done by
Colin Barker... apparently it was all Barker's fault. I do not mind
my revisionism being denounced, that is splendid. It is the duplic-
ity that bothers me. If I am good enough to copy out, I am good
enough to acknowledge... I did withdraw the letter in deference to
Cliff's nonexistent reputation.[1]

Ken Coates' story rings true, and Cliff's tale that the book was a
committee product over which he had no final control is unalloyed
rubbish. In any collaboration between Cliff and Colin Barker there
is no question that Cliff would be the senior partner exercising a
total *droite de seigneur* over the final text and, as a matter of fact,
over Colin Barker if he got at all uppity.[2]

What was abundantly clear was that, given the strength of IS
and the divisions on the left, the IS Group did not have the resources to carry out these formidable but necessary tasks. It was
also becoming clear that there were no other organisations that
were even thinking on the right lines. The pressure to come to
terms with what the group was and what we wanted it to be was
becoming urgent. It was in these circumstances that ill thought
out and far reaching decisions were taken. It seemed that the
needs of the hour called for dramatic growth that transcended
the steady but slow recruitment experienced so far. Unity of the
left forces could bring in the numbers if nothing else. At the same
time the groups closest to us were dedicated to a tradition that
rejoiced in the trappings of Bolshevism. Like some middle aged di-
vorcée seeking a fresh partner, IS ponced itself up in the outdated
cosmetics of its youth.

---

1. Ken Coates, *Workers' Liberty*, #18, Feb 1995
2. For further evidence of Cliff's carelessness with texts, see the
Appendix, 'Cliff on Luxemburg', p. 207.

Old Factions

We cannot revive old factions
We cannot restore old policies
Or follow an antique drum
T.S. Eliot, *Gerontion*

Throughout the latter half of the 1960s, there were not just the fragmented but developing struggles in industry, there was also CND, the Vietnam Solidarity Committee (VSC) and the smaller Campaign Against Racial Discrimination (CARD): in all of these IS played a part. These were campaigns that mobilised the enthusiasm and the idealism of the best of a generation, not least those most idealistic and enthusiastic people, the students. What was particularly heartening was the fact that, by 1967, the Viet Cong were actually on the advance. American imperialism was getting the sort of bloody nose that Russian imperialism would subsequently suffer in Afghanistan. The year 1968 contained enough excitement and activity to stretch the resources of a mass party, never mind a group of about 500 members. Abroad, there was the Tet offensive, the May events in France, Dubcek's 'Velvet Revolution' in

Ho Chi Minh Make revolution. in your own country.

Were Leeds Vietnam Solidanty Campaign What have you done with Ta Thu Thau?

Czechoslovakia and at home Enoch Powell's racist speech, with dockers marching in his support. In October there was the tremendous VSC demonstration, with more than 100,000 on the street. On top of all that there were occupations and sit-ins at campuses throughout Britain. IS already had a number of student members and was thus willy-nilly involved in their struggles. This was the British end of a Europe wide student revolt that reflected a number of sociological changes in the universities in response to the changing requirements of capitalism. These students did not conform to the standard characterisation as over-privileged, flannelled fools anxious to drive blackleg trains in the general strike, nor of aesthetes in the Apostles getting ready to do freelance work for the KGB. That was a thing of the past. The Stalinists no longer had much pull and the universities housed a much higher proportion of working class people than any revolutionary group could boast. The universities were no longer required to produce the administrators of a dead empire, or staff the higher reaches of the civil service and the City. Graduates were needed in large numbers to meet the needs of a much expanded and more complicated capitalist machine. Student actions were the strike and the sit-in, the same as militant trade unionists. If they added a certain theatricality, that was just a function of youth and added to the entertainment value.

This was the first student generation to be genuinely influenced by revolutionary ideas and a minority took to them with relish. Of those that did join revolutionary organisations, a majority joined IS, with the International Marxist Group (IMG) next and the rest also ran. Of course most students did not join and of those that did many have now moved on, but the renegacy rate has been remarkably low. The 1968 levy was in large measure responsible for the radicalisation of the white collar trade unions in the 1970s. It is also a fact that the media is a lot less staid and reactionary than it would have been without the creative input of the people of '68. Among those who joined IS at this time were, Christopher Hitchens, James Fenton, Martin Shaw, Ruth Nelson and, one of the best organisers IS ever had, Steve Jefferys.

The May events in France added immeasurably to the excitement of the time. Cliff and Ian Birchall, in their pamphlet, seemed to be saying that all that was missing from the French scene for the revolution to succeed was a Bolshevik party. In fact, France like most other countries in the West had its quota of pretenders to the title of 'Bolshevik saviour' but the fact that they did not measure up to the pukka thing actually begged a few questions as to why not? Questions to which, unfortunately, Cliff and Birchall did not address themselves.

In this rather overheated atmosphere, especially shocked by the dockers support of Powell, Cliff successfully urged for a unity of the left campaign against the urgent menace of fascism. The 'Vacuum on the Left', which is how Cliff characterised the period, could not disguise the fact that we were returning to the old Trotskyist formulation: 'the crisis of the working class is the crisis of leadership'. The unity campaign inevitably needed to reflect some coming together of the likely fusees. The political basis for unity, IS suggested, was:

1. Opposition to all ruling class organisations and policies.

2. For workers' control over production and a workers' state.

3. Uncompromising opposition to all forms of racialism and to all immigration controls.

Clearly the basis for unity was broad enough to encompass anyone to the left of the Communist Party, who would probably jib at the 'workers' control' section. Although all the left groups were written to, in reality this meant the International Marxist Group (IMG).[1] The Revolutionary Socialist League (RSL) was immured

in the Labour Party, the Socialist Labour League (SLL) was implacably hostile and Solidarity was busy trying to poach the IS's own

1. The International Marxist Group, originated in a split from the RSL and subsequently became the British section of the USFI.

left wing. The IMG were heavily engaged in student work, the USFI guru, Mandel, was currently rewriting Marxism to accommodate the 'foci' and 'Red Bases' in the colleges, and IS and IMG members were working well together. In the Vietnam Solidarity Committee, the IMG provided the full time workers and IS a lot of the on the ground organising for demonstrations. The IMG, however, was not playing; it was less than half the size of IS, had been formed for only two years and had just recently been appointed the British franchise holder by the United Secretariat of the Fourth International. After all, who wants to be a bit more effective in Britain when you can strut about in a T-shirt with the legend, 'World Party of Bolshevism' across the bosom. A unity campaign that was turning out to be a failure, was turned, at the last minute, into a total disaster. Sean Matgamna's Workers' Fight group, said 'yes'. Here was a tiny group with a handful of members in Manchester and a scattering in a couple of other places. They had been expelled from Healy's group, but there is nothing wrong with that; so had Cliff and, come to think of it, so had I. The story goes that Sean, who is hard of hearing, was forced, by Healy, to remove his deaf aid at the expulsion hearing, for fear it might be one of those Dick Tracy, two way radio, deaf aids. As if to prove that this expulsion was not a fluke, Sean and his comrades joined the RSL, only to find that they were up for expulsion once more. They let Sean keep his deaf aid, but they expelled him just the same. Now here he was signing up for IS. Having first established friendly relationships with Colin Barker, who lived in Manchester, Sean met up with Cliff and the two of them, without recourse to anyone else, arranged for the Workers' Fight to enter IS. The admission of Workers' Fight was essentially to acquire an ally in the move to democratic centralism and to help Colin Barker in Manchester, where the majority of the branch leaned to libertarianism. In the event it helped neither of these objectives but Matgamna was able to help himself to a few members.

It was not democratic centralism; it was not democratic and it certainly cast doubt on the effectiveness of Cliff's intuitive nose. The first the IS Group at large knew was that we had acquired a fully fledged faction, now performing under the banner of the 'Trotskyist Tendency' (TT). Cliff would have liked to remove the Trotksyist Tendency with all the negligent ease that he let them in.

Unfortunately, he had just enshrined the rights of factions in his version of democratic centralism and his unity proposals raised no barrier to thinking Russia was a 'workers' state', a characterisation that Sean adhered to with great fidelity for some years, until in the 1980s he suddenly succumbed to the dusty charms of bureaucratic collectivism. This is, at first sight, an unlikely conversion considering that bureaucratic collectivism had been around for over 40 years, without any response from Sean. Indeed, Sean's great idol at the time was James P. Cannon, probably the most adamant opponent of bureaucratic collectivism and its main theorist Max Shachtman. There are those, of an uncharitable disposition perhaps, who take the view that Sean is indulging here in a bit of consumer socialism. There are all manner of workers' statists about, and lots of Cliff state capitalists, but apart from a few ageing Shachtmanites in the States, bureaucratic collectivists are as rare as bacon butties at a bar mitzvah.

The next three years with the Trotskyist Tendency were not at all like that great university of life, where the work may be hard but the experience has lots of educational value. There was much posturing, a deal of plotting and neither side comes out of it with much credit, although Workers' Fight came out of it with rather more members than when they entered, which is as well for them because they had run out of groups to join and must needs operate independently. We will meet them again later in this narrative.

It was about this time that Duncan Hallas, who was teaching in Wandsworth, rejoined the group. His 14 year long sabbatical might never have happened he settled in so well and almost immediately became part of the leadership of IS. With his wide trade union and even wider political experience he gave added weight to the Political Committee's deliberations, at a period when such qualities were in particular demand. If he was a strong advocate of group theory and politics he was not always so enchanted by Cliff's slapdash methods and inability to operate as part of a collective. Several of us saw this as an excellent additional qualification for his presence on the leading committee. At the end of the day he may have proved a weaker reed than one supposed, but in the meanwhile if you wanted to know something arcane, like the real reason for the dispute between Craipeau and Bleibtreu in the French section of the Fourth International in 1946, Duncan was the man to tell you in minute detail. Not only what were the stated, but also the real reasons for the dispute.

Until 1968, the Group had been modest in self assessment and patiently ready for the long haul. Now a number of events were coming together which seemed to indicate that mass, and potentially revolutionary, actions were possible in the not too distant future. With the benefit of hindsight, it is easy to see that this was a fairly serious exaggeration. Even if there had been a party, with impeccable Bolshevik organisational principles, there was no revolution to be had in 1968.

Nevertheless, from the midst of that exciting year, Cliff decided that the loose federal structure of the organisation was becoming a drag on the further expansion of the Group. Until Cliff's changes were put into effect IS had operated on the basis that its Executive Committee was made up of one delegate from each branch, meeting quarterly. A Political Committee looked to the organisation between Executive Committee meetings. It was ill defined and cumbersome and, for some of us, it left a great number of large holes in the democratic process for Cliff to do very much what he liked. For him reorganisation was the way to a group that more efficiently carried out his directions – the emphasis here was on centralism. For others in the leadership it was a way of submitting everyone to the discipline of a collective – the emphasis here was on democracy. This is one example, and there are lots of others, that shows the tensions that exist under the umbrella of democratic centralism, whose tenets are not carved on tablets of stone, that were carried down the mountain by Lenin.

The vehicle that Cliff fashioned to carry this important message to the members was two sides of a quarto sheet under the heading, *Notes on Democratic Centralism*.[1] It is difficult to imagine how such a short document could contain so many non sequiturs, misstatements of fact, half thoughts, truisms and flashes of sense. If read with care, however, it indicates that Cliff had now come round to the notion that IS was the basis of the party. In the same way that Lenin observed that *"Communism is Soviet power plus electrification"*, so Cliff now concluded that the revolutionary party is democratic centralism plus Tony Cliff.

---

1. Reprinted here as an appendix, p. 213.

Most significant, in the light of the later draconian regime in the SWP, is the recommendation for factional representation, which was standard form for orthodox Trotskyist groups, although it did not guarantee too much democracy there either. The first beneficiary of this particular provision was the Trotskyist Tendency who throughout their stay had at least two members on the National Committee.

When Cliff tossed his very small document into the pond he probably assumed that not much would be stirred by the ripples. Mistake. Oppositionists started to come out of the woodwork, as if someone had whispered the Rentokil man was coming. It was decided that the Political Committee had better expand on Cliff's document. This time on eight pages of foolscap they attempted to convince the members that, with a growing organisation, with an even faster growing list of tasks to be performed, and with great unevenness in the experience of the members, it was more effective and, more importantly, more democratic to have a non-federal structure.

If this stilled the fears of some members it was not universally acclaimed. Among the more disenchanted were the so called 'Micro-faction'. This term was taken from Castro's description of the ultra-Stalinist Escalante group in the Cuban Communist Party; it was really totally inappropriate because the IS Micros were libertarians, but it was an offensive description suggesting that they were small and lightweight. Small they may have been, there were only nine signatories[1], but their documents were definitely heavy. In the discussion on organisation they were attempting to open up Group politics to critical scrutiny, cast within the framework of a closely argued examination of the Marxist attitude to consciousness, an area of study, they suggested, where IS had got it wrong. Their intention they said was to:

> initiate a permanent debate whose aim will not be peaceful co-existence of important different ideas but the triumph of correct policies... to begin a ruthless evaluation of IS theory and practice... to convince comrades of the need to understand that objective circumstances are seen by people who **actively** [emphasis in original – JH] hold views on the particular, general and ideological

---

1. Joan Smith, Steve Jefferys, Laurie Flynn, Mike McKenna and Andrew Hornung were among the signatories.

levels; who have a history, whose understanding of the world is mediated by that ideology and who are constantly in the process of transforming those beliefs into practice through daily experience and activity...

If the first part of this sounds to you like Daniel DeLeon when he spoke of *"All the tyranny of truth"* and if the second part sounds

to you like a philosophy graduate telling you that a lot of people learn from experience, then there is not much wrong with your hearing. Although this gives something of the flavour, some bits of the documents are better, correctly criticising an ill presented case that was being pushed through without time for proper discussion.

Peter Sedgwick in York was another critic, and a Libertarian Marxist faction argued, with a quote from Raymond Challinor, that the proposals were bureaucratic, not democratic, centralism. In Manchester, a small group around Colin Barker formed a Fourth Tendency, whose main concern was that IS had not declared itself democratic centralist years before. It was a transitory faction probably influenced by Workers' Fight: certainly at least six of its ten signatories subsequently joined the Trotskyist Tendency, as did the micro-factionalist, Andrew Hornung, a strange young man who seemed to rather fancy himself in the role of tribune of the opposition. There was a certain theatricality about him that was quite endearing. On occasion he affected a flowing cloak and a silver topped cane, perhaps he thought they made him look Byronic. In fact it did, but after the fever took its deadly toll at Missolonghi. Hornung was the author of one of the more scabrous documents of the Trotskyist Tendency, called *Centrist Current*. The actual content was not much cop, but the little asides when he stopped to catch his breath were a hoot:

> *For thirty pages I am driven on by the steam hammer of polemic.*
> *For thirty pages the focus of my own thought dims the images that*
> *do not stand in the very forefront of my vision. And yet for thirty*
> *pages, now with diffidence, now with a persistence, a doubt nags*
> *at my mind. I write swept on by the momentum of political invec-*
> *tive till pausing for a moment a nagging doubt seizes and snares*
> *my mind. I wonder whether... I haven't perhaps overplayed my*
> *hand... I wonder if I haven't been unfair... But I tear myself away.*
> *The piston rod of determined argument forces me on... Unwill-*
> *ing to submit to doubt and unwilling to stop for scrutiny, the mo-*
> *mentum of the polemic takes me up again. Its own internal logic*
> *driving past any signposts of doubt, past any warning lights of*
> *circumspection.*[1]

I am told that, sadly, Andrew is no longer in politics: one surely misses his particular brand of guileless pretentiousness. Maybe he is writing scripts for Reeves and Mortimer.

Noisy but of even less significance was the Democratic Centralist Faction, composed of Constance Lever, Fred Lindop, Stephen Marks, Noel Tracy, Dave Graham and Roger Rosewell. The ideas, such as they were, seem to have been supplied by Constance Lever and, as usual, the bombast by Roger Rosewell. Laurie Flynn dubbed them 'Toy Bolsheviks'. A quote or two from their document *Towards a Revolutionary Party* may give a feel for its worth:

> *For the class to be victorious, its most conscious and militant layer*
> *must be conscious, united and organised.*

I often think thoughtfully that it would make me happily happy to be surrounded by consciously conscious workers. Or try this for size:

> *We are now entering a decisively new historical period. The cracks*
> *and disintegrations in the social democratic and Stalinist organisa-*
> *tions are developments of epochal significance... we may say that*
> *we are entering a revolutionary period... such an organisation [IS]*
> *must be exclusive, tightly knit, self disciplined and answerable only*
> *to itself collectively...*

---

1. Andrew Hornung, *Centrist Current*.

This kind of almost literate braggadocio is redolent of Rosewell's style. Take it in too large a measure and your colitis becomes general.

From the Hull branch came two brief but apposite documents that bore all the hallmarks of being written by one of that branches' members, Michael Kidron. The first and most significant was called *We Are Not Peasants.*[1] Arguing forcefully for the retention of the branch delegate Executive Committee, he claimed that because there had been a large growth in membership, those new members had not had the time or the opportunity to assimilate IS theory or experience. This then resulted in the leadership attempting to find answers to the problems from the revolutionary tradition and neglecting their most important task of monitoring the world about us, so that they could direct the membership in meaningful activity. Not only should they be exercising political leadership but also, *"keeping their eyes and ears open to what the new members are saying and doing"*. The necessary interchange between the Political Committee and the members could best be ensured by retaining the branch delegate structure for the Executive Committee. Paradoxically, and despite its opposition to the 'Leninist' forms, this was the most Leninist of the contributions to the debate, it started from an appreciation of the importance of looking outward, it assessed the forces available to us, their strengths and weaknesses, and then formulated a plan to get the best from everyone. It was serious politics and it was totally unsuccessful, because nobody was really paying attention.

At the next conference, the Political Committee's plan was carried. IS now had a National Committee of forty, elected at the conference. Factions would be represented on the National Committee according to the number of conference delegates they commanded. Branches sent delegations to conference on the basis of one delegate per six members, later raised to fifteen. The National Committee elected an Executive Committee of ten to arrange the day to day political and administrative organisation of the group. Another part of the package was the introduction of the panel system which allowed the National Committee to make nominations for its own election. The grounds for this were that widely spread members might not be aware of the merit of certain

---

1. Reprinted here as an appendix, p. 217.

comrades and, lacking this information, would elect some flashy demagogue who performed well on the podium. It is not particularly sinister so long as branches have exactly the same right to nominate for all positions and all nominees have equal weight. In any case, even the most libertarian constitution can be subverted by a determined leadership, given a less than vigilant membership.

No sooner had Workers' Fight been transformed into the Trotskyist Tendency than they set about a little internal colonisation and, by 1971, they could report they had increased their membership fourfold. This is probably rather better than they would have done elsewhere. One might think that this is confirmation of their frequently levelled charge that IS was a soft centrist organisation. What can be said with some certainty is that it was a great deal less soft after three years of their company.

Just a year after the fusion Colin Barker, their original sponsor, was bleating for the Manchester branch to be split politically, with Manchester No. 1 branch as a sort of holding cell for the Trotskyist Tendency and Manchester No. 2 branch taking everything else. The fact that this cunning ploy emanated from the erstwhile Fourth Tendency proponent of rigorous democratic centralism would have made a cat laugh if it had not been choked by the pathos of it all. The split was agreed and a similar one occurred on Teesside.

Matgamna and his friends were basically sectarians, conforming with deadly accuracy to Marx's definition. They did see, *"their point of honour"* in the *"particular shibboleth which distinguished them from the movement"*. They believed that Russia was a 'degenerated workers' state' and that all the other Stalinist countries were 'deformed workers states'. They believed that unity with the Fourth International (USFI) was the correct course. Matgamna himself was much taken with James P Cannon, whose party was a fully paid up member of the USFI. IS believed in none of these things, but there was an organisation in Britain that did; the International Marxist Group. They, though, had fewer members and would probably have kicked the Trotskyist Tendency out a lot sooner. The Trotskyist Tendency preferred to see what pickings there were in IS where, by concentrating on any genuine discontents, they might maximise their impact.

They were, to all intents and purposes, a separate organisation, with their own subs collections and private meetings, their internal constitution including a category of probationary membership unknown in IS. Even so, despite the fact that most of their criticism was tosh—IS was never 'centrist' in any meaningful sense—the way to deal with their aggravating presence was not the series of organisational manoeuvres that Cliff favoured. It was quite funny to see Cliff, who after all had invited them—for which sin he should have been demoted to candidate guru status—getting quite angry when one pointed out the constitutional niceties that had to be observed before they could be removed.

Once the disputed questions had been elucidated they should have been vigorously debated before the membership. It would have been quite instructive and helped to educate the new members into the essential theories of the Group. Certainly Matgamna ventured into print on a number of occasions retailing his critique with all the amiable good nature of a Gaboon viper. As in:

> In general the theory [Cliff's state capitalism] is ultra mechanistic, based on vulgar non-Marxist economics and is irredeemably pessimistic... Not the least shoddy part of Cliff's book is his attempt to deal with Trotsky's views... In general Cliff's book on Russia reads less like a Marxist tract and more like a moralistic 'primitive socialist indictment.' It is totally subjective and totally incoherent.

On a rainy day, with a head cold and one arm tied behind his back, Cliff could have dealt with the author in a debate that might have proved educational for everyone, especially Sean. Cliff, however, found all this beneath him, far better to alter the rules, or better still break the rules to get rid of the problem.

In the end a special conference passed a simple resolution, by a large majority, to the effect that the fusion had not worked and should be unravelled. The minority against was, nevertheless, quite sizeable and many comrades felt that it had not been fairly handled. From this point on Sean Matgamna and his grouplet would have to stand alone. Sean is no longer an expellee, he is an expeller; happily ridding himself of Alan Thornett and his co-thinkers and the ex-IS Left Faction. *Plus ca change plus c'est la meme chose.*

For all the seeming heat that was generated by the faction fight, the aggravation was largely localised and on the Executive Committee. IS grew during the period, neither despite, nor because of, but in complete indifference to the factionalism. A new Tory government was attempting to break the post-war Butskellite consensus, as so called 'Selsdon man' sprang fully formed from Ted Heath's left ear. The industrial struggle was about to be ratcheted up a notch or two.

The Problem With Marxism is Marxists

Under thirty a revolutionist, thereafter a wretch
French saying, quoted by **Leon Trotsky**

The problem with Marxism is Marxists. Having discovered this world system, they are persuaded they have acquired a hammer-lock on infallibility. Trotsky, in his least convincing mode, speaks of Marxism as 'science'. It is as if, having elucidated the laws of motion of observable phenomena, you just have to apply the formulae according to your preferred theoretician's instructions and hey presto, revolutionary success will come knocking at your door pleading to be let in.

Unfortunately, not least for Trotsky but also for the rest of us, it is not like that. Trotsky's errors in analysis are manifest and quite numerous but his score is still better than almost everybody else because he got a few things spectacularly right. It is, though, in the prediction department that Marxism needs get its act together. You do not, for example, win a major prize for your 1938 prediction, that capitalism will no longer develop the productive forces and that the *only* alternatives are socialism or barbarism, if capitalism subsequently not only expands phenomenally but invades new areas in a quite spectacular way, improving in the process the living standard of countless millions of people. It does no good to argue, as Trotsky's more besotted fans do, that nuclear war and its prospect are barbarous, or indeed that any improvements in standards have been very unevenly spread. Although all of this is true, it is not at all what Trotsky was talking about: he did not know about the first and denied the possibility of the second. He really did mean that, to all intents and purposes, capitalism was irrevocably knackered.

It was this failure of prediction that disoriented orthodox Trotskyism. The Trotskists screamed about the imminent general crisis of capitalism, hoping that one day, if they screamed it often enough, it would become true. And so it will, but we ought to do better than rely on the law of averages. What gave IS the advantage in the early 1960s, was the more sophisticated analysis which offered an explanation for capitalism's apparent stability and a perspective for rank and file activity with the prospect of revolutionary organisation.

With the benefit of twenty-twenty hindsight it is clear that while both of these insights were valuable, they were quite inadequate to encompass either the extent of the changes to the system, or the varied and unexpected responses to those changes. The student revolt was one such change, the women's movement, gay liberation and the campaign for racial equality, spearheaded by blacks, were others. These movements were militant and accompanied, and sometimes surpassed in intensity, the developing industrial unrest. They were militant in their own terms and took strength from and learned from each other. Because they were a natural response to the pressures of a changing world, the theorising about them was *post facto*, and often fanciful to absurd – as in the notion that to be white is *ipso facto* to be racist, or in the similar notion that oppressing women is an immutable feature of the male psyche. For Marxists this cannot be the answer, or their theory is completely invalid. Indeed, not only has 150 years of Marxism gone for nothing but the whole age of enlightenment has proved to be an illusion.

If the theories seemed to be largely composed of hot air, the movements themselves were real enough and they were all not just potential allies but an integral part of the struggle for socialism. With the possible exception of the International Marxist Group (IMG), this phenomenon was not much appreciated. From the outside, it seemed that the IMG's interest was a function of its lack of influence, and inability to acquire any in the working class movement, but that may be uncharitable. In IS, what were essentially new opportunities were seen as a diversion from the central task of recruiting workers. Women workers, black workers yes; women in general and blacks per se, no thank you. This could, in part, be attributed to the fact that a significant part of the leadership of IS, by age and experience, did not understand the significance of these new movements (as part of that leadership at the time, I would certainly have to plead guilty). Even more significant was the simple fact that once more we had got the future wrong. The general expectation among all the parties to the democratic centralist argument was of an increasing and rapidly deepening working class radicalisation. The experience with Workers' Fight was, especially for Cliff, a torture. He justified his increasingly draconian suggestions by reference to the great strides we could make without having to spend an inordinate amount of time arguing with Sean Matgamna. To contemplate the sort of reorganisation that would be necessary in building a homogeneous revolutionary group, with all that implied in the way of faction and dispute, was almost too much to bear thinking about. So we did not think about it and resisted when others did. It was not admirable but seemed sensible.

With our NHS adjusted hindsight, it is clear that in the long run the Group was denied an opportunity to build a more socially significant and bigger organisation and one that would have been able to have considerable influence on the newly emerging movements, to the benefit of all. To do so it would probably have been necessary to change the entire leadership, including Cliff, but a period of quiet contemplation would have been good for them, especially him.

In 1970, however, with all the myopia of the present, the whole emphasis was on the growing militancy of the organised workers and the chance to channel this into rank and file organisation. With the election of the Tory government, the trade union bureaucracy who had signed up for *In Place of Strife* under Labour were far less inclined to support Edward Heath's corporatism. If IS mistook this anti-Tory element in militancy, it is also the case that many rank and file workers were fairly fed up with the bureaucracy's too ready acceptance of the Labour government's wage controls.

First fruits of this were seen in the Nantional Union of Teachers (NUT), itself a manifestation of a new white collar militancy, where the rank and file teachers' organisation very quickly became an unofficial opposition within the union and a militant leadership in some of the NUT branches. With greater or lesser success, similar movements were beginning to develop among local government manual and white collar workers, in the London buses, the NUM, the Docks with a number of widespread and episodic efforts in the AEU.

The pattern was beginning to be set the lessons of the Minority Movement assimilated. The role of the revolutionary organisation was to initiate and service activity, to help develop the sort of programme that would help the workers concerned to build their own strategy for advance. It would be transitional, both in terms of the expansion of trade union demands and in raising and expanding political consciousness. The Group should provide the framework where this could take place, allocating the necessary resources wherever possible. The extreme unevenness of the workers' movement meant that in one place one might be dealing with individuals helping them to produce trade union leaflets to organise their workplace, and in another developing a rank and file paper to appeal to militants across a major industry. This was not organising across the whole spectrum of the alienated and recently radicalised, but it was something of which we had learned a little and were beginning to do, if not well, better.

The Heath administration saw it as one of its priorities to negotiate British entry into the Common Market and, on taking office, vigorously pursued this course. Naturally there was a powerful chauvinist and Little Englander response from the Labour Lefts around *Tribune* and the Communist Party. The argument, especially in the mouths of some Communist Party leaders became positively racist, and those of us working in the trade unions did our best to counter this in print and by speeches. In doing this we were bolstered by the fact that, in pursuing a defencist rather than oppositionist line, we were following a long established policy of IS, best summed up in *International Socialism Journal* #11, 1962:

> *In itself the Common Market cannot tilt the class balance against us, but if we get lost in arguments for or against, instead of ensuring that workers neither pay for the preparations nor suffer the consequences in employment, wages or prices, it can or might.*

This was the outcome of discussions in IS, stimulated by the Macmillan governments' stalled attempt to join the Market, that had gone on for some time during which a minority argued for direct opposition.

At the 1970 and 1971 IS conferences, Peter Sedgwick argued for outright opposition to EEC entry; the traditional line was reaffirmed, however, with a united leadership arguing against any change. As the prospect of Britain actually joining the EEC became likely, and just a couple of weeks after the conference reaffirmed its traditional position, Cliff – ably abetted by Chris Harman – began to worry about how this would affect our trade union members who found themselves on delegations to the TUC and Labour Party or their own union conferences, in the face of the emotive campaign worked up by the CP-*Tribune* axis and submitted a document to the National Committee calling for a change of line. This concern for IS trade union activists was touching if misplaced, trade unionists with some experience – such as Geoff Carlsson, Ross Pritchard and Jim Higgins – were concerned that they would be embarrassed by suddenly changing the line they had been pursuing for some time. That the question should arise at all was a measure of the inexperience of Cliff and Harman in these matters. That the National Committee should endorse such a policy shift from Cliff and Harman, whose total working class experience comprised the three days that Cliff spent helping a building worker in Palestine, although it may be that Harman once had a paper round, also measures how inexperienced in these matters was the National Committee.

To justify their position Cliff and Harman produced a document which concluded:

> *Our aim in union conferences and the like should be to fight for resolutions to this effect, thus making clear both our opposition to the Common Market and our separation from confused chauvinism of the Tribuneites, Communist Party, etc. However, if we are defeated on such a stand we should then vote with the Tribune-Stalinists in opposition to entry.*

As a document from several National Committee members reasonably responded in an article in the Internal Bulletin:

What must be clear to anybody who knows anything about the penetration that the IS group has managed to attain in the trade union movement is that the possibility for a principled intervention prior to unprincipled combination is practically nil.[1]

Having been foolhardy enough to place their criticism in the Internal Bulletin the opponents of the new line found that their article was cheek by jowl to a response from Chris Harman of Tottenham. Not for the first time, and certainly not the last, Cliff had arranged for Chris Harman to pop his head above the parapet, to see if the banging noises meant gunfire and, if so, was it really dangerous. Under the stimulating crosshead: 'What Should be the Attitude of Revolutionaries at this Conjuncture?' Harman expatiated in a style redolent of all internal bulletins, since the time when monks in cold cloisters decorated them with illuminated dropped capitals :

1. *We are against anything that rationalises or strengthens capitalism in an epoch in which the productive forces have developed sufficiently to make socialism an objective possibility…*

2. *We are for weakening the mechanisms by which the ruling class exercises political-ideological control…*

3. *We have to maintain completely our ideological independence on a class based standpoint. That means complete opposition to all chauvinistic arguments. It means a refusal to campaign alongside those who propagate such arguments. If approached to do so (eg., by the CPs in the localities) we have to demand as a precondition for any joint campaign that it be based on class demands and rejection of all talk of 'national independence'.*

The document goes on quite a lot in this vein and, apart from its spine wrenching convolutions, it serves to display a sublime ignorance of what happens at union conferences, not least in the suggestion that the Communist Party might have felt so short of allies as to approach us to form a united front on the Common Market. Assuming that some aberrant Stalinist did so, we have further to believe that even though we suggested our rejection of all the Communist Party's chauvinist arguments in favour of prin-

---

1. Nagliatti, Foot, Higgins, Pritchard, Edwards and Carlsson, *The Common Market and the IS Group.*

cipled class based opposition to capitalist rationalisation, at the end of the day we would vote for a fatally flawed resolution, our mythical Stalinist would be bowled over by the stunning power of our dialectic and amend his own resolution to our complete satisfaction. On the other hand he might have told us to 'go take a flying kick at a rolling doughnut'. In the final vote on the question at the National Committee, the Cliff-Harman axis were once more successful by a narrow majority, augmented this time by the vote of Paul Foot, whose undoubted talents were, unfortunately, not accompanied by intestinal fortitude when under pressure from Cliff.

The developing militancy in the working class and the organisational changes in IS were also accompanied by developments in the physical resources open to the Group. By instituting a fighting fund and leaning heavily on the members, the Group was able to purchase a decent sheet-fed Heidelburg press and offices in Cotton's Gardens, just off the Kingsland Road near Shoreditch Church, that served as both a print shop and an administrative centre. Ross Pritchard manned the press, Michael Heym manned the reproduction camera and made printing plates. Roger Protz edited the paper, with its name changed from *Labour Worker* to *Socialist Worker*. Diane Nair operated as admin secretary and Jim Nichol, a member of the Newcastle branch and a clerk in the National Coal Board, was employed to look after the books. Despite the cramped space in the press room, it was not too long before an East German web press was installed. It had a rough hewn aspect, rather as if it had been chewed from the solid metal by GDR craftsmen using their teeth and an old file. This machine required the attention of Ross Pritchard, only someone of his considerable skill could deal with its temperamental eccentricities and so Jim Nichol's brother Paul was introduced to operate the Heidelberg.

A bit later, a wealthy and extremely dedicated and generous comrade was prevailed upon to put up quite a substantial sum of money to buy commodious premises at the Oval, between the Hackney Road and Cambridge Heath Road. Here in a more spacious press hall, it was possible to place the presses and install folding machinery and other ancillary bits and pieces. The Group had acquired a nice little earner. It is to this particular development that some critics, among them Joan Smith, point as the significant fact in the degeneration of IS. There can be no doubt that the profit from commercial printing subsidised the Group's own publications and provided the money to employ a number of full time organisers. In general, but not invariably, the full time workers were uncritically loyal to the centre and to whoever suggested their appointment, usually Cliff. It is also the case that the profits were partly a function of the extremely low wages paid in the printshop and the flouting of a number of union rules.

Even so, it does not follow from this that socialists should deny themselves the opportunities of building a cadre of professional revolutionaries to increase the effectiveness of their work. If we are to assume that all such surplus is in some way unmerited or tainted and that its possession will inevitably lead to an autocratic regime, policed by glassy-eyed apparatchiks, then I fear we must also concede the truth of original sin and start making our peace with the Almighty. In other, and happier, circumstances I would recommend employing organisers of the calibre of Granville Williams and Steve Jefferys. I would also recommend employing Chris Harman, providing that he spent at least five years in gainful employment first. So far as Cliff is concerned, it is certain that, paid or not, he would want his own way and do everything possible to get it. I am told that Peter Taafe, of Militant, when they finally got rid of Ted Grant, breathed such a heartfelt sigh of relief that even people who knew Taafe well felt retrospectively sorry for him.

THE "SMALL MASS REVOLUTIONARY PARTY"
Ernest Erber

Duncan Hallas also became a full time worker as National Secretary, a job that had not really existed before. In the sense that he was a man with a high degree of political knowledge and sophistication, an ability to speak well and to write simply, but as well as he spoke, he was a good choice. As a man to look after the administration and to monitor the work of the branches and the organisers, less good. Nevertheless, it was a significant advance.

Of much more dubious long term value was the appointment, at Cliff's urging, of Roger Rosewell as Industrial Organiser.

Rosewell was recruited in Kingston in the early 1960s by Mick Teague and John Palmer (They have both apologised profusely several times but I still feel that something painful and mediaeval by way of penance is appropriate). He was a member of the Young Communist League and then the Labour Party Young Socialists, and a member of some very small craft union – the Society of Metal Mechanics I believe. The most notable thing about him was his conceit: despite the fact that he was a rather short, slight of frame and, even when quite young, going prematurely bald, he strutted about as if he were a cross between Robert Redford and Arnold Schwartzenegger. So that he would stand out amongst the casually dressed IS members he wore pin-striped suits complete with waistcoat. At Cotton's Gardens one might, on occasion, come across him practising some kind of martial art in a noisy and theatrical fashion.

In direct imitation of Gerry Healy, whose style he much admired, he would orate with his thumbs tucked behind his red braces. This admiration for Healy, who he knew not at all – and certainly Healy would have eaten him for breakfast – was of a piece with his 'toy bolshevism'. This image of the hard man that he presented to the world was a smokescreen to a timid fellow, given to indolence and cowardice. The high-point of his alleged stewardship of the industrial work was when he shared a platform for a few meetings with Bernadette Devlin, who was close to IS at the time. Bernadette, who possessed all the qualities that Rosewell lacked, including modesty, was the one who drew the crowds and made the significant speeches, while Rosewell provided the braces-snapping demagoguery. After a time, to listen to Roger, one might have thought that the hundreds who turned up came to hear, and could not get enough of, the man in the red braces and the embarrassing oratory.

If he felt unloved, which must have been often, he would retreat to some provincial funkhole and sulk. If really upset and unable to cope, he would go and stay with Cliff. Together they could watch children's television, maybe to catch up on Blue Peter, in case it gave a specification for building the revolutionary party out of some sticky backed plastic, an egg box, a Squeezee bottle and a pair of Val's old knickers. On one occasion I was invited by Cliff to talk to the distraught Rosewell. He was tearful and told me that he was unhappy, unsuccessful and unworthy, and he wanted to go to Israel and live on a kibbutz. Perhaps inside every hard man there is a Roger Rosewell trying to get out. To my regret, I talked him out of this piece of nonsense (Half a million Hail Marys and twice round the Vatican). On another occasion he was sent to Teesside, where the first strike at the steelworks since the General Strike was taking place. One of the leaders of the strike was Arthur Affleck, a very impressive militant and an IS member on the National Committee. A meeting was arranged at which Rosewell was billed to speak in support of Arthur. He failed to turn up, giving as his excuse that he had to watch the *Maltese Falcon* on TV. What a prince that man was.

For some reason, which escapes me, Cliff would protect Roger from the consequences of his derelictions. At one stage, thinking it would be good for him to settle down, he suggested to at least one young female comrade that she might like to marry Roger. This concern for Rosewell, up to and including marriage broking, was not extended to others and, Roger being Roger, the affection was not reciprocated. Having resigned from the Industrial Organiser post, he was, for a time, Liverpool organiser. Here in concert with Andreas Nagliatti – he always needed somebody to supply the brains – he operated as the British end of the Italian, sub-Maoist, Avanguardia Operaia group.

Having left IS he went to Ruskin and thence to Oxford and, having acquired his degree, worked closely with Frank Chapple, the far right General Secretary of the ETU. He also wrote an exposé of IS in the *Daily Mail*, in which he claimed, among other lies, that Cliff had forbidden him to marry the lady of his choice. From ultra-right wing Labour he moved in with the Jenkins-Owen SDP. This, however, was just a way-station with no future, and the logical next step was the Tories. Here he met Lady Porter, the eldritch creature who ran Westminstrer Council like some branch of the penal system. In great, but ineffective, secrecy Rosewell was whisked into an anonymous room at Westminster Council offices, to help her to plot and to gerrymander, for the Tories benefit and to disenfranchise the poor and the homeless, all at the ratepayers' expense. An appropriate symbol for a wasted and worthless career.

Rosewell, of course, was not active in the IS Group's work on Ireland. That was largely down to John Palmer, Jimmy Greeley, Brian Trench, Paddy Prenderville, and Paul Gillespie. As a result a number of the People's Democracy people were brought in to the Group, among them Michael Farrell and Eamonn McCann: in their turn they brought IS in contact with Benadette Devlin prior to her election as an MP. It was quite natural that she worked closely with IS when she came to Westminster and, famously and quite splendidly, fetched Reggie Maudling a clout. As part of that association, Bernadette supplied the attraction and IS supplied the organisation and the people to set up meetings. These were the biggest meetings that IS has had, either before or after. Her meeting in Dagenham attracted an audience of 4,000, with hundreds unable to get in, and was also addressed by Eamonn McCann, John Palmer and Terry Barrett. A similar meeting filled Wimbledon Town Hall to the gunwales.

Despite the success of these big set piece events IS did not succeed in building an organisation in the six counties, although Brian Trench and Paul Gillespie did succeed in setting up the Socialist Workers' Movement, very much on IS lines. Through its press, through public meetings and internal education, IS did influence the British left to a clearer understanding of the Irish struggle. It certainly avoided the sort of 'left Unionism' of Militant and the IRA-tailism of the IMG. IS was especially influential in the anti-internment campaigns.

One of the more controversial stands of the Group was to resist calls for the immediate withdrawal of British troops, after the pograms in the Falls road and Derry brought them in, to the evident relief of the Catholic population they were, at the outset, protecting. This particular stand was one of the subjects for extreme criticism from the Workers' Fight. One might have taken this a little more seriously if Sean Matgamna had not, at an IS conference, circulated a photocopy of a map from the *Economist*, showing the location of the different religious sections of the population. This distribution, Sean suggested, showed how exchanges of population and territory between the North and South, could be facilitated and thus overcome sectarian difficulties. I understand that today his Irish policy implies a new partition.

For all that the Group was aware of its shortcomings in face of radical developments that it predicted and confidently expected , nevertheless, IS seemed to be best able to take advantage of those changes. Whatever its shortcomings, IS now thought of itself as the nucleus of the revolutionary party. That needs some clarification, because it did not mean for IS, as it did for so many messianic sects, that it was the party in miniature in – the Shachtmanite – Ernest Erber's immortal phrase: *"the small mass revolutionary party"*. There were developments to come that we could not foresee that would impose their own necessary changes on the organisation. In particular, it was well understood that a revolutionary party is one that organises a significant number of workers. It is one that can operate autonomously and begin to set a working class agenda. For example, if and when it calls a one day general strike, neither the members nor the workers will go to work that day. There was a long way to go before that could come to pass but in the meanwhile, the organisation could learn to campaign and to develop its strength in industry.

A Minute's Mirth

Who buys a minute's mirth to wail a week?
Or sells eternity to get a toy?
For one sweet grape who will the vine destroy?
Shakespeare, *The Rape of Lucrece*

The growth of IS can be measured fairly accurately by the increase in the number of branches between the 1971 and 1972 conferences. In April 1971, the number of branches was 87, by the following April that had increased to 113. It is interesting to note that over the twelve months the two Manchester branches had merged, following the exit of the Trotskyist Tendency. It was also apparent that the organisational set up of the Executive Committee and National Committee, with various sub-committees, was working with reasonable efficiency.

Over the year, the National Committee members had put up an impressive attendance record and if, ideally, it could have contained more worker members, at least it had some. It had issued eleven policy statements on subjects ranging from 'Political and Organisational Perspectives' to 'The Campaign against the Industrial Relations Bill', taking in 'IS and the Labour Party', 'On Unity' and several other items.

The Executive Committee was composed of Ian Birchall, international; Tony Cliff; Duncan Hallas, National Secretary; Nigel Harris; Jim Higgins, Chairman; Jim Nichol, Treasurer; Frank Campbell, a building worker; John Palmer; Roger Protz, Editor *Socialist Worker*; Roger Rosewell, Industrial Organiser and Chris Harman, Editor *ISJ*. It was a reasonably balanced committee, Harman invariably voted with Cliff, as did Jim Nichol, who – at least in my presence – never gave voice to a political utterance, but seemed to understand finance. Ian Birchall had a mind of his own, if given to moodiness and a tendency to resign from IS if at all unhappy. The most difficult thing, and one in which nobody succeeded, was to convince Cliff that his latest idea was not some kind of revealed truth, in the pursuit of which everything else should be set aside. To get across the simple fact that the workers' movement has certain norms of conduct and definite procedures that are there precisely because it is a collective movement, at its best involving all members of the collective, proved impossible. For Cliff the 'brilliant' insights of an individual (himself) could be submitted to popular approval on two conditions: one; that they agreed with his proposal in double quick time, and two; that if they did not agree he won anyway. This cast of mind is one he shares with some trade union leaders. It drives most militants into paroxysms of rage which is why, whenever the bureaucracy is pulling a fast one, the Conference Arrangements Committee report at trade union conferences is one of the most passionate debates. The existence of this phenomenon is one of the reasons why a genuine revolutionary party has, by definition, to include many experienced militants in its ranks because, among other things, they are the best guarantee against bureaucratic manipulation and capricious, high handedness. The failure to grasp this simple fact of working class life is evidence of a fundamental and debilitating ignorance and an absolute bar to revolutionary success.

In 1971, a rally organised by Jenny Davidson attracted 550 people to Skegness. The assembly was addressed by Cliff, Palmer and Hallas speaking respectively on: 'The International Movement', 'The Developing Crisis of Capitalism' and 'Towards a Revolutionary Party'. This was an impressive turnout by any standards and while it was also a social occasion, with dances, films and Alex Glasgow (an IS member) entertaining, most people came for the solid political core of the weekend. A touring day school on 'Imperialism and the Third World' and 'Revolutionary Work in the Unions' was popular as were weekend schools on 'State Capitalism' and 'The Revolutionary Party'. During the summer of 1971, a week long cadre school for young and comparatively new members was held with 37 attending to learn about public speaking, Marxism, Trotskyism, IS traditions, politics and industrial strategy. The *Internal Bulletin* was edited by Duncan Hallas and appeared every month, in almost enough copies for each member to have one (1350 copies distributed).

The increase in the proportion of workers in IS, did give rise to some problems for the Treasurer. With a largely white collar and middle class membership, most subs were paid by bankers' order, which led to a pretty slack attitude to collection in the branches. Manual workers, however, were generally 'unbanked' and paid subs in cash, except that branches were not geared up to collect them. This was to give rise to some heart-rending appeals from Jim Nichol. The only other time I felt sorry for him was when he was run over by a distracted nurse – I swear I did not know the woman – outside St Leonard's Hospital in the Kingsland Road.

There were industrial factions in ten unions, and six industrial sections. There were four rank and file papers, with a total print run of just short of 12,000. It was a disappointing outcome considering the level of militant trade union activity and a growing fight against the Industrial Relations Bill, but it may reflect the fact that Rosewell, who preferred talking tough to the nitty gritty of organising, was coming to the end of his tenure of this particular office and spent most of his time bunking off and catching up on afternoon TV.

HARRY WICKS' VOW

The real success story of the year 1971-72 was *Socialist Worker*. Over the period the average print order had gone up from 13,000 to 28,000, with a paid sale of around 70 per cent. It was calculated that the readership was in excess of 50,000. Most satisfying were tokens of success such as the fact that Dockers' National Stewards Committee decided to issue press statements only to the *Morning Star* and *Socialist Worker* and the fact that, during the miners' strike that year, the paper had been taken and enthusiastically sold by miners. *Socialist Worker* was staffed by Laurie Flynn, Chris Harman, Peter Marsden and Roger Protz full time, with

Nigel Fountain, Dave Widgery and Chris Hitchens giving part time help. Despite the characteristic philistinism of revolutionary socialists, most of the members were quite proud of the fact that the paper looked well designed and professionally produced. The paper was the public face of the organisation, one that a growing number of people recognised and a small but growing number considered required reading.

One small event that was particularly heartening in 1971, was that Harry Wicks joined the Group. Of course he was only one among several hundred, but he was a founder member of the Communist Party and an active member at that. A railwayman by trade, he was, in 1927, sent to the Lenin School in Moscow for a three year course in revolution. While in Moscow he became aware of Trotsky's arguments and, on his return to the UK in 1931, he met up with other oppositionists such as Reg Groves and Stuart Purkes. In due course they formed the Balham Group, were expelled from the Communist Party and produced a paper *Red Flag*. In 1932, Harry went to Copenhagen, where Trotsky was to address the Social Democratic Youth on the anniversary of the Russian Revolution. Harry was to take on the dual role of bodyguard at the meeting and delegate to an informal international meeting of Left Oppositionists. Harry took with him as a present for Trotsky a model of Hamburg, which was used at the Lenin School to instruct the students in street fighting. Trotsky was, apparently, quite pleased to get this gift and, flinging his arms around Harry, he cried, *"My dear Comrade Wicks"* and kissed him. This secretly pleased but also embarrassed Harry and when I asked him which cheek, so that I too could kiss the spot kissed by Leon Trotsky, it took some time for him to admit that it was both cheeks and he was going to have no more of that sort of behaviour. His decision to join IS was, for me, an indication that the Group was becoming an organisation to be reckoned with.

Later, in 1972, Duncan Hallas became Political Secretary, in addition to editing *ISJ*, and I was appointed National Secretary. The idea was to improve the communication in the group, to direct the increasing number of full-timers and to make the organisation more responsive to the changing situation. Duncan and I would complement one another in the national office. As one would suppose, the idea for this came from Cliff and I assumed that, having

known me for 13 years, he knew something about me and my
strengths and weaknesses, in the same way that I had a fair idea
about his. In the course of discussing the job with him, I felt that
he, at least, was convinced that it was worth taking me out of a
job I had been in for 25 years, and from my union, where I was
a branch secretary, on the Executive Committee and fairly well
known as a left winger up and down the country. Only an idiot,
I thought to myself, would expect me to chuck up what was, in
effect, half a working life's endeavour on a whim. At this remove,
of course, it is much easier to see who was the idiot and who was
the whimsical old prankster.

Between March 1972 and March 1974 the membership of IS
increased from 2,351 to 3,310. The number of manual workers
increased from 613 to 1,155 during the same period. This welcome improvement in the social composition of the Group was
not the whole story: during the membership campaigns of 1973
about 750 additional workers were recruited but could not be
integrated into IS. During this same period, the Group was trying
very hard to develop a factory branch structure. By July 1974,
there were a total of 38 workplace branches, organising some 300
members. A measure of the difficulties, and of IS inexperience,
in this work can be seen by the fact that from March, 73 to July,
74 a total of 56 factory branches had been recognised, but 18 of
them disappeared or were dissolved. Another problem was that,
while IS understood the theory of factory branches – Cliff had
written an *IS Bulletin* of 24 pages (A4 size pages in 8/10 point
type) that dealt with the matter exhaustively and paid lip service
to patience and caution – its experience in the field was zero. In
practice the job was rushed and half the time botched. Setting
up such branches with politically inexperienced workers, many of
whom were young, requires both patience and a commitment of
resources that were just not available. The intelligent thing to do
in the circumstances is to slow down the process and make a good
job where you can. As Lenin said, *"Better less but better"*. The excellent Industrial Report in the *1974 Pre-Conference Report*, which
bears all the marks of having been written by Steve Jeffreys, details the experience of several factory branches:

> *Branch A reports:* "The Branch was formed with eleven
> members. This rose to fourteen members. Three or four

dropped out after about one and a half months. Others left later on. The branch now has seven members. The majority left because they thought IS was something else. There was no real discussion or education. The branch was set up (in the opinion of the members left) too quickly. We knew very little about Marxism and even less about revolutionary politics. We therefore think it would have been better if we had joined the local branch and got to know the workings of the branch and got educated on Marx and Lenin..."
Branch J writes: "We have five members now and had eight at one time. The three were not interested in trade union work. They were full of criticisms but refused to fight for positions in the factory or trade union...' Branch D reported: '... To be frank meetings are terrible".

Practically all of the reports indicated high hopes at the beginning, followed fairly quickly by membership loss, with a low level of commitment and education. That is the sort of picture that calls for caution and remedial action. Not a bit of it, the report goes on:

> *Maintaining a revolutionary presence in the factory, training new and young socialists in revolutionary, working class politics, steadily becoming the real leadership of the left in the workplace – these are the sorts of aims that if achieved this year in our first forty factory branches, and over the coming year in another 80 factories, will mean we will be able to give real leadership to significant sections of the working class within the course of the next 18 months. We will have become a working class party.*

This is the kind of vainglory that makes one cringe retrospectively. From evidence that shows fairly clearly that what the factory branches have done over the year is to survive, we extrapolate to 40 factories with a fully fledged revolutionary leadership, then with a perspective of another 80 such paragons, we will be leading the working class in 18 months.

It is probably true to say that the factory branches were a preordained failure, no matter how much was put into them they would not have succeeded, because IS just did not have enough factory members. More significantly, the IS Group did not have, and was not aware that it needed, the sort of infrastructure that would enable it to assist these fledgling branches to develop into functioning industrial and political entities Such patient development was precluded because IS policy was predicated on a quite false perspective of an imminent general crisis of the system. A fortunate conjuncture of circumstances had given the Group the opportunity to grow to thousands, rather then the hundreds it had been a few years before, and the tens it had been a few years before that, but that should not have been seen as a promise of uninterrupted growth. It is all too easy for socialists to believe that the thing they most earnestly desire is just one big heave away – that we could pull ourselves up by the bootstraps, if only we pulled harder, while failing to observe that we have no boots.

In the early 1970s, just around the corner from the National Office, was Tina's Cafe, a small but pleasant dining room. It was here that comrades from the centre would partake of a little light refreshment. As is the nature of the beast, the comrades would discuss politics as they dined. Often what started out as an outlandish suggestion would, in the time taken to drink a cup of tea and consume a plateful of sausage, egg and chips, be transformed in discussion into an eminently reasonable and practical proposal. Extensive research reveals that Tina's Cafe Syndrome afflicts revolutionaries, with deadly effect, whenever they start to believe their own rhetoric, even without a high cholesterol diet.

Another quite debilitating complaint is the virus that infects people with the *Collected Works of Lenin* on their bookshelves. This particular malady manifests itself in the patient's inability to observe any present day situation without bending it into an analogy from the history of Bolshevism. In the chronic phase, Cliff is a text book example, the sufferer turns into a secular Thomas A Kempis writing *On the Adoration of Lenin*. If you read the history of the Russian Revolution, you will notice that the Bolsheviks were strong in the factory districts of Petrograd, particularly in the Putilov Works, the largest factory in the world in 1917. Reading further, we will note such occurrences as the Bolshevik central committee discussing plans for an armed manifestation on the streets. A decision is taken and the agitators are dispatched to the factories. And, in due course, just such a manifestation takes place. Now that is power and in a few short weeks they actually took it all. In Britain, of course, we were not in a position to have any armed demonstrations, but we could have factory branches and we could dream that, in the not too distant future, we might be sending in the agitators for an assault on our own Winter Palace. What could not be hidden – despite a primer by Rosewell, three undercoats by Steve Jefferys and a twenty-four page gloss from Cliff – was that a few factory branches are not necessarily the prelude to storming anything. Activity that was correct if it was done in a careful and structured way was performed in a silly slapdash rush. Factory branches have to have a basis in political experience and a proper group infrastructure. A rank and file movement is absolutely necessary but it cannot be built by edict and a rudimentary factory branch structure.

What did exist was hopeful but tentative, something that could, with tender loving care, grow but could just as easily wither and die. On top of all this was Cliff's overweening ambition and soaring imagination; the two coexisted in a dialectical relationship where ambition fed imagination and vice versa. If problems existed, they could not be part of objective reality, there was always a human culprit, or culprits, lurking in the background. Cliff's unease at the pace of recruitment which neither matched his ambitions nor, as he saw it, the opportunities available, were expressed in a series of half baked schemes for building the group in a hurry. Cliff arranged to have himself appointed Membership Secretary. The first fruits of this brainstorm was to set up the full time local organisers for a bit of socialist emulation in the recruitment stakes. At each National Committee, a league table of organisers was produced with the big time recruiters at the top and the no-good'niks at the bottom. What it did produce, apart from sound and fury, was an accelerated turnover of new members into ex-members and some creative accounting by the organisers. An ace recruiter and *Socialist Worker* seller was John Charlton, from Yorkshire. John was an amiable chap, with a quite touching belief in Cliff's infallibility, whose friendly disposition did seem to attract people to IS. On one embarrassing occasion, at Cliff's request, he delivered a quite lengthy exposition, at the National Committee, on how to sell *Socialist Worker* on the knocker. First was the need to be reasonably well turned out; it was also pretty vital to shut garden gates; sellers should not bang too hard on the door; when the door was opened a smile was mandatory, as was the offer to shake hands and the need give one's name. Having observed all the social amenities, only then could *Socialist Worker* be proffered for sale followed by a bit of a chat. John's talk was rather like a Kleenezee salesmen's seminar, delivered with all the wide eyed enthusiasm and certainty of a Seventh Day Adventist. He was, nevertheless, a very serious and dedicated comrade who, because of his leading position at the top of the recruiting league table, earned the right to whisper in Cliff's most impressionable ear – that is, if the space was not already occupied by the forked tongue of Roger Rosewell.

For a brief time it was these two sterling recruiters who exercised the maximum influence on Cliff and it was from their example that Cliff invented the 'Leading Areas' theory of organisation. It was in some ways an interesting theory, that prefigured the ideas of Margaret Thatcher – I have nowhere seen her acknowledge the debt, but that's Tories for you – it was simple, it was backed by preconception rather than evidence and it was, in practice, quite ineffective. According to this thesis you put maximum effort and resources into the leading areas, leaving the smaller and the less hopeful to experience a trickle down effect. A failure to appreciate the profound wizardry of this stratagem condemned you as a conservative element beyond hope of Leninist redemption. The accusatory finger inexorably pointed at the Executive Committee. Here, for Cliff, was the root of the problem, a committee endlessly obsessed with the Group as a whole, concerned that even the least among us should get their due measure of attention. This kind of negative thinking proved conclusive so far as Cliff was concerned, the personnel at the centre had to go. He absented himself from meetings for weeks on end and his initiatives would materialise in the leading areas, without passing through the committee set up specifically for this purpose. When eventually called to account, Cliff's response was that he was not sure if his initiatives would succeed. In fact he did have a low success rate, and he feared that the Executive Committee would oppose what he thought to be the correct course. A moment's thought about all of this will indicate that what we are seeing here has nothing to do with democratic centralism, but something much more akin to anarchism. In all of this it seemed to some of us that there was not much Lenin and a lot of Louis XIV; as in, "*L'État c'est moi*".

The debate that surfaced in the Executive Committee was on the question of the Rank and File Movement. As recently as the 1973 IS conference in April, the Group had reaffirmed its intention of working toward the setting up of such a movement. The Executive Committee, including Cliff, were convinced that the propitious moment was approaching and all were agreed that such a movement was an essential prerequisite for the development of a mass workers party. It was not something that the IS could, or should, control, but it would need the resources and initial input of the Group to set it up. It was the method of transitional politics that we expected to be a bridge to the party. With our Factory branches and the industrial and trade union fractions, the rank and file organisations together with their journals, it seemed that we might, with a lot of effort, set the Rank and File ball moving. The optimistic hope was, that the Rank and File movement would grow, after the initial kick-start, into a movement in which IS would be the predominant, but not the only, political tendency.

This pleasingly unanimous view on the Rank and File conference did not outlast the opposition expressed by Rosewell and Charlton at the National Committee meeting. Their arguments were not at all convincing and the National Committee rejected their call. Cliff turned up to the next Executive Committee meeting with a resolution to scrap the Rank and File Conference and substitute a recruiting rally at Bellvue, Manchester. After a lengthy and exhaustive discussion, the Executive Committee voted down the resolution with, I think, only Cliff and Harman in favour. At this setback, Cliff demanded three months leave of absence. He intended to retire to Nigel Harris's country cottage and finish his book on Lenin.

None of us, of course, imagined that Cliff's leave was a gracious admission of defeat, to be followed by three months of industriously clipping Lenin's *Collected Works* in the sylvan surroundings of Nigel's dacha. Not a bit of it. This was to be three months of frenzied activity, with Nigel's telephone almost bursting into flames through the heat of long winded, long distance lobbying, as Cliff badgered, bludgeoned and persuaded as many people as he could to overturn the National Committee. Fearing for Nigel Harris' solvency when the phone bill came in, and also to avoid an unnecessary fight, I managed to persuade a majority of the Executive Committee to agree to a compromise: Cliff should have his rally in November 1973 and the Rank and File Conference would be held in early 1974.

Strange as it may seem, so long as he had his rally, he no longer required a leave of absence, but his animus towards the 'conservative' Executive Committee remained undiminished: the night of the long knives was fast approaching. The putsch, when it came, found its justification in the leading areas theory. In this case, if the Executive Committee did not go to the leading areas they must come to the Executive Committee. In a proposal that was almost boring in its predictability and stupidity, the old Executive Committee was to be dumped, to be replaced by a body comprising Cliff, John Charlton, Roger Rosewell, Roger Kline and Jim Higgins (National Secretary), Roger Protz (Editor of *Socialist Worker*) and Andreas Nagliatti (Industrial Organiser). Non-voting places were offered to Chris Harman (Editor of the *ISJ*), Jim Nichol (Treasurer) and Nigel Harris (Chairman of the London Region). Nigel declined this dubious honour. John Palmer, Ian Birchall and Chris Davidson were excluded because they were unable to attend meetings in working hours, which is when Executive Committee meetings were held.

Readers who have followed this story with care will have noticed that someone is missing from the cast list. Duncan Hallas had become an unperson. This seemed odd: Duncan was one of the most experienced and talented comrades in IS, he was the leader writer for *Socialist Worker* and, at least nominally, the Political Secretary of the Group. Despite his obvious qualifications, he did manifest a serious failing—he often acted as if not every word of Cliff's had been ticked by God and given ten out of ten. As Roger Protz and I took a similarly blasphemous view, Duncan's presence on the committee would play havoc with the Executive Committee's voting arithmetic. Nagliatti was generally sound from Cliff's point of view but he might prove a loose cannon when it came to the Rank and File Movement. This is not at all to say that, apart from Cliff and his coterie, anyone else was behaving in a factional manner. Duncan was as likely to disagree with me as he was with Cliff, and similar considerations applied to Roger Protz. Nevertheless, when I raised the question of Duncan's inclusion on the Executive Committee, I was astonished at the degree of opposition and the vehemence with which it was expressed. His presence, I was told, would ruin any chance of the changes working and lead to frustration and loss of efficiency. Such was the extent of his disenchantment with Duncan that Cliff was proposing to sack him from full time duties. I felt that this was a case less of throwing the baby out with the bath water than of hammering the poor little bugger down the plug-hole. I proposed, and the National Committee accepted, that Duncan should become Deputy National Secretary.

This assertion of a small degree of independence seems to have been rather like handing over a signed and undated suicide note for safe keeping. Cliff and Rosewell began to canvas for a new National Secretary, offering the job to John Charlton for one and then Dave Peers for another. As the campaign mounted, a sort of parallel centre was established in Cliff's home, the National office was sidestepped and marginalised. The tasks of administration that a growing group, or even one that wants to grow and to monitor its success, or even one that wants to measure how leading are the leading areas, requires some sort of admin. For Cliff in his Nechaev mode all this was anathema: 'smash the duplicator' was his merry cry. According to this school of thought, or rather non-thought, the members did not require minutes or Internal Bulletins, they just needed to be told what to do; better still just, enjoined to follow the example of the leading areas. After a few months of being bypassed, marginalised and worn down by a steady drip of slander, I began to get the distinct impression that I was at a party where the invitations could be retrospectively withdrawn and mine was long overdue for the shredder. The final straw came when Executive Committee meetings always started late because Cliff and his faction had to meet, in Tina's Café, to decide what decisions would be imposed upon me without discussion. I resigned and took a job as a reporter on *Socialist Worker.*

Over the years several people have asked why, given the undeclared factionalism of Cliff and his satraps, I had not utilised the position of National Secretary to organise a more effective opposition. Operating from the Centre, it would certainly have been possible to organise quite a few of the neglected non-leading areas and, as a matter of fact, a couple of leading ones too. The reason for what I now see as a neglect of duty was that I was convinced of the favourable climate for IS to grow and break out of the frustrations and idiocies of sect politics. A serious faction fight would have, I thought, put in jeopardy the hard won gains of the last couple of years. Effectively having two competing national offices was a recipe for a split and I shrunk from such a prospect. Unlike Cliff, I was not prepared to devote every waking hour to getting a mean advantage to falsify the past and lie about the present. The 'leading areas' thesis, I now realise, was not seriously worked through but was a tattered fig leaf Cliff hoped would cover his rather sordid manoeuvring. It was successful in that limited objective and was then dropped, never to be heard of again, except from the disgruntled and disappointed.

So little was I interested in factional advantage, rather than what I conceived to be the good of the Group, that I was instrumental in getting Steve Jefferys, then the Glasgow Organiser – and a very good one – to come down to London, to replace Andreas Nagliatti who had resigned, as Industrial Organiser, with a seat on the Executive Committee. This was a mistake because his organising talents were used to the full in the later fight against us.

On all the other counts I was also wrong. There was a great deal more dissatisfaction than I realised and it was a mistake to forego whatever advantage one might have had. One had to assume, as Cliff always did, that there would be collateral damage, but that is in the nature of such struggles and may be minimised with more evenly balanced forces. In the event, the faction fight that did eventually break out displayed a smaller minority than might otherwise have been the case. Even then, the majority found it necessary to use their control of the Centre to gerrymander the decisive conference. The Opposition thought they were fighting for the soul of the party, while Cliff struggled for his permanent casting vote.

Worse than Maxwell?

How dare you speak when I'm interrupting.
Gerry Healy

he Bellevue *Socialist Worker* Rally, in November 1973,
was successful, with 1,200 people attending. The following April, the Rank and File Conference was held in the
Digbeth Hall, Birmingham. Some 600 trade unionists applied for
credentials, and it is possible to gauge the effectiveness of the
previous work with rank and file papers by the fact that of 32
TGWU branches participating, eight of them were from London
bus garages where Platform circulated. *Hospital Worker* encouraged nine NUPE branches, two TGWU and one COHSE branch
to send delegates. *Carworker* was influential in getting twenty-one
AUEW and TGWU branches in the motor industry and twenty-
seven shop stewards' committees to the conference. In all more
than 300 trade union bodies applied for credentials, including 249
trade union branches, 40 combine and shop stewards' committees,
nineteen trades councils together with a few strike committees
and occupations.

If this did not look like the Petrograd Soviet in 1917 – or 1905,
come to that – it was a very creditable event. It is true that a majority of the contributions from the floor were from IS members;
it was still a matter of consequence that they were all experienced
trade unionists with something credible and apposite to say. Better still was the fact that there was a not insignificant number
of non-IS militants who spoke in support of the programme and

in favour of a continuing organisation to develop the rank and file movement. Outstanding among these was George Anderson, chairman of the joint shop stewards' committee at Coventry Radiators, and Joe McGough, convenor of Dunlop Speke and chairman of the Dunlop National Combine Committee. It was an impressive start that proved to be another false dawn. Cliff, influenced by Rosewell and Charlton, was not at all enthusiastic. It was clear that a deal of resources would need to be put into the building of the Rank and File Movement. That work would have to be self denying and dedicated to the proposition that the independence of the Rank and File Movement was one of the most important conditions for its eventual success. The benefit to IS was in the long term and the only guarantee that IS would be at the far end of the bridge to the revolutionary party, when the workers started to pass over it, was that we would establish our credentials, incontrovertibly, against all other comers. It was, in a word, an affirmation of our confidence in the work of the previous 25 years that IS politics were correct. To those of us who had some small part in developing those policies and passing them on to others, this seemed to be the ABC of Marxism in the 1970s. For Cliff's faction it appeared as a step too far in the dark. Precious resources that might be expended on immediate rewards should not be exchanged for something that might ultimately be more richly rewarding. By some quirk of fate, the opposition found itself defending Cliff's politics against Cliff's policies. If his faction had argued outright that the Group and the real world were as yet unready for the sort of long term ambitions represented by a successful Rank and File Movement, then there would have been a serious discussion that might have completely reoriented the Group. That, however, was not possible because for Cliff social upheaval, as in France in 1968 and later in Portugal (where according to Cliff the future was fascism or revolution led by a Portuguese IS), were the portents of the Europe-wide revolution. To take, perhaps, years to build a solid working class base would, for him, be some kind of Menshevism. Before then a period of experiment would divert the comrades and might even work.

With the Executive Committee now a pliant extension of Cliff's enthusiasms and the National Committee an extension of the Executive Committee, all the democratic structures of the Group failed to function, and other forces with different needs started to fill the vacuum. The full time organisers, the medium through which Cliff could give substance to his latest schemes, not only blossomed in the warm glow of Cliff's attentions, they also acquired a measure of power in their own right. This was neatly exemplified in the otherwise risible 'Buyers into Sellers' campaign.

In the course of writing his hagiography of Lenin, Cliff found himself examining afresh the institutions of IS in the light of his researches. Having wrought his Leninist magic on the Executive Committee with less than stunning success, he looked around to discover that the 'conservatives' were now ensconced in *Socialist Worker*. That the paper was still putting on circulation, while the membership remained static, was not something that an irrelevant diversion could not put straight. The first shot in the campaign was fired in the March 1974 issue of *ISJ* followed, in the April *Internal Bulletin*, by the second barrel.

The piece in *ISJ* #67 has some mildly interesting things to say in a general historical way. That, however, is not its purpose. It is designed to sell a policy on the basis of inadequate, partial and distorted evidence. Its authority rests on the fact that it is bolstered by quotations from the great Lenin, in the same way as, on occasion, Cliff will quote from Trotsky if the context could be made to look appropriate. Let us see how this works in practice. First we have to bear in mind that Cliff has a hidden agenda to dispense with some of the *Socialist Worker* journalists. Cliff writes:

> *Pravda was not a paper for workers; it was a workers' paper. It was very different to many other socialist papers, written by a tiny group of sometimes brilliant journalists. Lenin described one such paper as a 'journal for workers', as there is not a trace in it of either workers' initiatives, or any connection with working class organisations"*

The alleged Lenin quotation, within single quotes here, is from the *Collected Works*. The real quote actually reads as follows:

> *Trotsky's 'workers' journal' is Trotsky's journal for workers, as there is not a trace..., etc.*[1]

---

1. Lenin, *Collected Works*, vol. 20, p. 328.

It is quite amusing that Trotsky does not get named here because in the companion piece in the *Internal Bulletin* (April 1974) he is quoted approvingly on his views of the workers' paper. The deceit of course is that this doctoring of the text is to fool the reader, in whose eyes Lenin's authority might be reduced by the amount of weight accorded to Trotsky, if the report had been accurate. It does not end there either, because, while Cliff is suggesting that Lenin's *Pravda* was 'a workers' paper' the great man himself is actually not claiming anything of the sort. The article, with the pedestrian title, 'Disruption of Unity Under Cover of Outcries of Unity', is basically an attack – rather a sectarian attack as a matter of fact – on Trotsky for starting another socialist paper, *Borba*. Cliff fails to mention that *Borba* was intended as a journal to foster unity in the party, not to report strikes; it was a weekly not a daily, as was *Pravda*, and it only appeared for seven issues between February and July 1914. Once you appreciate that *Borba* and *Pravda* are as different as chalk and cheese, you might further think that *Socialist Worker* and *Pravda* are not particularly fruitful subjects for comparison. If you did come to this conclusion, you would be right and you would also have learned something about the Cliff method: history, for him, is a vast archive rich with precedents; he decides what he wants to do and then, like some shyster lawyer, pillages the past for something that can be made to fit his case.

Let us shed a little more light on the *Pravda* of 1912. It was a daily paper circulating mainly in Petrograd, half was sold on the street and the rest in the factories. Although as Cliff claims, the Bolsheviks in 1912 were smaller than IS in 1974, they had been a major force in 1905 and even in 1907 had 46,000 members. There was, therefore, a numerically small working class, a significant proportion of which had been in the Bolshevik ranks, employed in large enterprises – at the time the Putilov Works was the largest in the world. The Bolshevik's periphery was much bigger than anything the IS could dream of in 1974, because it contained literally tens of thousands of ex-members, their friends and workmates. In Tsarist Russia, there was a well established tradition for workers' groups to club together and collect a little money to help finance the founding of a paper. In the first months of 1912, workers' groups, overwhelmingly in Petrograd, made 504 collections for *Pravda*. That is not 504 distinct groups, it is the total. For instance in January 1912 there were fourteen group collections and 34 in June, the high point was in April with 227. Similar collections were made for Menshevik papers, although Lenin claimed not as successfully. With this in mind one can see that the statistics are not quite as impressive as Cliff presents them. Indeed, using similar arithmetic, the SWP could today claim 30,000 members, among whom, it could number Bill Ainsworth, Sid Bidwell, Stan Newens and Jim Higgins. One should be doubly careful in this case because not only is Cliff doctoring the statistics but also Lenin had already done a little sleight of hand himself. Cliff writes as follows:

> *During the whole of 1913* Pravda *received 2,181 contributions from workers' groups, while the Mensheviks received 661. In 1914 up to 13 May,* Pravda *had the support of 2,873 workers' groups, and the Mensheviks of 671. Thus the Pravdists organised 77 percent of the workers' groups in Russia in 1913 and 81 per cent in 1914... And Lenin correctly drew the conclusion: "Thus four-fifths of the workers have accepted the Pravdist decisions as their own, have approved of Pravdism, and actually rallied round Pravdism.'..."*

None of this stands up to examination. *Pravda* organised four-fifths of the total of Menshevik and Bolshevik worker support groups, there were workers' groups for other legal papers. For example, if you aggregate the total number of groups for *Pravda*, Mensheviks and Left Narodniks from January to May 1914, *Pravda* actually had 70 percent, Mensheviks seventeen per cent and Left Narodniks thirteen per cent. And still Lenin is only aggregating three sets of adherents, not the entire working class. With breathtaking nerve Lenin quotes these figures and then says:

> *The Pravdist newspaper is the only working class newspaper. Both the liquidationist* [Mensheviks, Trotsky, etc.–JH] *and the Left Narodnik newspapers are bourgeois newspapers. No lie can refute this objective fact.*

Don't you just love that 'objective fact' bit for what is actually Lenin's opinion? No wonder Cliff thinks so highly of him.

If the historical analogy is bent beyond repair what are you left with? Bald unsupported assertion, I fear. Cliff concludes his article:

> Workers who are not in IS should be asked to sell the paper to their workmates, to their neighbours on the estates, at trade union meetings, in the local pub. In addition, collection cards for regular donations to Socialist Worker should be issued on the widest possible scale. Last but not least the paper needs thousands of workers to write letters and reports for it... Members of IS will often find that involving nonmembers demands enormous persistence and perseverance. But without that involvement the gap between our organisation and the growing militancy of sections of the working class will remain... difficulties will arise again and again as we develop the network of Socialist Worker seller-supporters. But Marxism as a guide to action is not only a science it is also an art... Hence it demands improvisation and daring when it comes to organisational forms...

The last two sentences quoted here are such richly steaming products of the byre they almost make your eyes water. Marxism as a scientific art form guiding us to action is a concept only Cliff could dream up. His apotheosis into the Leonardo da Vinci of the dialectic is rather like the man who was astonished to discover that he had been speaking prose all his life. As the connoisseurs marvel at the beauty of line, the elegant dissonance of mixed metaphor and the grace of composition in the buyers into sellers campaign, the workers can explain how they don't know anything about scientific art but they do know what they don't like. Not only that, the concept can be extended to organisation where artistic Marxist science appears as daring improvisation. The coded message here is: The more barefaced and arbitrary my diktat, the more Marxist it becomes.

In his enthusiasm for the Buyers into Sellers campaign, Cliff variously estimated between 1,000 and 5,000 buyers becoming sellers, with a lot more becoming *Socialist Worker* supporters. Cards were printed to enable supporters to have their contributions marked; they were of a somewhat bulky design and became known as 'revolutionary beer-mats'. If 11,000 items written by workers could appear in *Pravda* in 12 months, Cliff maintained (although without reference or attribution), why not 50 each week, 2,500 a year in *Socialist Worker*? As Cliff put it, *"It is much easier for Paul Foot, for instance, to write a whole page on his own than to edit five or six stories that will also fill a page."* This, of course, was one reason why Paul Foot would not have done it.

The policy announced in *ISJ*, subsequently rubber stamped through the National Committee, was then put before a meeting of full timers. Here, as if to confirm Joe Stalin who said, *"The cadres decide everything"*, the policy was greeted with a resounding raspberry. That day, Buyers into Sellers bit the dust, a sad confirmation that historical analogy is always of limited value and may be counter-productive if you are tampering with the evidence to bolster a bad case.

What remained was the revolutionary beer-mats and the worker-writers for *Socialist Worker*. The first fizzled out very quickly – another mountain that turned out to be a small depression. The worker-writers were not so easily lost and had real factional value for Cliff and his satraps.

The leading areas Executive Committee was not a disaster at all, it was nothing less than a damp squib. Its sole purpose seems to have been to engineer the exclusion of Jim Higgins and Duncan Hallas. In short order, two of its members resigned and the full body met once or twice a month, hardly close attention to the activity it was supposed to promote. To make up the numbers, Nigel Harris was brought back, so was Chris Harman, then Granville Williams, another exceptionally good organiser with an ability to get close to and recruit experienced workers, and then Paul Holborow, Wolverhampton organiser. He was a great Cliff fan who I once heard described as, *"A Stakhanovite sycophant who has overfulfilled his grovelling norm"* – a nicely rounded phrase I thought, and accurate too. Rosewell was by now back in Liverpool, where he established a fiefdom from which he would sally forth occasionally to abuse the National Committee and Executive Committee. Having cashed in his one way El Al ticket to the land of sad oranges, he resumed his pose of granite hard bolshevism, the theory fashioned for him by the fine Italian hand of Andreas Nagliatti, supported by Glyn Carver, the Manchester organiser. They talked so tough even their tongues were muscle-bound.

In his April 1974 *Internal Bulletin* article Cliff had been quite complimentary about *Socialist Worker*:

> *There is no question that* Socialist Worker *has improved radically over the last few years in terms of involvement of workers in writing for it. There is no question that it is by far the best socialist paper on the left for decades.*

It is strange, therefore, that he was shortly giving tongue to the thought that he found the paper unreadable, let alone the workers. So obvious was the whispering campaign directed against Higgins, Hallas and Protz that, on Duncan's urging, a few National Committee members met informally to discuss the problems. They were Ross Pritchard, a leading left wing member of the NGA and a machine minder in SW Litho, the Group's printshop, Roger Protz, John Palmer, Jim Higgins and Duncan Hallas. Of these the most alienated and bitter was Duncan who, not unreasonably, had a particular animus for Cliff. It was decided to produce a document detailing our disagreements with the campaign against *Socialist Worker*, the political and industrial perspectives, especially the Rank and File Movement and the nature of the regime in IS. At the end of the day the document received additional support from other members of the National Committee; Wally Preston, Manchester power worker, Ron Murphy, Manchester AEUW, Granville Williams, Birmingham organiser, Rob Clay, Teesside organiser, Arthur Affleck, steelworker Teesside, Ken Appleby, draughtsman, Keightly and Tony Barrow. This was then sent for inclusion in the April 1974 *Internal Bulletin*.

If our intention had been to upset the Executive Committee, we could not have calculated more accurately. The signatories available in London–Hallas, Higgins, Palmer and Protz–were summoned to meet the Executive Committee. Arrayed before us, rather like a French Committee of Public Safety in a Baroness Orczy novel, were Cliff, Harman, Peers, Harris and Nichol, who had obviously chosen the role of Citizen Chauvelin–he is the character who rubber stamped the death sentences. We had been sent for, it turned out, to withdraw our document in the interest of Group unity. There was, unfortunately, to be no meeting of minds: Nichol's presence on their side probably precluded that. There was no quid pro quo offered, no attempt to engage us in some dialogue, or to accept our seriousness and sincerity that we too had some concerns about IS. Our role in all this was to roll over and play dead and the Executive Committee would then roll over us without a second thought. We took the view, like all serious Marxists or anyone else with an ounce of principle, that we would not withdraw our document. At this Nichol swore violently and flung his chair against the wall. We took this as his way of saying that the meeting was terminated and left, all the while wondering if there was, after all, some truth in the old canard: 'a Geordie is a Scotsman with his brains kicked out'.

The response to our document in the Group as a whole was encouraging and depressing at the same time. It was nice to know that we were not alone, but it was alarming to see the number of angry, puzzled and increasingly disaffected members in virtually every part of the country. Predictable, but tedious, was the campaign mounted from the Centre against the 'conservative elements'. The full flowering of this became apparent at the May National Committee.

The first thing that one noticed on entering the meeting room, over a King's Cross pub, was the presence of a small detachment of Liverpool Proletarian Light Horse, whose task it was to act as a claque, jeering any oppositional speakers. One of their number, clearly an Alan Bleasdale prototype, intervened at one point to explain wittily at full bellow, *"We're the workers we'll march all over you"*. To get the full flavour of this try it in as broad a scouse accent as you can manage. Cliff was nervous, and why not; he was just about to jettison a large lump of IS theory.

He informed us that *Socialist Worker* had entirely the wrong focus, the emphasis on advanced militants was misconceived. The people moving to revolution were the young and traditionless, while their elders were bent, having established comfortable niches for themselves in the shop steward's committees and union branches. This, he said, was the meaning of the theory of the *Changing Locus of Reformism*. For the new levy of revolutionaries what was needed was a paper that exposed the scandals of the system in short pithy *Daily Mirror* style journalism. If only the journalists would apply themselves to this new layer and adapt to sub-edit the workers' copy, then 80,000, nay 100,000, copy sales of the paper could be ours.

In the discussion that followed it was quite difficult to have a sensible debate. The Proletarian Light Horse noisily indicated their displeasure with anything less than fulsome agreement with Cliff, while Jim Nichol entertained the claque by making grossly offensive interjections from the sidelines. It was unedifying, it was ridiculous and it made a mockery of twenty-five years of IS politics

Of course, the chance of doubling the *Socialist Worker* circulation was, for the innocent, a beguiling prospect and at the time I failed to realise that Cliff did not believe in his prescription any more than I did. A moment's reflection would have indicated that not only would a Rank and File Movement be useless with a generation of bent stewards, but Buyers into Sellers would look pretty silly as well. If the 'changing locus of reformism' was not about the importance of the shop floor and the advanced workers, then Cliff's books on Incomes Policy and Productivity Bargaining were an exercise in daydreaming, not to speak of a more or less total denial of Leninism. If it meant that the whole trade union machine, both official and unofficial, was rigged, then our first task would be to see how we could assist in building new revolutionary syndicates, an essay into dual unionism, another Industrial Workers of the World.

The matter goes further. If we were seriously convinced that one of the fundamental, and most securely based, Group theories was really about the corruption of the shop stewards, then *Socialist Worker* should have exposed it in every issue. Paul Foot, who was always a dab hand at the shock, horror, scandal type story, might have written something like this:

> *James Roberts (34) convener at United Grumblewuzzits, Acton, was heard calling the Works' Manager, Frederick Fredericks, (54) by his first name. According to union member Jack Spriggs (18),* "There is a great deal of anger in Grumblewuzzits at this unprincipled class collaboration. These old men are rotted by the fruits of office, he won't even become a *Socialist Worker* buyer let alone a seller. When the new interpretation of the 'changing locus of reformism' has had time to bed down properly, I will run against him, if I can find a seconder. I reckon that I'd be pretty good once I find out what mutuality and measured day work are all about".

Of course no stories of that kind appeared in any IS publica-tion, under any signature, let alone Cliff's. The whole thing was a set up. Cliff saw an opposition that was almost as much a part of IS as himself; it could not be shrugged off as an alien intrusion. To fix it he was prepared to deny vigorously that which a few weeks before he had affirmed wholeheartedly. It was a sad spectacle and an earnest of worse to come.

Immediately after the National Committee, an emergency Ex-ecutive Committee meeting was convened at which it was decided that Dave Peers and Jim Nichol should seek Roger Protz's res-ignation from the editorship of *Socialist Worker*. It will surprise nobody that Roger, who was a voting member of the Executive Committee in his role of *Socialist Worker* editor, was not invited to this meeting. Having secured Roger's editorship, the Execu-tive Committee then organised the sacking of Jim Higgins from *Socialist Worker*. The whole episode was conducted with such well rounded and polished cynicism that one was left awestruck at the sheer cheek of it all. It has to be said, though, that the National Secretary's letter to the branches purporting to explain matters had all the veracity and half the credibility of a snake oil salesman. It combined unctuousness and menace in a way that had not been seen since Uriah Heep.[1]

The response from the branches was surprise, bewilderment and, in some cases, anger. Many sent resolutions demanding rein-statement and calling for a full discussion of the disputed ques-tions. At the May National Committee, the Executive Committee was censured for its decision to force Roger out and to sack Jim Higgins, but the call for reinstatement was not carried. A similar result was obtained from the conference. Cliff, of course, is quite happy to lose the odd vote so long as he gets his own way and, as he would probably have ignored a resolution to put them back on *Socialist Worker*, it did not make much difference anyway.

For my own part, although I had enjoyed working on the paper immensely, I found that in some ways it was a relief not to have to work any more with Foot. Prior to his metamorphosis into Cliff's cats-paw, I had thought of him as a bit of a weak sister, given to buckling under pressure, as his antics over the Common Market

1. Reprinted here as an Appendix; 'Dave Peers: Letter to IS Branches', p. 221.

debate showed, but I had not judged him so feeble as to be unable to work with somebody who disagreed with him. Since then, of course, he has been able to work, for a king's ransom – albeit a small Balkan kingdom – for Robert Maxwell without damage to his delicate psyche, although he did find the dubious Ulster charm of David Montgomery more than even he could stand. Now there is a useful marker for a chap to measure himself against. I am worse than Maxwell but on a par with Montgomery. Another entry for the old CV?

Completely Changed

If desired a man can be completely changed
... and after such a change has been accomplished,
he will be suitable for any purpose.
Bertolt Brecht

Arising from the furore about the changes in orientation and staff on *Socialist Worker*, it was necessary for the leadership to establish the theoretical basis for their antics. For a job like this Cliff was outstandingly well qualified, and he obliged in the May 1974 *Internal Bulletin*, in a piece entitled 'The Way Ahead for IS'.[1] The central political point was effectively answered by Ruth Nelson.[2] What she did not take up was the essential dishonesty of Cliff's article. It starts with a weary reference to this, 'petty squabble', as if 'nasty types' or 'weak nerved dilettanti' had forced the quarrel on him. After all it was he who rewrote theory on the hoof to justify dubious and ultimately unsuccessful organisational proposals.

Like so many of his articles it starts with a quote from Lenin without reference, a sure sign that a full reading of the text would probably indicate the reverse of what he was attempting to prove. Certainly he never produced a quote from Lenin in which the great man damned experience and tradition in mature workers.

The reference to Kidron's article in *International Socialism* #7 is to a piece entitled 'Reform or Revolution: Rejoinder to Left Reformism'. It is essentially an exposition of the Permanent Arms Economy (a theory, readers may recall, repudiated by Kidron in

1. See appendix: 'Cliff: The Way Ahead for the IS', p. 229.
2. See appendix; 'Ruth Nelson: Who is Our Audience?', p. 233.

1977) with just one page devoted to *"the diffusion of the locus of reformism"*. In a very abstract manner, it is true, Kidron confounds Cliff's notion that there has been a *"depoliticisation of the mass of the workers"*. He wrote:

> *For him [the worker] reform and revolution are not separate activities, enshrined in distinct and separate organizational loyalties; his transition from reform to revolution is natural, immediate and unhampered by the vested interests of a reformist organisation and one eminently responsive to changing circumstances.*

Kidron is making the point with some force that the new politics of shop floor reforms have the possibility of going over to revolution in the pursuit of their aims. The form of organisation is the one that the worker can relate to closely and control. It is the shop stewards' committee or whatever is the rank and file form that fits the job and is best able to carry on the fight. Hardly a recommendation for the young and traditionless.

The discussion on the Cliff-Barker pamphlet, *Incomes Policy Legislation and Shop Stewards*, is even less apropos. This was a thesis which, somewhat optimistically, counterposed the linking of rank and file committees to the government and trade union leaders' collaboration in Incomes Policy laws. When it was published, the very notion that it was directed to the very young would have been laughed out of court. Indeed, the fact that it contained an introduction by Reg Birch, at the time a long standing and leading Communist in the AUEW and who was adopting an oppositional line to King Street, shows that it was a pamphlet addressed to mature trade unionists. Further still, the work that succeeded the Incomes Policy book was the Productivity pamphlet. This was a work that presented a detailed plan for productivity bargaining which included a sliding scale of demands. It had been written after a long series of discussions with shop stewards and rank and file workers in a number of industries, especially engineering. Suffice it to say that the general run of Cliff's informants were not particularly young or inexperienced, or that the book's prescriptions for militant struggle were primarily directed to those who did not fill a shop stewardship or other rank and file representative post.

Perhaps the most telling refutation of Cliff's new insight into the wellspring of workers' revolution is in the experience at ENV. Here, Geoff Carlsson, a well established and talented IS member had, over time, been instrumental in bringing to the organisation a number of militants, many of them ex-Communist Party members, to form an IS branch that was Cliff's pride and joy – the apotheosis of his theory about the locus of reformism. It was the living denial of his later nonsense.

He was right to say that IS recruited more young workers than older ones, but absurdly wrong to suggest that they were in some way more pure because unsullied by trade union experience. It is always the case that the young are more readily persuaded to revolutionary politics and it is equally inevitable that revolutions are not made without a lot of revolutionaries across the whole length of the age range. If being over twenty-five is, by definition, to be reformist, then Cliff is already a three time loser.

To compound this error Cliff went on to cast severe doubt on his own judgement by suggesting that these paragons of youthful virtue should be contesting for shop stewards' positions. Had they got enough workers to vote for them to ensure election, then they would have then actually have had to carry out some stewardship, like representing discipline cases, allowances, rates and favourably implementing national agreements, not all of which are susceptible to an excited cry of, 'all out'. Which, of course, is why the youngster would not get the workers' votes.

If words mean anything, the 'workers' newspaper' was to be written by, and the 'workers' leadership' was to be drawn from, this youthful band. This pathetic rationalisation piled absurdity on absurdity, concluding in a great heap of mystical nonsense. Because they were workers, they could write about industrial matters in an agitational way, relating it to the overall politics of IS. Fresh from this synthesis, they could work their magic on the politics of IS. This they would do not on the basis of their experience in leading workers in struggle, but because they were workers. Using the same fractured logic, every Tibetan male could be the Dalai Lama.

As a matter of fact, inexperienced these youths might be, but they certainly would display less ignorance of the workers' movement than Cliff and his middle class cadre. Of course, neither these nor any other workers wrote for *Socialist Worker* in any significant numbers, nor did they have any leadership role in IS politics. They had become, like the ark of the covenant, an object of veneration, fulfilling a purely decorative function. Their inherent revolutionary merit could be measured in voting positively for anything Cliff proposed.

The very idea of a Rank and File Movement that transcended single industries, unions and enterprises, but did not have a solid base of shop stewards and lay union officials, is a contradiction in terms. No matter how Cliff and his minions squirmed, rewrote IS theory and misquoted Lenin, the contradiction remained. With the benefit of hindsight, it seems clear that Cliff did not believe that IS had the capacity, even with the correct orientation, to build a Rank and File Movement. It is, of course, perfectly honourable to hold such a view. What is totally dishonourable is to conceal that thinking and to dredge up some half baked theory, adherence to which will ensure the failure of any Rank and File strategy. When one considers that the Rank and File strategy was formally the focus of IS activity for several years – despite the fact that after a promising start it very rapidly became moribund – only to find fitful life as the vehicle for the Right to Work campaign, one can see that it was a facade to conceal some very tattered credibility.

For a number of us, who had spent some time in IS congratulating ourselves on its comparative sanity, all of this came as a nasty shock. We did not believe that IS was teetering on the brink of becoming a party, but we did believe that it had grown sufficiently to become a force of attraction to militants and a source of embarrassment to the union bureaucrats in several industries and unions. At around this time, for example, Clive Jenkins, the General Secretary of the ASTMS, became quite paranoid about IS and its attacks on himself and his Stalinist allies.

The signatories to the document 'Socialist Worker Perspectives and Organisation' realised they were faced with more than a bureaucratic attempt to do a clear out on the Executive Committee and *Socialist Worker*. Here was an attempt to rewrite the working class content of IS politics, to write minus where before we had written plus. The theory of State Capitalism was a persuasive explanation of what had happened in Russia, Eastern Europe and

China and it was that analysis that helped us to keep our eyes off the 'socialist forms' of state property, etc., and to concentrate on the working class content on all the relevant political questions. Even so, it was not essential to adhere to State Capitalism to accept the notion of the centrality of the working class and to analyse and build on contemporary working class experience. For us, it would have been a lot easier to swallow if Cliff had engaged in an agonising appraisal of State Capitalism – so long as he did not replace it with any guff about workers' states or bureaucratic collectivism, the Permanent Arms Economy and Permanent Revolution – than the grievous bodily harm that was done to hard won insights on trade union and industrial work. To wrench the group

about in this cavalier fashion required not only a compliant leadership, but also a complete about face on the question of the regime.

With a fairly heavy heart, a majority of the signatories decided that it was necessary to form a faction to defend the essential core of IS politics. The name IS Opposition was deliberately chosen to indicate that we stood on the basic traditions of the *Socialist Review* and International Socialist's past theory and practice. It was then that we lost Duncan Hallas. After a lengthy discussion with Cliff, Duncan informed us that he no longer wished to be associated with our opposition. It has to be said that this was disappointing. Not only was he one of the more persuasive speakers and writers in the group but he was also the most vigorous proponent of our original protest, and it seemed to me that, having willed the struggle, it was only proper to bear the consequences, if and when they came.

Duncan took a different view, bolstered no doubt by the promise of continued full time employment, the return of his seat on the Executive Committee and the promise that the sunny side of

Cliff's countenance would shine forth upon him in the future. What is responsibility, solidarity and political principle compared to these treasures? Not very much, apparently. Cliff's cynicism in all of this was quite breathtaking. Duncan Hallas, whose presence on the Executive Committee a few month's before would, according to Cliff, have completely vitiated its work, was now welcomed back with open arms. We were aware that the dialectic is about contradiction but this sort of hypocrisy was a contradiction too far.

The new Executive Committee – Dave Peers, National Secretary; Paul Foot, *Socialist Worker* Editor; Steve Jefferys, Industrial Organiser; Chris Harman, ISJ; Jim Nichol, Treasurer; plus Duncan Hallas; Nigel Harris; Tony Cliff; John Charlton; Ross Pritchard – was split into two camps: the majority had degrees and the minority, Cliff, Nichol and Pritchard, did not. This was the committee that was to represent the leading areas and enshrine worker leadership. It was not bad, just no better than any other six possible committees – certainly not such an assemblage of talent that it was necessary to set the Group in a turmoil to seat them. Ross Pritchard was, of course a worker but did not fit Cliff's ideal prescription in that he was in his mid-thirties, a very experienced trade unionist and had been in the group since the early 1960s. He atoned for these errors by not staying on the Executive Committee for long. Truly the mountains had been in labour, having forgotten how they got pregnant in the first place.

The basic document of this IS Opposition was called, *The International Socialists: Our Traditions.*[1] In ten duplicated A4 pages it set out to call the members' attention to serious problems developing in the group. It attempted to show that the disputes were not about a couple of old party hacks being nasty because they had been fired. It spoke of the growth of IS and the need to consolidate and avoid spurious get rich quick policies like the Buyers into Sellers. It criticised the youth vanguard thesis. The document went on to oppose another stratagem for putting on members, the white collar branch and the student branch. This last laughable piece of froth had all sorts of comic consequences. Teachers branches were formed under the tutelage of the junior Industrial Organiser John Deason, who seemed to think that they could op-

---

1. See below, p. 391.

erate rather like the ENV branch might have done, taking the national agreement and building on it in the localities. Never mind that, in teaching, agreements are reached and all the i's dotted, and all the t's crossed far away from the reach of any rank and file teachers, even those being hectored by John Deason. The student branch notion was even more risible, with Chris Harman giving voice to the proposition that, to save the workers being swamped in student excesses, the student branches should be given only half the votes of other branches. At the time, this particular sally almost convinced me that he had a sense of humour.

The greatest of the offenses committed by the IS Opposition document was the brief section, 'Cliff's Influence Within the Leadership', which detailed a few of the more glaring faults displayed by Cliff. It did so in muted tones that I now think to have been altogether too restrained, saying inter alia:

> *Cliff has great and probably indispensable strengths... Unfortunately, they are accompanied by a number of less desirable traits. Unlike Trotsky or Lenin, he finds detailed work of organisation or administration boring unless it is directed to his own immediate preoccupation. His rigid certainties, so long as the passing enthusiasm lasts, brooks no contradiction... Cliff is not a disciplined member of a collective and leading committees are good to the extent they agree wholeheartedly with his ideas and bad to impossible to the extent that they do not.*

These few thoughts on Cliff – a commonplace amongst those who knew him well – were received in the same spirit as one imagines the devout Christian would display if he caught someone using the Holy Grail as a chamber pot. Nobody actually shouted 'sacrilege' but it was made clear that Cliff and his coterie found this kind of open critique deeply offensive and a spur to increasing their covert campaign of slanders against the IS Opposition.

A note on the IS Traditions document reported that it was supported by, "*The following National Committee members: Ken Appleby, Rob Clay, Jim Higgins, Ron Murphy, John Palmer, Wally Preston, Granville Williams*". As if to prove the twin adages that it is best to be at the top of the ballot paper and that it pays to advertise, Ken Appleby was offered and accepted a job as Assistant Industrial Organiser, to work with Steve Jefferys. Ken was, incidentally, a very nice chap; a very capable and experienced militant, a draughtsman who had conducted long strikes and been victimised by employers. His new job also involved lengthy struggles and ended with him being victimised by the ambitious and hyperactive John Deason. Not a pleasant story but there was a lot of it about at the time.

At the September 1974 IS conference, the disputed questions were not clarified and, due to the vagaries of the agenda, hardly discussed. A few of the IS Opposition comrades were elected to the National Committee – John Palmer, Granville Williams and Rob Clay. The fact that the IS Opposition would not go away and still insisted that it was defending the IS tradition against the existing leadership proved to be one obstacle too many to the vanguard of the workers' vanguard. One fairly hefty straw in the wind was the appointment of Jim Nichol as National Secretary in place of Dave Peers. While one might view with some trepidation the outcome of the deliberations of a jury of one's Peers, it would be a foregone conclusion that, with a jury of Nichols, you needn't bother with the prosecution case, the bastard's already been found guilty.

IS now had what might be called a balanced political leadership. Paul Foot produced the sort of paper Cliff wanted, Hallas and Harman produced the justification for Cliff's latest wheeze and Nichol could sort out organisation questions to the detriment of the IS Opposition. In pursuit of this objective an Organisation Commission was formed. Cliff delved deeply into the 1922 Dutt-Pollitt report for the CPGB and regurgitated it

RODIN'S OPPOSITIONIST

practically whole. As Harry Wicks wrote to me in April 1975: "*It is not an exaggeration to say how heavily they have borrowed from Dutt. Christ they have even pinched the punctuation.*"

Here we have the emphasis on locals and district committees, on security and the imitation of the Bolshevik model. Cliff was unaware, or chose to forget – even though Harry Wicks who had been in the Communist Party at the time could have refreshed his

memory – that the Dutt-Pollitt report was not just a reorganisation of the party. It had far more important objectives: to displace
the leadership of ex-Socialist Labour Party members such as Mc-
Manus, Paul and Bell and to install a leadership more compliant to
the Russian party. The year after its implementation it had to be
severely amended, having achieved its original objective.

For Cliff and Nichol the historical question was beside the
point, it provided a ready made solution on how to minimise the
presence of the IS Opposition at the conference. Delegacies to the
conference were to be increased from one per fifteen members to
one per thirty members. Elections were to take place at District
meetings instead of branches. In very few places did the opposition have a majority in Districts, although it did in a number of
branches. Contrary to Cliff's 1968 ideas for minority representation, the elections were to be on a winner take all basis. The net
result was that the IS Opposition, who had significant minorities
in a number of Districts was denied its fair representation.

The existing structures of a National Committee – theoretically
in overall political control and electing an Executive Committee
to carry on the business of the Group between monthly National
Committee meetings – was to be jettisoned in favour of a Central
Committee elected at conference and an advisory National Council with delegacies from districts and fractions, that essentially
reverted to the federal system of yore. What was clear was that
a system that had only fitfully been able to restrain the full time
apparat was being replaced by a system of absolutely no control
at all.

To add to the general air of hysteria it was decreed, on the
grounds of security, that the coming conference would be open
only to delegates. This was a significant break with the past and
one that was definitely not in the spirit or practice of Bolshevism
where, even at the height of repression, members were entitled to
attend such gatherings whether or not they were delegates. The
venue was to be kept secret and this particular stratagem, to keep
the IS Opposition even further at bay, led to the ludicrous situation where delegates wandered about Finsbury Park looking for
the comrade who would guide them to the conference. Whether
the guide wore a red carnation in his button hole I cannot remember, but I do recall that it took about five minutes to discover in

which hotel the conference was being held, a puzzle that would have taken even the dumbest agent of state repression not much longer to solve. All of this high drama – which was, in reality, even higher farce – was made more absurd by the fact that, while the members were kept away, guests at the hotel and those availing themselves of its public facilities could indulge themselves with the pleasure of listening to Cliff in full rant. As it happens, not many of them did so. Perhaps he was off form that day.

The thing that is of passing interest about all this constitution changing is that it was unconstitutional. Clause fourteen of the IS Constitution says categorically: *"These rules shall only be amended at Conference"*. In a neat reversal of the democratic norm, the delegates were elected under a set of rules that constitutionally did not exist, which they could, as unconstitutional delegates, then proceed to validate, at an improperly constituted conference. If it does not hurt your head, you can begin to realise the deep creativity of Cliff's Marxism. One is reminded of the ruler in the Brecht story who found that the people were deeply repellent to him and resolved to elect a new lot.

The publication of the document *Platform of the IS Opposition*[1], elicited a quick response from the Central Committee. That it was not long delayed was not at all surprising, and in a way I suppose it was equally unsurprising that the author of the reply should be Duncan Hallas. There is a certain dreadful symmetry in the picture of a man who had a short time before subscribed to most of the IS Opposition's criticisms and, indeed, had been the first to articulate many of them, should now be pressed, or maybe volunteered, to fill the role of hammer of the opposition. Suffice it to say that it was the signal for a stiffening of attitude to the Opposition.

In the West London District, the full time organiser, a nervous incompetent called John Rose, was flushed with loyalty to the Central Committee and produced a tendentious document denouncing the Twickenham branch for its association with the IS Opposition. His intention, it seems, was to make Harry Wicks articulate his own political position in the debate. Harry was always

---

1. See appendix, 'Platform of the IS Opposition', p. 237, and also 'Reply to Duncan Hallas by the IS Opposition', p. 263.

willing to oblige – and so that there was no dubiety, this polite but politically tough man expressed himself with some vigour:

> *It has never occurred to me before that anyone was in any doubt as to where I stand: For those who do nurture such doubts, let me say as clearly as possible;* **I go all the way with the IS Opposition and further** *[emphasis in original]... The organisational changes introduced on the eve of the conference I consider are an impermissible violation of the norms of democratic centralism... Let me make it clear. All the time I am in IS I shall fight against any concession to the Maoist and neo-Stalinist conception of the monolithic party.*[1]

These signs of opposition from Harry Wicks were most unwelcome and Rose took steps to isolate the Twickenham branch and to pursue a kind of vendetta against them. Ted Crawford, who was a member in the West London District but not the Twickenham branch, was moved to write to John Rose:

> *I find your treatment of comrade Wicks quite insolent. You cannot answer him politically. Having jacked up somebody to stand against him and canvassed the vote, your young proto-Bolshevik could not even attend conference... Do you really think in your factional zeal that comrades could not learn from Harry? He might be wrong but would you be able to tell unless your employers told you?*[2]

In the same letter, Ted describes how in two years, "*I have seen the membership [of West London District] halve from nearly 100 to 44… in your position I would hand in my cap and jacket as a fulltimer*". At the September District Aggregate, Rose had reported that, as there was an imminent wave of repression and the Group would be semi-underground, all standing orders to the Group should be suspended and subscriptions paid in notes to the treasurer. This may have been a directive from the Centre, but far more likely an excess of zeal on Rose's part and, given the already reduced membership, played havoc with the District's income. This may

---

1. Harry Wicks, Letter to the IS Executive Committee, 24th April 1975.
2. Ted Crawford, Letter to John Rose, West Middlesex Organiser, 11th September 1975.

be why, two months later, the policy was reversed. Eventually the Twickenham branch and Ted Crawford were suspended at a meeting they were not permitted to attend.

At the Northern Home Counties Aggregate, in May 1975, IS Opposition resolutions on Democratic Centralism, the Rank and File Movement and Women were carried by two to one majorities. Unhappily they had insufficient time to discuss the political perspectives and so a further meeting was arranged for a week later with a speaker invited from the Executive Committee. As a mark either of their contempt for the District, or for their own political perspectives, the Executive Committee sent down Jim Nichol. True to his reputation as the first non-political National Secretary of IS, Nichol took up his allotted time attacking the Harlow Branch, which supported the *Platform of the IS Opposition*. It emerged that he had spent his day happily perusing the files of the local press at Harlow public library. As a result of this research he claimed the branch had not acted on strikes, redundancies and public expenditure cuts. It just happened that the Harlow branch, which contained such excellent members as Hugh Kerr, now an MEP, Barbara Kerr and Sue Lambert, was one of the most active on local issues and had fought on all of these questions. It takes more than being absolutely wrong to faze Jim Nichol, and he went on to attempt to force a reelection of the conference delegates who were supporters of the IS Opposition. No success there either.

By May of 1975, some 135 members had declared their support for the *Platform of the IS Opposition* and others were known to exist. At the April National Committee, fourteen voted against the proposed organisational changes, twelve of them workers. A collection of representative bodies within IS (Industrial and geographic branches and some District Committees) protested the new rules. At a number of district aggregates, debates between Executive Committee and IS Opposition speakers frequently resulted in a win for the Opposition. John Palmer was particularly active and successful. Of course, the debates were usually held where the IS Opposition had some presence because in totally loyalist areas they made certain that IS Opposition speakers were not invited.

In the event, the leadership's gerrymander was effective and only seventeen IS Opposition members were elected as conference delegates. Not surprisingly, the organisational proposals were endorsed by large majorities. All that was required now was tidying up operation. The IS Opposition were told to disband; its arguing license was being withdrawn. As if to reinforce the fact that there was no longer a place for 'conservatives' who clung to the old traditions that had animated, sustained and built IS over the years, the new orthodoxy required a dramatic gesture, a real blood-letting sacrifice of the past.

In Birmingham – where, incidentally, the IS Opposition probably had a majority – the organiser, Granville Williams, had been an excellent recruiter and builder of the Group and was particularly good at bringing experienced trade unionists and stewards in to membership. Naturally enough, and this is another reason why Cliff and his dopey youth thesis was wrong, shop stewards do not come washed and shriven to the movement, a blank consciousness on which the leadership can write its revolutionary software. They come to revolutionary politics through their own experience and, precisely because they are experienced, they live in a real world where they have commitments and alliances that are not easily set aside because someone on the Central Committee has had a rush of blood to the place where his brain ought to have been. In this case, the cerebral haemorrhage was in pursuit of the desirable, but long term, ambition of replacing the Communist Party as the recognised left in the AUEW. It seemed like a splendid wheeze to run an IS member in the upcoming election for National Organiser. So overcome were the Central Committee by the manifest splendour of the new policy that they did not feel the need to discuss it with the AUEW fraction. After all, only a beast argues with revealed truth.

Largely as a result of Granville's efforts, there were more than twenty IS members in the AUEW in Birmingham, organised in two factory branches and an industrial branch. Among them there were ten shop stewards, two convenors of big factories, six members of the AUEW District Committee – one of whom was the District President – and several Trades Council delegates. All of them had been in IS for at least two years and some for up to eight years: most of them were veterans of hard fought and hard won strikes and other militant actions. All in all you might think, it was a collection of workers that any revolutionary group would have been anxious to recruit and retain. Wrong. In a combination of the maladroit and the malicious, the Central Committee conspired to rid IS of the embarrassment of the best industrial hope they had had since the high days of ENV.

The background to this piece of primitive dis-accumulation of the cadre is straightforward. In the unity moves of happier times in 1972 and 1973, IS had attempted to involve the Communist Party in joint activity on a limited programme. This had not happened nationally, but in the unions where IS had any sort of presence its members would involve themselves with what was the generally recognised left caucus. In the AUEW, the Broad Left was the most developed forum for discussion and debate on tactics and policy. The strong representation of the Communist Party ensured that the Broad Left had a predilection for election-eering – in a union with an election for one post or another going on practically all the time – but for anyone with any pretensions to revolutionary work that was more than posturing or phrase-making it was a serious area for activity. Indeed, at the 1974 IS conference Andreas Nagliatti and his faction had been denounced as 'syndicalists' for opposing IS Broad Left policy in the AUEW. As serious militants and as loyal members, the Birmingham engi-neers were involved in the Broad Left and as part of that involve-ment they had agreed to support the candidature of a Communist Party member, Phil Higgs, convenor of the Rolls Royce factory, for the National Organiser job. This, it has to be said, was before the Central Committee or anybody else thought of running Willie Lee, an IS member and a well thought of AUEW militant in Glas-gow. Willie's credentials for the job were fine, the question was: is this the way to most fruitfully pursue work in the AUEW? If the notion was to build a serious challenge to the Communist Party in engineering, would it not have been better to fight on policy, where they could be put on the defensive, rather than electorally where they had their greatest strength?

To endorse the Lee campaign the IS leadership called an AUEW fraction conference in Manchester. Along with quite a few others, the Birmingham comrades turned up to explain their circumstances and to oppose the candidacy. Vic Collard, a Senior

Steward at Lucas in Birmingham, put the case against running an IS candidate and won an overwhelming vote in his favour. Now comes the clear indication that the move was less related to a particular policy initiative and more towards getting the Birmingham engineering workers. At the IS Conference, the Central Committee organised a meeting of any delegates who also happened to be AUEW members and secured a favourable vote for running Willie Lee as candidate for National Organiser. This ad-hoc meeting apparently outranked the national AUEW fraction meeting because, the Central Committee claimed, it was held at Conference which was the supreme policy making body. Presumably if Cliff had a vision that he was V.I. Lenin reincarnated, it would be true so long as it occurred at the Conference venue.

Steve Jefferys was sent to Birmingham to call the AUEW members to order. They attempted to explain to him and the Central Committee that long term work in the unions and the rank and file would always have its drawbacks this side of the revolution, and that we would have to forego the luxury of suck it and see policies if we were ever to be taken seriously by more than a handful of workers. As Mick Rice, a leading Birmingham IS engineer, wrote:

> *comrades may ask, why did the Birmingham AUEW comrades not submit to the discipline of IS? Do they hold their association with a bunch of CPers, Tribuneites and other left elements more dear than membership of the revolutionary organisation? The answer is simple, in fact the comrades have considerably more respect for IS than they have for any amorphous body like the Broad Left. They also, incidentally, have a great deal more respect for IS, its tradition and standing in the labour movement than does the current crop of IS leaders. They pursued what was IS policy for several years, their misfortune is that they have succeeded and unlike those with no record of success they cannot just jettison the work they have done. Let us give an example. Just recently a leading IS member Cde Arthur Harper, was reelected AUEW District President. This was achieved because; A. Arthur is a respected long standing militant, with a proven record of struggle; and B., because he was in receipt of Broad Left support. He would not otherwise have been elected. Having effected an alliance on that election the Birmingham comrades were being instructed to break*

with the Broad Left on the question of Willie Lee's candidacy.
Such antics may go down well in Cottons Gardens, but in the real
world where active workers measure your worth on consistent per-
formance rather than the ability to perform flip-flops it is a recipe
for disaster. Five years of work would have gone down the drain, is
it little wonder that the Birmingham comrades saw a higher duty
to IS than jumping through hoops held up at the caprice of the
Central Committee.[1]

There followed some truly bizarre behaviour on the part of the
leadership. Opposition supporters in Birmingham were not allowed copies of the Internal Bulletin, they had to read it in the
IS Bookshop and then hand it back. Steve Jefferys had attempted
to reach some compromise, but when that failed, he went about
his grisly work with all the enthusiasm of Conan the Destroyer.
He met Mick Rice in a pub and, on learning that he maintained
his support of the Birmingham AUEW comrades, suspended him
with a promise to move his expulsion at the next Central Committee meeting. Mick Pedley received the same treatment. As if
to prove that his time at the London School of Economics had not
been wasted and that he could still do simple arithmetic, Steve
then went off to a meeting of the Birmingham IS District Committee, of which august body Mick Rice and Mick Pedley had
been members until their suspension. At the meeting there still
needed to be a bit of fine tuning to ensure that the sums came out
on the right side, so Roger Griffiths was suspended as he came
in the door to take his seat. For those of us who had been in the
WRP/SLL, or one of its earlier manifestations all of this had a
dreadfully familiar ring. Disagreement was disloyal, arguing was
disloyal, marginal doubt was disloyal, even the inability to keep up
with the chameleon-like speed with which the line changed was
disloyal and disloyalty had to be extirpated with the utmost dis-
patch and never mind the constitutional niceties. Mick Rice's last
despairing paragraph puts the case very well about what might
have been:

> *IS is more, much more than a command structure, with an im-*
> *maculate leadership uniquely gifted with the authority of decision.*
> *Marxism is about mutual development, of interaction and syn-*

---

1. Mick Rice, *The Birminham AUEW Expulsions*, an ISO document.

thesis. The Marxist party should enshrine the principles of free discussion not from bourgeois ethics but because without it there can be no serious practice and no party.[1]

The Group continued to scamper to the left; trade union work was seen as routinism; the real class struggle according to the leadership was on the street. The Rank and File Movement was an abject failure which was now totally controlled from the Industrial Department, an IS shell that would shortly be dissolved into the Right to Work Campaign and its associated march. IS was back to doing what a small sect can do with comparative ease, the one shot noisy campaign: it was a form of activity that Gerry Healy was particularly adept at organising. The comrades are kept busy and the sheer pace of activity disguises the fact that the organisations is marking time. The less rewarding the prospect, the more boastful the promises. The promise now was for the Socialist Workers Party in 1976. The basis for this piece of vainglory was neither clear nor explained. IS, with fewer than 3,000 members, perhaps a third of whom were manual workers, was not a party. What was expected in the next two years that would transform it into a force capable of operating autonomously in the labour movement, as any organisation claiming party status must do? If what was wanted was to replicate the CPGB of the early 1920s, a very modest ambition, it would be necessary to transform the social composition and to build an infinitely bigger periphery. If it was to make Duncan Hallas feel that he had recreated the RCP of its best days, that was more an indulgence than an ambition and, in any case, it would have been necessary to amend the regime drastically so that it did not go around decimating the industrial cadre and abusing the norms of revolutionary leadership.

In the less than two years from Spring 1974, the IS group had lost 500 members and suffered a considerable fall in the circulation of *Socialist Worker* to 24,000, with a paid sale of half that number. The number and size of the factory branches was down, the circulation of the rank and file papers had taken a nosedive. When taxed with this fall Cliff replied, *"Formal accounting is a social democratic notion"*. Funnily enough, we did not reply, *"and brass*

---

1. *Ibid.*

necked cheek is usually employed by conmen and crooks". As I have indicated, we were much too polite and soft in our criticism.

The shadows were definitely lengthening on the IS Opposition. In November 1975, representatives of the opposition were called before the Control Commission (an 'impartial' tribunal comprising Jim Nichol and Dave Peers) where they were taxed with the fact that an IS Opposition document, 'The Crisis in IS', had got into the hands of a *Morning Star* journalist, Rod Caird. He had detailed the IS Opposition criticism and pointed out:

> *It is not long since IS built its reputation on a carefully constructed image of openness and back-breakingly studious respect for democratic procedures; its appeal, like that of other ultra-left groups, rested in the way it pointed with virginal horror at the supposed mistakes, divisions and muddles of other organisations.*[1]

The truth of this Caird piece should not obscure the fact that any Stalinist hack has not much right to point accusing fingers at anyone. Nichol could not prove that the IS Opposition had passed the offending document on to Caird any more than the IS Opposition could prove that they hadn't. What was certainly true and no doubt weighed heavily with the Control Commission was the fact that if you do not have an IS Opposition you do not have any IS Opposition documents.

At the December 1975 Party Council, Duncan Hallas argued that factions always lead to a split and were impermissible in a combat organisation. The IS Opposition, he said, had more allegiance to their faction than to IS and were only on the fringes. In one of those moments that are so deliciously revealing, Cliff said, *"Factions could be allowed in the Bolshevik Party but not in IS"*. Later on he added that the Bolshevik factions were good ones. Naturally enough we wanted to be a good faction, but could not for the life of us see that there was any justice in submitting our character to Cliff's judgement. Call us wrongheaded if you will, but we thought he would be prejudiced. The Party Council majority, clearly swayed by Duncan's oratory and impressed with the fact that Cliff had just written one bad book on Lenin and was about to write another three, carried overwhelmingly a resolution demanding that the IS Opposition dissolve its faction.

---

1. Rod Caird, 'Between the Lines', *Morning Star* 22/11/75.

The Steering Committee of the IS Opposition, after discussion, sent a statement to the Central Committee:

> *Our position with regard to the Party Council resolution on the IS Opposition is exactly as was stated at the meeting with the Control Commission on Sunday 30th November. The criticisms that we raise go right to the heart of IS's political traditions, orientation and democratic structure. We are concerned that the current lurch to ultra-leftism will destroy any realistic working class base, while it may generate the kind of self perpetuating irrelevant work we associate with the WRP. We feel that it is to the detriment of IS that the National Council has decided to terminate the discussion on the basis of hastily passed resolutions on permanent factions; on the issue of the Right to Work Campaign and the launching of the SWP, it has found it appropriate to disregard or overrule the decisions made at the conference. For these reasons we are not prepared to disband the faction, though we will continue to act as disciplined members of IS.*

In reality it was just going through the motions. On receipt of the ISO letter, Nichol telephoned Hazel Mandrell, the faction secretary, to say that all the members of the IS Opposition Steering Committee were suspended and their expulsion would be moved at the Central Committee that day. Sue Baytell, an office worker at the Centre, received the full treatment. Nichol fired her, suspended her from IS membership and undertook to move her expulsion at the Central Committee. That man was all heart.

It was the end of the road for the IS Opposition: if its members were not expelled they left in sympathy with those that were. For them the great IS experiment was over. The dynamics of the sect had won again. Many of the tormenters of that time became sooner or later the tormented. I cannot say that I agree myself, but my old mum used to say: *"God doesn't collect his debts in money"*. If so perhaps he could consider sending in the heavies because even after all this time there are still a few notable outstanding debtors. Only the morally defective have no point beyond which they will not go. Unfortunately there are some of those and they naturally gravitate to the court of the emperor, where they can congratulate him on his political raiment, applaud his latest flight of fancy and jeer in unison at those ill mannered enough to point out that the emperor is quite naked. It is some kind of life, but not much of one and it bears no relationship to the socialist emancipation of mankind. That is an altogether more serious undertaking and one that will be performed by people who are more truthful, more dedicated, more democratic and more loyal. More truthful about what they are and what they can do. More dedicated because they operate without illusions and without lying to themselves or anyone else. More democratic because tricks and gimmicks will not work; it is only with the maximum democracy that a mass movement for socialism can be built. More loyal to theory and politics, more loyal to the members and above all more loyal to the working class. None of these are optional extras, to be tacked on as a rousing peroration to a May Day speech; they are the essential pieces to the jigsaw that will one day all fit together to reveal the socialist commonwealth. History is not over, it has yet to begin.

Unstormed

Speak one more time
About the joy of hoping for joy
So that at least some will ask:
What was that?
When will it come again?

Erich Fried

I n the early Christian church there was a continuing problem of Bishops who were surplus to requirement. They might be removed from office or even excommunicated by the Pope: nevertheless, through the mysterious ways of the apostolic succession dating back to St Peter, who laid on hands to create the first Bishop, they remained bishops with the power to lay on hands and create more bishops themselves. This caused a deal of anguish to various Popes who took the view that if they could make 'em, they could break 'em. However, no less an authority than St Augustine proclaimed the continuing validity of orders once conferred. The result was an embarrassing surplus of redundant, incompetent or malfeasant Bishops, who wandered about behaving like princes of the church despite the fact that they had no See. They were known in the trade as *Episcopi Vagantes* (Vagrant Bishops). This obscure historical fact was little remarked on in church circles, but was noted by a 19th century Church of England parson, A.H. Mathew, who cunningly managed to get the Church of Utrecht to adopt him as their Bishop for Britain.

No sooner had the apostolic hands graced Mathew's head than he was off forming his own church. There is nothing like a Bishop's mitre and crozier to make a chap look posh and become the object of envious glances from other would-be Bishops. Where one man has ventured others will surely follow, if not always by the same route. J.R. Vilatte and Vernon Herford were made Bishops by the Nestorian Church of the Malabar Coast. Thus it was that the good work continued: the new bishops built their churches and, in time, felt the need for additional bishops. Need being father to the deed, they laid their hands on suitable candidates, who oftentimes, in their turn, developed doctrinal differences which necessitated them breaking away to form their own church. With each split there was a new accretion of theological exotica. One vagrant bishop blended Catholicism with theosophy and built his cathedral around a massive brass funnel through which God sent down beneficent rays to the faithful, who stood underneath the blessed metal conduit to receive them. Another, perhaps unsure of the effectiveness of one ceremony, was consecrated on numerous occasions in various vagrant churches and when last heard of was styled Mar Georgius, Patriarch of Glastonbury, the Episcopate of the West, and his subsidiary titles covered ten full lines of twelve point type. Among this small but sparky firmament, one with real star quality was the French 'Bishop' who combined Catholicism with druidism. He conducted baptism, weather permitting, in the sea off the Normandy coast. This splendid chap styled himself, 'His Whiteness the Humble Tugdual the Second'. May his God preserve him from pneumonia. The most recent count, in 1961, of the number of such 'Bishops' was over 200, and I sincerely hope that Tugdual II, who was one of them, is still with us.[1]

It does not require a particularly profound knowledge of the Trotskyist tradition to notice certain similarities between Marxist obscurantism and an addiction to Christian arcana, together with shared fissiparous tendencies. There is Trotsky, like Peter, the first and the best of the disciples and then there is the ever growing proliferation of sects, sectlets and insects claiming direct descent from the master. Each one of them has a cast iron reason for standing against the rest. If the class nature of Stalinist Russia seemed of vital import to Trotsky in 1940, then it must be at the centre of our thoughts in 1996. Never mind that country no longer exists; the maintenance of the argument is the maintenance

---

1. For further information on this fascinating subject see: H.R.T. Brandreth, *Episcopi Vagantes and the Anglican Church*, and P F Anson, *Bishops at Large*.

of the tradition, it has become an end in itself. So powerful is this yearning for the certainties of the past that even the way some of us talk and write is redolent of Commintern jargon of the 1920s, freshly translated from the Russian by an incompetent. Quite a few years ago there was a member of the Revolutionary Socialist League whose fluency with the jargon exercised an awful fascination. A typical example went something like this: "*In the coming period, the various amalgams will concretise into programmatic agreement on limited and partial plans for statification and so on and so forth.*" The last five words of this quote are, although not mandatory, usually there because they give the quite spurious impression that you have a great deal more of importance to say. The uncritical, not to say idolatrous, veneration for everything Bolshevik, until 1924, and the obsessive desire to see everything through the prism of Russian precedent, has resulted in far too many people suffering a self induced inability to communicate with workers in a language they can understand without an A level in Russian Marxism.

In 1938, the Fourth International was formed. If generous, or gullible, you can believe the Founding Congress's claim of approximately 6,000 members world wide. Little enough you might think for a 'World Party of Revolution' – and that was probably its high point. It was an aggregation of tiny groups drawn together by the attraction of Trotsky's historic role and his powerful intellect. Here was the force that was to lead the working class to power when capitalism and Stalinism succumbed to the irresistible force of the coming war. In fact, came the war and the Fourth International, along with Gracie Fields and W.H. Auden, went to the US for the duration. When all is said and done, the likelihood of the Fourth International actually taking power would ensure that William Hill gave you odds against of such length that if the bet came good you would, as a multi-billionaire, be opposed to the result.

Trotsky had seen the future working in 1917 and all his scepticism, independence and willingness to contemplate change was heavily circumscribed by that event. The Bolshevik success and its ability to replicate itself were reduced to organisational forms rather than their content. As one, along with Luxemburg, who had on occasion correctly criticised Lenin before the revolution, in his struggles against Stalinism he became an ultra-Leninist, which paradoxically ensured that he denied the essence of Lenin. For Lenin the form was always subsidiary to the revolutionary content: he would see nothing wrong with developing a new strategy and tactics to meet the changed reality and the suitable organisational form would derive from that experience. At least, however, the pre-war Fourth International lived in a world where the Russian Revolution was of recent memory and Trotsky's perspectives had yet to be invalidated by unexpected changes in the script.

Nowadays, there are lots and lots of Fourth Internationals, each one claiming fidelity to the thought of the founder. It may be that some of them do actually believe that they are uniquely qualified and prepared to lead the workers to power. Perhaps you have in your mind's eye a vision of a worker continuously on the lookout for a Fourth International, preferably one with a democratic centralist constitution, a clean copy of the *Transitional Programme*, a battle cry of *"forward to the first four congresses of the Communist International"*, and nothing later than 1940 in the way of political theory. There may be such workers about, but they have almost certainly been in another group for at least ten years and will, therefore, think you are a bit of a prat. Your average newly radicalised worker will not find the somewhat mystical, on occasion almost hysterical, attachment to an abstract International attractive. Like Guinness and Chris Harman, it is an acquired taste that the overwhelming majority of people never acquire.

One thing that all the groups on the left share is a dedication to democratic centralism. This goes for those from the Trotskyist tradition and from the survivors of the Stalinist shipwreck. Democratic Centralism is something that is taken as read, that is now so manifestly appropriate for all occasions as to be beyond discussion. Why this should be so is difficult to understand. It is not a form of organisation that can be easily deduced from a close examination of the classical Marxist texts. On the other hand, it can be readily understood as a necessary organisational response to the oppression of Tsarist autocracy and the intrusions and exactions of the Okhrana. That it grew out of the 1903 debates in Russian Social Democracy, on who is and who is not a member of the party, and subsequently developed piecemeal into a set of rules, is because it was a reaction to events as they occurred and not as a result of a preconceived plan of action. In the Communist and Trotskyist tradition, democtratic centralism has now acquired a universal validity beyond time and context. It is like some deviated cargo-cult where the strict observance of certain complicated rituals will result in the great four-engined bird flying in, loaded with a nourishing mass revolutionary party just for us.

It is frequently claimed that democratic centralism makes the organisation more efficient, enabling it to become a more effective combat organisation. I have often heard this claim; indeed I confess to having asserted it myself on occasion, but I cannot recall any time when it was manifestly so, and unsupported assertion is seldom accepted as conclusive evidence before impartial tribunals. Let us suppose a democratic centralist organisation is split 49 per cent to 51 per cent on whether or not to adopt a particular course of action. Will the magic of democratic centralism ensure that the 49 per cent fling themselves into activity with little squeals of enthusiasm equal in intensity to those of the 51 per cent? Will they together be as effective as another organisation, unblessed with 'Leninist' rules, where 100 per cent of the members are agreed on the course of action to be taken? The answer is No. For even the most 'Leninist' organisation has only volunteers for the overwhelming majority of the membership. No matter how forcefully the Central Committee promulgates its instructions, the only sanction available against those who refuse to follow them is that they will not be allowed to carry out any future orders, to pay the extortionate subscription and to attend meetings. Not much of a frightener when you come down to it: indeed, it sounds more like a promise than a threat. It is true, however, that for some people the 'party' becomes a way of life, an extended family in which to feel at home. It is the cause in which all of the idealism and enthusiasm has been invested and where a complete social life can be found.

Precedent suggests that the most enthusiastic partisans of democratic centralism are, more often than not, the most authoritarian in their control of the party regimes. One thinks of Cliff and Healy and the old Communist Party. They are, of course, the top tenth of the centralist iceberg; beneath the surface there is a proliferation of smaller centralised sects where democracy is the absolute right of the people who agree with the leader, their freedom of speech in praising the guru and his works is not only guaranteed, it is mandatory. There are those who claim that their version of democratic centralism is heavy on democracy with just a soupçon of centralism. It is open to anybody to believe this story, but before signing up for the duration it might be wise to seek out any recent expellees to see if the claim is universally accepted.

Is the democratic centralist organisation secure from the attentions of the organs of state security or malign political opponents? Not really. Anyone who wants to know the inner working of the leading committees just needs join the group and hang around the centre making himself useful and frequenting the right pubs. In not too long a time he will be supplying his spy masters with information about who is doing what to whom, who is in and who is out and, if he has any *nous* at all, whether any of it matters a toss. In an organisation like the SWP, the pool of experience is limited to the members of the Central Committee because the Group is not structured to utilise the experience of the membership. That such a system can maintain a sort of organisation is proved by the continuing existence of the SWP; but for those of us who support Rosa Luxemburg's contention that the mistakes of a genuine workers' movement are infinitely to be preferred to the decisions of the most immaculately conceived central committee, there can be little community of interest with Cliff and his minions.

In Prague before the First World War, Jaroslav Hašek, author of the *Good Soldier Svejk*, founded The Party of Moderate Progress Within the Bounds of Law. The aim was to ridicule the imperial authorities, abuse other parties and especially to bring custom to his pal, a landlord in whose pub the new party held its meetings. An early resolution laid it down that anyone who liked could sit on the Central Committee – the number of members was limited only by the capacity of two tables stuck together in the dining room. For my part, if that seems a bit restrictive, we can always move to a bigger dining room and add tables. Certainly it is closer to a sensible ideal than the toy Bolshevism of so many of our democratic centralists.

Naturally enough, all of this organisational fetishism is justified, like practically everything else, by reference to the works of the great masters. Pre-eminently, that means Lenin, with Trotsky as a useful seconder of the Leninist proposition. Thus infallibility acquires such power that the substantive motion has an irresistible force for the faithful. This argument by quotation ascribes god-like qualities to individuals. It assumes that Lenin, who died in 1924, and Trotsky who died just 16 years later, encompassed in their lives and thought through all the permutations of the answers to the problems afflicting revolutionary socialism that might arise after their deaths. It is a pity, really, that they were unable to apply the same powerful insights to the time when they were alive: it would have saved us all an awful lot of subsequent pain and suffering.

Such is the frequency with which some of the Lenin quotes are used that I would like to make a modest proposal that would save ink and paper – a vital consideration in these ecologically sensitive times. In the logging camps of North America the lumberjacks were isolated for months on end and before long they had heard one another's jokes so often that they gave each one a number. Thus, just by calling out the number – so long as you avoided number 37, which was too disgusting even for lumber-jacks – you could get the laugh even though you had forgotten the punch line. By the same token, why not give these Lenin quotations special codes? Using a modi-fied Dewey system we could arrive at

THE CORRIDORS OF POWER.

LC17/430/2/1-5, which would indicate a reference to Lenin's *Collected Works*, Vol 17, page 430, paragraph two, lines one to five. As it happens, this is a very boring denunciation of the fake liberalism of the Cadet party in 1905, but it might have been an absolute cruncher like LC 56/54/1/4-10. To which the only reply, and that a purely defensive one while you regroup, is LC/24/623/1/1-4. This might just catch on and it would have the immeasurable benefit of reducing the length of Cliff's books to manageable proportions.

Failing such a sensible reform, the hucksters will continue to root about in the *Collected Works* looking for apposite quotes to add a little class to some sordid manoeuvre. Inevitably someone else who opposes the move will, given the right of reply – clearly these are not members of the SWP – find an equally apposite and opposite Lenin quote.

The history of the Marxist movement is a storehouse of useful information and can provide many lessons for current practice, particularly if we are looking for things not to do in the future. What, however, we should never do is lose sight of the need to set every historic work and every quote from an historic work into context. That means not just the context of its surrounding sense, but also the time and the world to which it was addressed. Lenin wrote an awful lot, and some of it is clearly of more lasting significance than other bits. The man himself recognised this when he recommended that certain works should not be republished without a commentary to explain their peculiarly Russian application. He was, after all, not God sending down messages incised in stone; he was a fallible human being, albeit one of genius, whose more obscure factional spats and rows can be safely allowed to rest easy in uncut volumes, with absolutely no loss to the workers' movement.

Of course, those who impose a dreary democracy on Lenin's work, where his collected laundry lists are of equal significance with major theoretical contributions, will continue to quote him in and out of season. Robin Blick, for example, was once a bright young man in Gerry Healy's group. Since he fell out with Gerry he has gone quite a long way in rejecting his own past. He is, nowadays, an inveterate quoter from Lenin, but where once he wrote plus he now writes minus. He does this with some skill, selectively and blissfully free of context. His intention is to prove Lenin was an unmitigated scoundrel, not just the only begetter of Joe Stalin but a true descendent of the Tartar hordes, an associate of the German Black Hundreds and an all round jolly rotten person. Cliff, on the other hand, quotes Lenin with some skill, selectively and equally abstracted from context, with the intention of proving him to be a jolly decent person who, by happenstance, seems to have written incredibly prescient material that justifies anything Cliff wants to do, no matter who he wants to do it to. The only defence to this quotation offensive is to have your own copy of the *Collected Works*, although these days that is quite expensive and Cliff sometimes tries to fool you by using the 4th Russian edition. Better not to be impressed by anything that reads as if Lenin has been sitting at Cliff's feet soaking up the sheer Marxist wizardry of his latest enthusiasm. For Blick and Cliff, Lenin is a milch cow of full-fat quotations, allowing them both to remain smugly plump with their own certainties – an awful double X certificate sight that should be kept from the young and innocent at all costs.

The SWP is the paradigm of the worst possible application of democratic centralism and a *reductio ad absurdum* of Lenin's politics. The supposedly key role of the revolutionary party has become the whole object of the exercise. The only measure of revolutionary advance is the membership figures – never mind the quality feel the width. Presumably, the workers are assigned the role of foot soldiers in the revolution, the vanguard will be there to lead them in the sweet by and by. In this scheme there is no need to recruit workers now, they might spoil the autocratic anarchy of clique leadership.

The party that was formed in 1977 was not predicated on great upheavals and political differentiation; it was less capable of mounting its own initiatives in the workers' movement than it had been three years before. Its founding was for purely internal reasons, to give the members a sense of progress, the better to conceal the fact that there had actually been a retreat. The social composition was now worse, the circulation of the papers reduced. The sheer pretentious absurdity of the move resulted in long-standing and valuable members like Peter Sedgwick, Richard Kuper, Mike McGrath, Martin Shaw and quite a few others deciding that another journey into Cloud Cuckoo-land without maps was more than tolerance and sweet reason should be asked to bear. They headed for the exit convinced that the performance was over. The fractions and factory branches were declining in number and influence. The rank and file papers were quietly dying. Of course there were noisy campaigns – a right to work march here and some anti-fascist work there – but they were one off campaigns which were allowed to live just as long as they produced new members: when that stopped the life support system was switched off. As with all such sect inspired activity the campaigns were not worthwhile in their own right, just creatures of the party, jealously guarded against alien intruders. One almost heard the cry, *"this is our recruiting agency, if you want one go and build your own"*.

An organisation like the SWP can continue to exist despite its sectarianism and behaving, outside its own ranks, like a gatecrasher sneering at the hosts but nicking anything that is not screwed down. It will go on so long as a few conditions are met. That its print-shop continues to generate sufficient profit from its commercial work to subsidise the party press and contribute toward the full time wage bill. The apparatchiks, in their turn, will organise the subscription return and ensure a reasonable recruitment rate at least equalling the membership attrition. Long ago the SWP established a policy of minimum debate that is now so firmly embedded as to be part of the tradition. Dissent is stamped on and the norms of revolutionary justice ignored. The Central Committee is uniquely qualified to pronounce on anything and everything, containing as it does that renaissance man, that Marxist Leonardo da Vinci, Chris Harman. Not long ago he pronounced, *ex-cathedra*, as it were, on the question of anthropology and now that is the line, although why the SWP should require a line on anthropology is beyond me. The anthropologist member of the SWP – there could even be more than one of them – who accepts the modern academic wisdom on the subject, now contradicted by Harman, is under a vow of silence on his own specialisation. One recalls Lysenko, who, at Joe Stalin's command, stood Darwin on his head, inducing genetic changes in plants over a few generations by altering their environment. Thus he claimed he could grow winter wheat and tomatoes north of the Arctic circle. Nobody was ever allowed close enough to actually examine his plants – for all I know they were made of plastic. Eventually he was shuffled off into early retirement, but not before he had ended the careers of a number of more conventional geneticists. The SWP's cultural climate is strangely reminiscent of those halcyon days when Zhdanov wielded the cultural hatchet for Joe Stalin, a triumphant outing for philistinism.

A leading committee with this kind of suzerainty over all it surveys is unlikely to fall apart from within its own ranks, because dissent from one or two members can be stifled by the rest. Nor will it succumb to a nonexistent democratic pressure from the party. It will, however, be most unstable if its leading figure is removed. One hopes that Cliff has, like Lenin, written his Testament. It would be distressing to see any unseemly squabbling in the future, although the Lenin precedent does not give us too much hope for a smooth transfer. The metaphorical blood-letting may well put us in mind of a Dashiell Hammett novel but without any of the style and none of the artistry. It would be unchristian to wish any unpleasantness to the current holders of authority in the SWP. On the other hand, of course, I am an atheist.

The unseemly scuttle to the wilder shores of obscurantism that Cliff started in the early 1970s was made possible by the fact that, in the previous twenty years, a group had been built of sufficient size to maintain some momentum, in large measure by ignoring or rejecting large chunks of the Bolshevik and Trotskyist tradition. The attractive force was in the somewhat laid back and nonsectarian way in which IS viewed revolutionary politics without being at all light minded about it. If the work on state capitalism, reformism, the long boom and Luxemburg were tentative and incomplete they showed sufficient coherence to indicate that there was some life in revolutionary politics after Trotsky's death in 1940. The serious work of completing this was not done, although the Incomes Policy and Productivity books were the progeny of that period of earnest and worthwhile enquiry. The 'Leninist' phase was Cliff calling a halt to new thinking; a retreat to the certainties of history that can be rewritten on the hoof. There is, for example, more Marxism in Cliff's productivity pamphlet than in all four volumes of his Lenin. The first was directed to building a presence in the working class movement and the second is a primer for a party that is allegedly Leninist and in practice is formed in Cliff's image. That party will never be built.

The SWP is an example of the worst kind of recidivism; it represents the past not the future. Over the years nearly all those who knew the group in better times have either been expelled or have left in disgust: the few who do remain have cultivated that 'genre of silence' recommended by Isaak Bebel at the height of Stalin's purges.[1] New members are generally new to all politics,

---

1. Actually even his silence did not save Bebel. He was arrested and sentenced to a long period of incarceration. He died in prison. Perhaps

with no background in other organisations in the socialist movement. The closed confines of the SWP is the fortress from which
they sally forth episodically to pursue the organisation's limited
campaigns. They are encouraged to believe, and some manifestly
do believe, that outside the party there is just desert, unrelieved
by oases – not even a glass of cooking lager. Fortunately for the
rest of humanity there is a real world outside the SWP and, despite what it may say in the party press, the revolutionary party
has yet to be built.

When it is built it will not be on the basis of inappropriate Russian organisational forms, expressed in a language deriving from
badly translated Russian. Nor will it be built by the SWP engaging
in a stepped up version of the Cliff method of primitive socialist
accumulation. For the SWP to be part of the process there will
have to be a sharp differentiation within its ranks and a decisive
break with its current practice. Similarly, the traditional 'unity'
offensive that has marred the Trotskyist movement in the past,
and has invariably been the prelude to one or more splits, will not
be of much help in the party building stakes. It is almost possible
to despair when recognising the fact that the groups – who have
in membership fine, intelligent comrades – should cling so fanati-
cally to their differences with everybody else. The irony is that
those differences operate as an effective bar to them growing to
the point where they could do anything about their defining principles. Either they will stop behaving to other groups like thieves
in the night, believing them fit only to be plundered, or they will
effectively lock themselves away from the possibilities of real advance. There is nothing in the record that says that they are likely
to reform but the lesson of those long grinding years of failure
must eventually filter through to all but the most closed minds.

The small mass revolutionary party idea does not just animate
the Socialist Workers' Party. Arthur Scargill hopes to position
himself so that he is handily placed to offer a home for the socialists who will be cast adrift after Tony Blair's New Labour takes
over the ship of state. That Arthur's Socialist Labour Party bears
a strong resemblance to the pre-1956 Communist Party is one
reason why it will not succeed. Another, of course, is the comic
spectacle of the SLP's party machine being controlled by mem-

---

Stalin had, like the British army, a crime called 'dumb insolence'.

bers of the United Secretariat of the Fourth International (almost as many members as letters in the name) who are dedicated to the task of denying admission to Trotskyists of any other persuasion.

The real grounds for hope rests on the changes that have taken place in the past few years. In the past, the revolutionary movement found itself crushed between the upper and nether millstones of Stalinism and social democracy. Both of these excrescences on the body politic proved incapable of matching the strength and dynamism of capitalism. If they were not outgunned and subdued they were absorbed. Their collectivism, far from mirroring and building on workers' solidarity, became a force for exploitation, squalor and inefficiency. And now they are both gone: social democracy by its own hand and Stalinism by some advanced ageing process that set in before it had even grown up. Although these events took all the groups by surprise – and their first response was to be even more strident in their projection of their defining difference, especially their attitude to the class nature of the now non-existent Soviet Union – it must surely follow that while we are wishing Stalinism a raucous sailor's farewell, we must also recognise that we are living in a post-Trotksyist world. The disappearance of the two millstones, far from liberating Trotskyism from its constraints, seems to have removed those features by which it defined itself.

The party will not be built with the disillusioned followers of Stalinism, or the socialist refugees from social democracy, because there are none any more. It is back to the working class, where we ought to have been all the time.

There are those who claim, like Edward Bernstein before them, that capitalism has so changed that not only are Stalinism and social democracy redundant, but the very notion of socialism has passed its sell by date. We are told that manual skills are little needed and what we have is lots of technology and a lot fewer technicians. The growth area in employment is women on part time contracts. The buzz word of the 1980s and 1990s has been downsizing and manufacturing has been irrevocably exported to the Pacific rim and Central and South America. According to this story in the old capitalist world the working class has been beaten and decimated. Of course there is some truth in all this but it is, like every other snapshot of a complicated world, a static and inadequate view. Everything is there but, because it cannot be seen in movement or its elements interacting one with another, it is misleading. It is true that there are more women in the labour force than before, and so much the better. It is true that downsizing enabled companies vastly to increase profits without selling more products, but as the guru of downsizing, Stephen S. Roach, now confesses: *"Tactics of open ended downsizing and real wage compression are ultimately recipes for industrial extinction… If all you do is cut then you will eventually be left with nothing, no market share"*. The question about manufacturing is not whether it will grow again but when. The growing workforce will need trade unions – either those available or others yet to be built. They will also need, as they have always done, a socialist movement that speaks a language they can understand, that is not self-indulgent and sectarian, that is comfortable to live in and that will grow with its members. All of this will take time and patience and forbearance, but when you remember how long we have gone getting nowhere without these qualities, it seems reasonable to give it a chance.

It is clear that the task of regroupment and renewal will not be an easy one and it is not difficult to become disheartened before the magnitude of the task. Nevertheless, it has to be tried because there is still no other course to follow. We have to educate, agitate and organise, applying those things to ourselves as well as others. There are no guarantees of success, not even the promise that the pursuit of socialism will make you happy, although the happiest times of my life have been in the movement. The one enduring certainty is that the future will not be won by attempting to recreate the past. It might be as well to reverse Lincoln Steffens famous phrase, to make it read, *"I have been over into the past and it does not work"*. New forms, new forces and new ideas that accord with the world in which we live are far more important than yesterday's failed certainties. Heaven and earth remain unstormed, and we still have a world to win.

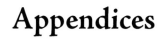

Appendices

Origins of the Theory of State Capitalism

From the standpoint of socialism, the bureaucratic collectivist State is a reactionary social order; in relation to the capitalist world, it is on a historically more progressive plane.
Max Shachtman, 1941

...the alternatives facing mankind are not so much capitalism or socialism as they are: socialism or barbarism. Stalinism is that new barbarism
Max Shachtman, 1962

The problem for the student of the early years of the Group is that there is no written account anywhere and memory is at best fallible and often partial. In this context, we can discount Ian Birchall's small devotional work in *IS Journal* #75/76, old series and, while Martin Shaw's 1978 *Socialist Register* article, 'The Making of a Party?', is very good, it restricts its coverage to the period 1965 to 1976.

Thus it is that speculation on the influences at work which were to produce the particular state capitalist analysis Cliff set out in his RCP *Internal Bulletin*, can be as far fetched as the imagination of whoever wishes to diminish that achievement. It is in this context, I am told, that Sean Matgamna, than whom no-one's imagination ranges further or overreaches wider, takes the view that Cliff lifted his analysis from the 'Shachtmanite' theory of bureaucratic collectivism. In fact, there is no good reason to believe that this was the case. Obviously, there are similarities in any two theories that are based in the conviction that Stalinist states are class divided societies, but it is not at all obvious that Cliff would have found these specifically in Bureaucratic Collectivist analysis more than anywhere else.

At the time, between late 1946 and 1948, when Cliff was making his sea-change from 'workers' state' to state capitalism, there was no fully set out coherent work on the bureaucratic collectivist case, merely a handful of articles by Shachtman and others in the *New International*. So far as I know, there is no such work published to this day. If, however, you know of such a work, please keep it to yourself. Of course, all the competing theories that purport to define the class nature of the Stalinist states leave an unsatisfied feel in the stomach, rather like a three course meal that is a starter, a pudding and no main course, but bureaucratic collectivism does not even get to the pudding.

A far greater influence on Cliff was Jock Haston and it is true that Jock was a very attractive personality whom Cliff often referred to as his father in the movement. For whatever reason, Cliff was unusually impressed by the arguments of Haston and Grant during the brief time these two were pursuing a state capitalist analysis. We know this to be the case because they changed his mind. This unprecedented achievement has yet to be repeated. What is quite clear is that Cliff is perfectly capable of putting together a workable, or an unworkable, theory: he has done both in his time.

There was, in any case, no good reason for Cliff to find his inspiration in the dubious verities of bureaucratic collectivism, when he was convinced in an argument, specifically about state capitalism, on which there was a long history of work, going back to before the October revolution. In his book, *The Theory of the Imperialist State*, published in 1916, Bukharin discussed the general trend to *"militaristic state capitalism… a new Leviathan, in comparison with which the fantasy of Thomas Hobbes seems like child's play"*. He was to return to this theme several times in the 1920s. Also in the 1920s, the exiled Mensheviks produced a state capitalist analysis, as did Osinsky and Sapronov, of the Democratic Centralist faction of the Russian party.

Various members of the Trotskyist movement adopted state capitalism, Yvan Craipeau for one. Anton Ciliga, a Rumanian oppositionist, also defined Russia as an exploitative society where the bureaucracy controlled all the levers of power.

Bureaucratic Collectivism probably has its origins in the work of an Italian, Bruno Rizzi who, in the 1930s, published his book *The Bureaucratisation of the World*.[1] The essence of the volume was

---

1. Rizzi is usually known as Bruno R. He was a strange chap, an ex-member of the Left Opposition, reputed to be anti-semitic and

that the world was being transformed into societies ruled by a new managerial class based in state institutions. Evidence for this was adduced not only from Russian Communism and German and Italian fascism, but also the American New Deal. The book did not make much a of a splash at the time, but it does seem to have come to the attention of Joe Carter (Joseph Friedman), who was a leading member of the Burnham-Abern-Shachtman faction in the (American) SWP. Carter convinced Burnham, but not Shachtman – who incidentally, always denied that the Independent Socialist League theory had anything to do with Bruno Rizzi's work, that he was correct and together they developed the theory.[1]

After the 1940 split in the SWP, Shachtman and his faction took nearly half the members and formed the Workers Party – it became the Independent Socialist League (ISL) in the late 1940s. Burnham almost immediately deserted the new party, subsequently producing a non-Marxist version of the theory in his book *The Managerial Revolution*.

In not very much time, Carter had convinced Shachtman and the Workers Party majority that bureaucratic collectivism was the theory for them. At first Shachtman took the view that bureaucratic collectivist society was superior to capitalism, but later he decided that it was the ultimate barbarism. Eventually, he supported the US in Vietnam and at the Bay of Pigs. At the end of his life he was supporting Senator 'Scoop' Jackson, a rabid cold warrior with a penchant for nuclear war. One should add that although Shachtman was the best known exponent of bureaucratic collectivism, it is not the case that adherence to the theory leads inevitably to support for capitalism against Stalinism. Carter, Hal Draper and many others remained revolutionaries and supporters of the theory until they died.

Perhaps of some significance for Cliff was the work of C.L.R. James (JR Johnson) who led a state capitalist group in the Workers' Party, the Johnson-Forest Tendency, that included Grace Lee

---

apparently able to move fairly freely in and out of fascist Italy.
1. Although it is quite unfair to Joe Carter, adherents of his theory have traditionally been referred to as 'Shachtmanites' after the charismatic leader of the group. If only because it is a familiar usage, I will stick to this form of description.

and Raya Dunayevskaya (Freddy Forest). It was James, a man with a well developed sense of humour, who characterised bureaucratic collectivism as 'Carter's Little Liver Pill'. Both James and Dunayevskaya's work appeared in *New International* and, according to Ray Challinor, Cliff met Dunayevskaya at an Fourth International meeting in Paris in 1948.

What is certainly the case is that one of the theoretical underpinnings of the Socialist Review Group at its formation was Cliff's article against the theory of bureaucratic collectivism. It is, of course, true but unsurprising that some of the critical framework used to describe Stalinist society in bureaucratic collectivist writing is much the same as that used by the theoreticians of state capitalism. Indeed, much of the data also fits a critique made by a conscientious Marxist who saw Russia as a 'worker's' state'. Analysis of the texts does not suggest that Cliff's state capitalism was either lifted from, or a deviated species of, bureaucratic collectivism.

This is not to say, however, that the Independent Socialist League did not have its effect on the British group. For example, the Shachtmanite journals *New International* and *Labor Action* were distributed in the UK by the Socialist Review Group; Stan Newens acted as the agent for some years. The slogan, 'Neither Washington Nor Moscow But International Socialism', was appropriated by *Socialist Review* from the ISL. In the 1960s, several of the younger ex-ISL comrades came to Britain and joined IS, but the only significant visitor from the ISL I can discover was probably Felix Morrow. Bill Ainsworth recalls such a comrade arriving in Birmingham in the very early 1950s. Unfortunately, the comrade was suffering from a severe case of diarrhoea. Bill writes: "*I think it may have been Felix Morrow. We tried to discuss with him over* the lavatory wall, but without success – he was totally obsessed with the state of his bowels. Departed on the next train".[1]

As we have already noted, in the early days, the Socialist Review Group was a standard Trotskyist group with heretical views on Russia and Eastern Europe. The ISL was a much more relaxed organisation, whose disputes and discussions were carried on in the open press. After 1948 (when they realised what a sorry pass the Fourth International had come to), the ISL became progressively less Trotskyist. In 1958 they dissolved the League and joined the Socialist Party-Social Democratic Federation, the pale corpse of the Norman Thomas socialists. The dissolution statement was embarrassing in its submission to social democracy and the disowning of any revolutionary past. In the meanwhile, however, they had passed on the outlines of the theory that was to become the Permanent Arms Economy.

Under the title *The Permanent War Economy*, six long articles appeared in the *New International* between January and December 1951 by T.N. Vance (one of the pseudonyms of Ed Sard). The first article begins with the bold announcement, "*With the beginning of World War II, both American and world capitalism entered a new epoch – the era of the Permanent War Economy…*" Here, Vance was asserting, was a new and decisive factor in world economy that would seriously amend economic theory, "*both bourgeois and Marxist*". In his articles Vance quotes lavishly from government statistics but the main burden of proof rests on his ingenious projection of these figures into the future. Quotation from other sources is minimal, with just the odd reference to Marx and Keynes. Due, not to say fulsome, credit is afforded to Walter J. Oakes, author of a seminal article in *Politics* in February 1944, entitled 'Towards a Permanent War Economy.' Vance quotes Oakes approvingly as follows:

> A war economy exists whenever the government's expenditure for war (or 'national defence') becomes a legitimate and significant end purpose of economic activity.

Arms expenditure, he says, is responsible for a high level of economic activity and reduces unemployment to negligible levels. In addition, it provides for "*the maintenance of stable and safe economic*

---

1. Bill Ainsworth, Letter to Jim Higgins, April 1996.

equilibrium for the bourgeoisie…"[1] For Vance, the critical level of arms expenditure is when "*the ratio of war outlays to total output exceeds 10 per cent*".[2] Vance also speaks of Keynes' 'Multiplier' where indirect outlays equal and thus double the economic effects of arms production. All of this he says is so much more effective than public works, as in Roosevelt's Works Progress Administration (WPA), because the high levels of taxation required to finance arms production for defence against communism are politically acceptable to the capitalists, whereas the WPA, an expensive and ineffective Keynsian style mechanism for reducing the unemployed figures, was highly unpopular with the bourgeoisie.

Writing in 1951, Vance had in fact no contemporary statistics that supported his thesis. The latest he could muster were for 1948, were significantly lower than those for 1946 to 1947 and a statistically negligible amount higher for 1949.[3] In his tables, the really impressive increases are for the years 1950 to 1953, which are all based on Vances' own calculations.

One might feel more satisfied with all this if most of his conclusions had not been vitiated by time and experience, but also one feels a little suspicious when looking closely at his sources. The theory of 1951 rests heavily on the 1944 article by Walter J. Oakes; a prophet well before his time maybe, but authoritative as all get out. A close examination, however, reveals that T.N. Vance is not Ed Sard's only pseudonym. It appears that Ed's other nom de plume is Walter J. Oakes: perhaps he only used this one for writing authoritative, highly quotable articles in *Politics*.

This then is the theory appropriated by Cliff and rechristened the Permanent Arms Economy by Michael Kidron. In their hands, particularly Kidron's, it became an altogether more convincing piece of work. Duncan Hallas has a reference to arms economy in an article in the *Socialist Review* of April 1952, but the full version did not see light until Cliff's article, 'The Permanent War Economy', in the May 1957 issue of *Socialist Review*.[4] Until 1968,

---

1. *New International*, vol. XVII, #1, p. 41.
2. *Ibid*, p. 34.
3. See Table, *Ibid*, p. 35.
4. Incidentally, Cliff's table supporting this article is rubbish, even if it has a footnote "* *approximate figures*". It suggests, for instance, that Britain could prosecute the war for the whole of 1943 for £9.5 million.

when Mike Kidron published his book *Western Capitalism Since the War*, there was very little written about the theory, which is odd as it offered an answer to the problem of the long post-war boom, which was quite beyond the brains of orthodox Trotskyism. In preparing this book, I had occasion to speak to Mike Kidron, who told me in passing that the really serious work of validating the theory had at no time been undertaken. Perhaps, then, it is not surprising that Kidron, the man most associated with the Permanent Arms Economy, should, in 1974, have dismissed it with the telling phrase, 'Two Insights Do Not Make a Theory'. Oh well, PAE–RIP.

For that money you could not run a decent war for a fortnight.

Cliff on Luxemburg

Ha, Ha! what a fool Honesty is!
and Trust his sworn brother,.
a very simple gentleman!
Shakespeare, *Winter's Tale*

In 1959, some time after the promised publication date, Cliff's pamphlet, *Rosa Luxemburg* was produced.[1] Not only is it the best written of his publications, it is in a way also his most original. This was long before Marxism and Marxists enjoyed a literary vogue and some years before Nettl's two volume biography was published. It was a serious attempt to revalidate the spirit of libertarian Marxism in line with the Socialist Review Group's awareness of the growing importance of the rank and file. At the same time it distinguished the group from the exclusive brethren of orthodox Trotskyism. Inevitably, and necessarily, it set Luxemburg's work against that of her greatest contemporary, Lenin. It was refreshing to discover that Cliff had decided that Luxemburg was not invariably wrong in these exchanges and that, in any case, much of the differences reflected different experiences and conditions. Lenin's centralism was a reaction to the chaos and inexperience of the Russian movement and, whisper it softly lest the children be upset, as Lenin's homage to 'the Pope of Marxism', Kautsky; and Luxemburg's spontaneity was a response to the regimented character of German social democracy and Kautsky's formalism. This, interestingly

---

1. Tony Cliff, *Rosa Luxemburg: A Study*, London: International Socialism, 1959 – originally published as #2 and #3 of *International Socialism*, 1959.

enough, is the line rather more elegantly and entertainingly expressed by Max Shachtman, in the May 1938 issue of *New International*.

Here is Shachtman:

> *The 'professional revolutionists' whom Luxemburg encountered in Germany were not, as in Russia, the radical instruments for gathering together loose and scattered local organisations, uniting them into one national party imbued with a firm Marxian ideology and freed from the opportunistic conceptions of pure-and-simple trade unionism. Quite the contrary. In Germany, the 'professionals' were the careerists, the conservative trade union bureaucrats, the lords of the ossifying party machine, the whole crew who finally succeeded in disembowelling the movement...*

And here is Cliff:

> *Where Rosa Luxemburg's position regarding the relation between spontaneity and organisation was a reflection of the immediate needs facing revolutionaries in a Labour Movement controlled by a conservative bureaucracy, Lenin's original position – that of 1902-4 – was a reflection of the amorphousness of a vital fighting revolutionary movement at the first stage of its development under a backward, semi-feudal and autocratic regime.*
>
> **For Marxists in advanced industrial countries, Lenin's original position can much less serve as a guide than Rosa Luxemburg's**, *notwithstanding her overstatements on the question of spontaneity. [My emphasis – JH]*[1]

Don't you just love the pompous circumlocution of that, "*notwithstanding her overstatements, etc., etc…*"?

From this, at least, it is clear that in 1959 Cliff saw no reason to construct a party on 'Leninist' lines. Indeed, at the time, he considered that the party organisation called for in 1902-4, "*was copied and given an added bureaucratic twist by the Stalinists the world over*". This view was entirely consonant with his opinion then, that the Socialist Review Group was not a pre-Bolshevik, but a post-Bolshevik formation. By this he was clearly understood to mean that world had moved on quite bit since 1902, or 1917 for that matter. The maturity of the class and the form and content of

---

1. *Ibid*, p. 54.

its struggle would be the decisive factor in setting the forms of organisation.

So matters stood for some time, when Cliff, almost single-handed, reinvented the 'Leninist' concept of stick bending. It derives from a speech by Lenin at the Second Congress of the RSDLP:

> *The Economists bent the staff towards one side. In order to straighten it out again, it had to be bent towards the other side and that is what I did.*

You will notice here that Lenin is talking about a correction to the Economists, not a 180 degree turn from what he himself was saying a little earlier. On the one hand we have exaggeration in the course of a political struggle and on the other a capricious or opportunist reversal of policy.

In line with his rediscovery of democratic centralism, it was felt necessary to rewrite the past, specifically Cliff's past. In the 1969 reprint of *Rosa Luxemburg*, of the two paragraphs quoted above the second, *emphasised*, paragraph disappeared completely to be replaced by:

> *However, whatever the historical circumstances moulding Rosa's thoughts regarding organisation, these thoughts showed a great weakness in the German revolution of 1918-19.*

The sea change is even clearer on page 53 of the first edition, thus:

> *Rosa Luxemburg's reluctance to form an independent revolutionary party is quite often cited by Stalinists as a grave and an important cause for the defeat of the German revolution in 1918. They argue that Lenin was opposed to the revolutionary Left's adherence to the SPD and continuing association with Kautsky.*[1]

In the second edition this particular quote had somehow been transformed into:

> *Rosa Luxemburg's reluctance to form an independent revolutionary party followed her slowness to react to changed circumstances. It was a central factor in the belatedness of building a revolutionary party in Germany. In this, however, she was not alone. Lenin was no quicker to break with Kautsky than Rosa. There is no*

---

1. *Ibid*, p. 53.

> *ground in the Stalinist story according to which Lenin was op-*
> *posed to the revolutionary Left's adherence to the SPD and con-*
> *tinuing association with Kautsky.*

That is less stick bending than full frontal attack with a tomahawk. From being a better guide than Lenin she is transformed into a cause of the weakness of 1918-19. In 1959 the Stalinists were calumniating her and, by 1968, the Stalinists were apparently right.

The last quotation is also interesting because it suggests that Rosa had not sussed out Kautsky before Lenin. This is rubbish, Luxemburg had effectively broken with Kautsky in 1910, long before Lenin, as the great man acknowledged in a 1914 letter to Shliapnikov, "*I now despise and loath Kautsky more than all the rest… Rosa Luxemburg was right. She long ago understood that Kautsky had the highly developed 'servility of a theoretician'*". Everyone, of course, is entitled to change their mind, but there is such a thing as honest accounting. In particular, the theoreticians of a Marxist groups have a responsibility to acknowledge when and why they have changed their minds. This is especially so when their comrades have to defend them.

I recall a meeting in Merlin's Cave at which Nigel Coward, a pleasant young comrade who had earlier acted as full timer but somehow fallen foul of Cliff, said that Cliff had made unacknowledged changes between editions one and two of the Luxemburg book. As someone who already had the first edition and had not, because it was supposed to be the same as the first, read the second, although I had bought one, it was quite beyond my wildest imagining that Cliff would have done this. I assumed, quite unjustly, that Nigel was suffering his fall from grace with a fit of pique. "*Quote chapter and verse*", I challenged him. Fortunately for me, Nigel did not have a copy of the offending texts with him, nor did he recall the detail too clearly, otherwise I would have been extremely embarrassed in front of a fairly large audience. So too would my companion at the meeting, who sat next to me and noisily supported my contribution. It was none other than Tony Cliff. I do not think I have seen Nigel since then to apologise, an apology he richly deserved. The business was subsequently taken up by Sean Matgamna of the Trotskyist Tendency and the issue was then submerged in the faction fight. When I raised the question with Cliff he merely shrugged. It was not an impressive or an edifying performance.

In July 1983, the fourth edition of *Rosa Luxemburg* was published. It retained all of Cliff's revisions, with the added top dressing of an introduction by one Lindsey German. Imitation being the sincerest form of flattery, she writes in a style very reminiscent of Cliff's, cleaving closely to the leaden prose, but without the political sophistication. I assume she actually believes it when she writes:

> When first written it [Rosa Luxemburg] was an attempt to make the basic ideas accessible to a new audience... to present Rosa Luxemburg's ideas in order to reassert the revolutionary socialist tradition.

I fear she is a little naive in this. Cliff never wrote anything that was not intended to have some immediate relevance to building his group. The Luxemburg book was intended to present the Group as a Marxist haven for those repelled by Stalinism and hearing echoes of it in the Trotskyist groups around, especially Healy's. The main audience was envisaged as in and around the Labour Party, but it was not intended as a general validation of revolutionary socialism. It was part of developing a complete politics that went beyond the verities of the first four congresses of the Communist International and the transitional programme. If he had not seen Luxemburg as the logical development of the movement from which he and his group sprang, he would not have cast it in the terms of a dialogue between Luxemburg and Lenin. You take the spontaneity of the workers and the mass strike from Rosa and the revolutionary will from Vladimir Ilyich. If this sounds to you like the 'mix-n-match' from Woolworth's sweet counter, you have just hit on Cliff's stratagem for keeping up his political calory count.

One of the more risible items in Lindsey's introduction is the following:

> *in 1918-19 millions of German workers did look for revolutionary ideas. But they didn't look to Rosa Luxemburg and the new KPD, they looked to the old party and its leaders – people who were prepared to talk left wing ideas at such a time, but whose past words and deeds told a very different story. Rosa Luxemburg had been consistently principled in her revolutionary politics – but this fact wasn't known to the mass of the workers for she had remained largely hidden in the SPD.*

Where does Lindsey get this old cobblers from? Does she believe that the pre-1914 SPD was rather like the Harrogate constituency party in Tony Blair's New Labour? The workers were in the SPD in their millions, they virtually lived in the party. It was, as they said, 'a nation within the nation'. Rosa Luxemburg, wrote for its magazines and newspapers, she spoke at its congresses and she spoke at countless meetings, public and party, all around Germany. She would almost certainly be better known to the German workers than Lenin was to the Russian working class. She lost in 1918 because the workers stayed loyal to social democracy and because the SPD betrayed, as they had already done in 1914. Ebert, Scheidemann and Noske did not play the fool with left phrases; they played the counter-revolutionary game and they killed Luxemburg, Liebknecht and Jogiches just as surely as they killed the German revolution.

One assumes that Lindsey German's introduction was intended to iron out the wrinkles in a book originally tailored for a different client at a different time. I fear that it merely serves to call attention to some rather clumsy restyling to the fabric. The false antithesis between Lenin and Luxemburg that Cliff's antics have set up in the various editions has found an appropriately inept commentator in Lindsey German.

Cliff: Notes on Democratic Centralism
20/6/68

Things fall apart ; the centre cannot hold
Mere anarchy is loosed upon the world
The blood dimmed tide is loosed, and everywhere
The ceremony of innocence is drowned
The best lack all conviction, while the worst
Are full of passionate intensity
W.B. Yeats, *The Second Coming*

Our group has for a long time been purely a propaganda organisation – publishing books, theoretical journals, holding schools, etc. The structure fitting this situation was a
loose federative one; all branches were like beads on a string.

Over the last year or two we have moved towards agitation.
This demands a different kind of organisational structure. A
revolutionary combat organization – especially if it becomes a
party – needs a democratic centralist structure.

In the First International the Proudhonists and the Bakuninists
(both Anarchists) wanted a federal structure. Hence logically they
argued that the International was not a Workingmen's organisation, and only workers should be its members and representatives.

Marx argued that the prevailing ideology under capitalism, is
the ideology of the ruling class. As there cannot be a revolutionary movement without a revolutionary theory, the leadership of
the International would not necessarily be workers, and could not
be delegates on a federative principle (hence, Marx was the Russian 'Representative' on the General Council of the International,
although he was not a Russian nor had he ever been in Russia;
hence also the Central Committee of the Bolshevik Party had only
one worker and all members were taken from one city; the same
applied to Mensheviks, to Luxemburg's Spartakusbund, etc.)

The federal principle – the idea that the Executive of a revolutionary organisation should be made up of one delegate per branch is untenable:

a. It is undemocratic. If a branch has 50 members who divide on a central issue 26 to 24, what is democratic about one person casting the votes of 50?

If a minority of the whole organisation – let us say 20% – has one set of policies separating it from the majority – it will not be represented at all – or at most by a derisory number of people on the executive.

b. The inner-organisation struggle for ideas that is so vital, will be directed from issues to organisational frustrations and combinationalism.

c. The organisation cannot grow beyond a certain size: with 1000 members and let's say 100 branches, no executive could work.

d. It is incompatible with specialization and division of labour. As Marx and Engels, Lenin and Trotsky, Luxembourg and Liebknecht were too busy to be able to be involved in local branch activities they could never have been eligible for election to the executives of any Revolutionary Organisation.

e. In conclusion, the federal structure is unstable and inefficient. In our own terms, with the expansion of the group and the transition to a cell structure, half the Political Committee, including the editor of our agitational weekly, would not be able to be on the executive, as they might be inactive locally in a branch. A revolutionary organisation whose two top committees – the Executive and the Political Committee – are elected on opposite principles, could not work effectively.

A democratic centralist organisation is based on the following:

A delegate conference – meeting once or twice a year – decides the policies – the principles and strategy of the organisation.

An Executive, Political Committee, etc., are elected by the conference – as individuals, or on a list of candidates where there are factional groupings: each group of delegates is entitled to elect the number of people to the committees in proportion to their share at the conference.

All decisions of Conferences and between Conferences of the executive are binding on all members of the organisation.

A revolutionary combat organisation faces the need for tactical decisions – daily and hourly – hence the need for great centralization.

The most important decision for a revolutionary party – the decision to take state power – was taken by the Central Committee of the Bolshevik Party; in a revolutionary situation one cannot afford to waste a day (not to say a month – the time necessary to organise a conference). The decision on war or peace – the Brest-Litovsk discussion – was again taken by the Central Committee of the Bolshevik Party. Or again the historical statements of the First International on the Paris Commune were written by Marx and agreed by a handful of people who turned up to the meetings of the General Council – without reference to the national sections of the International, not to speak of their mass rank and file.

If a minority of the branches – let us say 20% – find it necessary to call an emergency conference – the executive is bound to carry this out. New decisions and new elections can ensue.

In practice because of the size and uneven nature of IS we have to have a transitory structure: from federalism to democratic centralism.

At present all branches with 10 members or more have a member on the executive except for three branches: East London, Croydon and Richmond. I suggest the addition of one from each of these three branches.

The London Regional Committee – covering some half of the members of IS – should be strengthened. (It could organise demonstrations, schools, etc. The fact that it is based on a delegate per branch does not guarantee its functioning).

Meetings of comrades in specific fields should be convened (as the teachers do regularly).

Two-way communication is vital: up to now there is much more information going from the Executive Committee and administrative committee to branches, than in the opposite direction. More theory is necessary, hence the need for more centralism. The worst 'economism' and organisational frustrations has come about in many local activities that were completely autonomous. Of course, any arrangement the September Conference decides should not run for a few months, as the IS – 800 or so at present – is bound, we hope, to grow considerably.

Mike Kidron: We Are Not Peasants

A Note – and Proposals – on IS Organisation, Hull IS, 10/10/1968

If our half yearly delegate meeting showed anything at all, it is that we are not yet a *political* organisation. The 'Centre' appealed to our sense of good, truth and beauty, but did not reveal which aspects of the capitalist system they thought most vulnerable to attack at the moment, how we are to mobilise for it and how approach our potential allies. They failed to do for IS as a whole what Roger Cox and Steve Jeffreys were doing so well for our engineering workers.

There are real problems in doing so. The world is not an open book. False consciousness abounds. In addition, and this is probably the most important factor for us, we have been growing so fast that many of our members have not had time or opportunity to assimilate IS experience and IS theory, or to get to know what different groups and individuals amongst are doing.

As a consequence, the more experienced members feel it necessary to colonise *within the group* for tradition and to repeat and then repeat again the fundamentals of socialist theory. They find themselves neglecting the necessary processes of monitoring the world with a view to affecting it, and of keeping their eyes and ears open to what new members are doing and thinking.

On the other hand, many new members plunge into activity without understanding its broader meaning, or being shown the relevance of the socialist political tradition to whatever they are doing.

The result is often a confused dialogue of the deaf, with the older comrades on the Political Committee trying to ram un-argued proposals down our throats and some of the throats reacting at full blast but without proposals.

It would be tragic to allow the issues to be confused in this sort of dialogue: we need operational political analysis; that is, a view of the world in the here and now which links our activities to our basic assumptions. And we need constant internal justification of that analysis and its assumptions. Only the Political Committee can do the job, and only a Political Committee which concentrates as much of our political experience in one place – that is, one elected nationally. Such a political committee must be allowed every facility to do its work: full control over the political content of our press, the right to appoint editors and spokesmen, the right to disengage from administrative detail.

At the same time, we need to have a very clear idea of our own strengths and weaknesses in a rapidly changing situation, or else our political prescriptions will never find practical expression. A body like the Political Committee which reflects neither our unevenness in experience nor our dispersal in function and space has not got, and cannot have, this clear view (so much, at least, we have learned from the way they presented – and then withdrew – their organisational proposals). To have such a view, to be able to decide on the practicability of the Political Committee's proposals, on what is possible for IS as a whole to undertake, the body must be more representative of the branches as they exist – a delegate Executive Committee.

Since such a body should always be trying to adopt a national view and so overcome the unevenness and parochialism which make it necessary at this moment, its members should be elected by the branches for the period spanning the half yearly delegate conferences (subject always to recall). To help it in its day to day operations, it should select a secretariat or Administrative Committee (not necessarily from its own number).

The result would be a clear division of functions between the political and educational centre of IS (the Political Committee) and the decision taking and organisational centre (the Executive

Committee). It is a division of functions that would prevent 'the Centre', to use the Political Committee's current phrase, from throwing out organisational instructions when we want political advice, or fundamentalist iconography when we want organisational guidance. They would know what they were supposed to be doing, so would we. And they would soon find themselves appealing to reason, not loyalty or faith.

We therefore propose:

1. A Political Committee elected by the half yearly delegate conference of about twelve members to formulate and publish IS perspectives, goals, policies and activities; to exercise control over the political content of our press; to promote our internal educational programme; to appoint editors and spokesmen; and to promote and harmonize in conjunction with the Executive Committee sectional and regional policy making in terms of our general goals and policies.

2. A delegate Executive Committee elected by the branches between half-yearly conferences to decide IS's activities in the light of the Political Committee's recommendations, such an Executive Committee to appoint an Administrative Committee to help in its day to day administration. Branch delegates to reflect the 'structure' of opinions in the branch.

Mike Kidron

Dave Peers: Letter to IS Branches

10th April 1974

> Matilda told such Dreadful lies
> It made one Gasp and Stretch one's Eyes;
> Her Aunt, who from her Earliest Youth,
> Had kept a Strict Regard for Truth,
> Attempted to Believe Matilda.
> The effort very nearly killed her.
> **Hilaire Belloc**, *Matilda*

D ear Comrades, it is with much regret that the Executive Committee has to announce that following the last National Committee meeting's decision on the future orientation of the *Socialist Worker*, Roger Protz has decided to resign as editor. This is particularly regrettable given the very long period in which he has guided the paper through the most difficult years of its growth. However, the Executive Committee respects the political positions advanced by Roger on the orientation of the paper and in view of the deep divisions the dispute has created within the staff of the paper sees no alternative but to accept this resignation, pending ratification by the National Committee. In the interim, the Executive Committee has recommended to Roger that he take a month's leave to think matters over.

If Roger's resignation is accepted by the National Committee, the Executive Committee will recommend at the end of that time that if he feels it possible to accept another appointment on the paper or on any of the other publications of the group – the Executive Committee would be pleased to discuss this with him.

At the editorial staff meeting of *Socialist Worker* on Monday the acting editor, Paul Foot, was instructed to write to the Executive Committee drawing to its attention the view of the majority of the staff on the position of Jim Higgins. In the opinion of the staff, it was not possible to reorient *Socialist Worker* if Jim was still on the staff. The letter said:

> *I told Jim that I thought it would be impossible for us to make a go of the paper along the lines argued at the National Committee if Jim was still in the office. His opposition to what had been decided was bound to interfere with the smooth running of the paper.*

The Executive Committee met Jim and discussed this in detail with him and without entering into the rights and wrongs of the issues at stake, it seemed to the Executive Committee that its responsibility to the group for the continued production of the paper made it impossible for the wishes of the staff to be ignored. This is particularly important given Roger's resignation as editor and the attempt of the staff to reorient the paper in difficult external conditions. In these circumstances it is absolutely essential that the members who have to carry the paper should be able to work together as a team without the divisions which have affected morale over the last six weeks. Therefore, after much discussion, it was decided that Jim should not continue as a journalist on the paper. However, the Executive Committee reaffirmed that in no way should this inhibit discussion of the political differences expressed by Jim and others on our future orientation, and its confidence that Jim's role on the National Committee and in the organisation generally will remain important.

Yours Fraternally

Dave Peers
National Secretary

Various: Letter to All IS Branches

circa 12th April 1974

Dear Comrades, we feel bound to bring to your attention a number of facts that are notably absent from the letter to branches, over the signature of Dave Peers, on the removal of Roger Protz and Jim Higgins from *Socialist Worker*.

At the last National Committee on Saturday 6th April a debate took place on the future role, orientation, style and character of *Socialist Worker*. The two different positions are more or less summed up in the document in the recent *Internal Bulletin*. The discussion was long and in the result the line of the Executive Committee was upheld by a two to one majority. At no time in the National Committee discussion did the Executive Committee or their supporters on the *Socialist Worker* Editorial Board give any indication that they thought there would have to be changes on the *Socialist Worker* staff.

Immediately after the National Committee, the Executive Committee held an emergency meeting at which Jim Nichol and Dave Peers were instructed to interview Roger Protz on the following day and to secure his resignation. About midday on Sunday 7th April the two Executive Committee members arrived on Roger's doorstep. They made it clear to Roger that there was no place for him on the paper. Roger saw some justice in the notion that he should not continue as Editor holding a different conception of the paper from that of the National Committee majority. He was, however, anxious and willing to continue as a reporter under whoever was appointed as Editor. This was turned down by the Executive Committee members. Finally Roger agreed in the interests of the paper to resign. Another interesting fact of this Sunday meeting was that Comrade Nichol told Roger that Jim Higgins would also be going.

It was therefore not surprising when the following evening a majority of the *Socialist Worker* Editorial Board called on Jim Higgins to resign on the grounds that his presence would make impossible the carrying out of the new orientation. In reply, Jim said that he would to the best of his ability carry through the new line. He undertook to continue in the post, not to raise the disputed issues in the office, but reserved his right as an IS member to raise questions at other more suitable forums, the National Committee, etc. He further stated that he would not resign.

Paul Foot, as acting Editor, wrote to the Executive Committee which met on Tuesday 9th to interview Jim Higgins. At that meeting all the Executive Committee contributions, with one exception, were directed to Jim's dismissal. After some deliberation he was informed that he was sacked with effect from that meeting. The Executive Committee then began to backtrack on their hard line regarding Roger Protz and offered him a technical job, either on the paper or on the rank and file papers. Roger refused the offer so long as it did not include the reinstatement of Jim Higgins.

There are you will see some significant differences between the facts and the tendentious account of Dave Peers' circular. But quite apart from the need for honest accounting, there is a crucially important political principle at stake. The point is democratic centralism, this demands full and free discussion followed by a decision which all the participants carry out loyally whatever their previous disagreements. It is the task of the political leadership to uphold this principle, whatever the subjective attitude of the *Socialist Worker* Editorial Board. It was in our view, the duty of the Executive Committee to patiently and sensitively point this out to those who had forgotten or never knew the principles of democratic centralism. The Executive Committee has behaved like a faction under siege rather than a responsible leadership. Comrades, who on the Executive Committee's own admission have some record of service to IS are removed without any attempt to test their willingness and capacity as disciplined revolutionaries.

That is the situation to date, we have little doubt that this simple recounting of the facts will illuminate for many our *Internal Bulletin* article. The way that change is effected in IS is more and more the prerogative of the select few at the Centre. Dissent comes to equal disloyalty. The members are effectively excluded from decision making. These are serious matters for serious people. The tendency in the group for abrupt and capricious changes accompanied by the sacrifice of comrades has got to stop. Only the membership can bring about the necessary changes in leadership style, it is high time that members were heard and their views seriously considered.

We urge branches to write to the Executive Committee protesting at their high-handed behaviour. We ask you to pass resolutions demanding the reinstatement of Roger Protz and Jim Higgins. We ask you to demand full information on both sides in the current dispute. The signatories to this letter are prepared to speak to branches on the issues raised in the *Internal Bulletin* document. We will be preparing other material for circulation in the near future. Please keep us informed of any action you or your branch may take – just write to the address at the head of this letter.

Yours fraternally

Duncan Hallas, John Palmer, Granville Williams, Rob Clay, Wally Preston, Jim Higgins, Hugh Kerr, Ken Appleby, Ron Murphy, Tony Barrow, Roger Protz

Roger Protz: A Funny Way to Go (Extracts)

D ave Peers came to see me[1]... and asked me what I thought
I should do if I lost the vote on the National Committee
on the future of the paper. I said that because I thought
the differences were wide that if I lost – and I did not assume that
I would – then I thought I would probably have to stand down
as editor in favour of a comrade who agreed with the new line.
Dave then asked me what my job prospects were like in journalism. I answered, prophetically, nil. He then said would I consider
continuing to work on the paper as a reporter under a new editor,
either permanently or until I found another job. *I said I would be
happy to do so.*

At the Executive Committee that week, the day before the
March National Committee, I argued vigorously for the issue of
the paper to be decided the following day because I felt the comrades on the paper would like a quick decision rather than drag
on for another month. The Executive Committee majority said
it would be wrong to rush the decision. There should be more
discussion and time for both sides to write documents. The documents duly appeared and were discussed at the April National
Committee. When the voting on the paper was concluded I expected the Executive Committee would raise the question of the
editorship. Nothing was said. Instead a special Executive Com-

---

1. In March 1974 – JH

mittee was held immediately following the National Committee (I was not told of this meeting) which, apparently, decided to send a delegation to see me. National Committee members will no doubt ask why the issue was not raised and settled at the National Committee.

The next morning Dave Peers and Jim Nichol came to see me... They said they thought I should leave the paper immediately. They ruled out the possibility of my staying on the paper in a different capacity on the grounds that it would be impossible for them to effect the changes if I were present... Later that day I had a long conversation with Paul Foot. His opinion was that I should definitely leave the paper... He thought time was needed to heal the wounds on the paper and that could be done only if Jim Higgins and I were absent (at this stage the Executive Committee had officially taken no decision concerning Jim Higgins)...

...Throughout the debate on the paper, Executive Committee spokesmen have suggested that Jim Higgins has *"poisoned the atmosphere"* on the paper, has turned a once happy office into a faction racked nest of vipers and has turned me from a happy craftsman into a conservative reactionary. This is utter rubbish. As editor I would not have tolerated one member of the staff acting in this way. But if the Executive Committee believed this grotesque distortion of the truth is it not curious that it took immediate steps to remove me from the paper and not Jim... A printshop meeting was told that I had agreed to leave the paper. A scapegoat was found in Jim. That evening the Executive Committee declared that it was not prepared to work with him any longer. The following evening the Executive Committee did a collective Pontius Pilate and sacked him. If any comrades are still unconvinced that this was a set up job, then perhaps they will ask themselves why after asking me to go and then sacking Jim Higgins, the Executive Committee then wrote to me, said it had reconsidered my position and would like me to take a month's holiday and then come back on the paper or other publications of the group. I was seen clearly by the Executive Committee as a pawn in their manoeuvring to get rid of Jim Higgins. Accordingly I told Dave Peers that I was not prepared to work on the paper without Jim...

Roger Protz

Cliff: The Way Ahead for IS

IS Internal Bulletin, May '74

Get thee glass eyes;
And, like a scurvy politician, seem
To see things thou dost not
Shakespeare, *King Lear*

Recent conflicts in the National Committee must appear to many comrades as simply petty squabbles. Alas as Lenin said, *"No struggle over principles waged by groups within the Social Democratic movement* **anywhere in the world** *[Cliff's emphasis – JH] has managed to avoid a number of personal and organisational conflicts. Nasty types make it their business deliberately to pick on 'conflict' expressions. But only weak-nerved dilettanti from among 'sympathizers' can be embarrassed by these conflicts, can shrug them off in despair or in scorn, as if to say it is all a squabble!"*

The quicker we clear the real political differences in the National Committee the better. The central issue we face is that of defining the workers' audience to which IS relates and has to relate.

Already 30 years ago we formulated the proposition that the locus of reform had moved since the Second World War to the factory floor. (for an elaboration of this idea see Mike Kidron, *International Socialism* No7, and *Incomes Policy Legislation and Shop Stewards*). From this we drew the conclusion that a wide and deep fragmentation of the labour movement had taken place, that there had been a depoliticisation of the mass of the workers. At present there is no live revolutionary tradition in Britain (of course we have a tradition enshrined in books, but hardly any workers alive and active from the fighting years of the 1910s and 1920s).

Hence our audience is largely made up of young workers with very little political tradition, and quite often even with very little trade union experience Only in these terms can our policies of the last year be explained and justified the membership campaign, the building of factory branches, the building of rank and file organisation, the change in *Socialist Worker*.

If the workers we related to were mainly those with political tradition, even if ex-Communist Party or left Labour the membership campaign would have been quite irrelevant if not damaging. People with long political tradition could not be recruited today in a campaign of a few months duration.

(The coolness of some of the members of the old Executive Committee towards the Membership Campaign was therefore basically rooted in a different evaluation of the audience we were talking to.)

The factory branches we built during the last year, that were part and parcel of, our membership campaign, also confirm our definition of the audience. The big majority of the members of the factory branches are young workers with very few shop stewards among them. (Self evidently, these comrades should fight for shop stewardship, and naturally have to learn politics and absorb revolutionary tradition).

Again if one watched the rank and file conference in Birmingham, one could easily see that it was composed of young workers, many of them very new indeed to socialist politics.

Again, when defining the nature of *Socialist Worker*, the question of the audience is central. If the audience is made up of Alan Watts, and Mickey Fenns, then the idea of the paper being largely written by workers is stupid. After all the above comrades would rather learn from the 'experts'. However, if the main audience are the tens and hundreds of workers around Mickey or Alan, then the main writers should be those two and their ilk.

Now that about half our members are industrial workers, our main task is to transform IS into an organisation led by workers.

We have to bring to the fore workers not as a token, a decoration, but as actual leaders. This we can do only on condition that the workers that come to the fore are those who have a constituency in the working class – outside IS – and inside IS.

A worker who has no influence in his place of work and/or trade union, cannot fulfil the role of a workers' leader in IS. On the other hand, a worker who has influence, but does not relate to any constituency in IS–whether a district, a fraction, etc.–cannot really play a leading role either.

The coming few months prior to the conference should be used for involving all members in the issues the organisation is facing... Making IS into a workers' party should be the theme of the September National Conference.

Tony Cliff

Ruth Nelson: Who Is Our Audience?

IS Internal Bulletin, June 1974

U nderlying the present dispute in IS is the question of our
central orientation: who is our audience? to which workers does the organisation relate, and whom must it aim to
recruit?

IS has always had a clear answer to these questions: We must
relate to the thin layer of politically experienced and class conscious militants, primarily shop stewards and convenors, who can
in turn relate our politics to broader layers of workers.

So comrades may have been surprised to find in the May Internal Bulletin an alternative answer provided by Tony Cliff: "*Our
audience is largely made up of young workers with very little political
tradition and quite often with very little trade union experience… only in
these terms can our policies of the last year be justified…*"

But no amount of retrospective rationalisation can alter the
fact that Cliff's position is a radical departure from our traditional one. Look at the Perspectives documents for the 1973 Conference:

> Over the last 18 months we have witnessed a whole number of
> battles of national significance which the working class had the
> determination and the power to win. But these were lost, or at best
> had an inconclusive outcome, because that determination was not
> matched by the existing leadership of the organisation. A revo-
> lutionary organisation with a few hundred **militants of some**

standing [All emphasis in the original – JH] *in each of the major industries could have produced a different conclusion in these struggles, putting forward strategies and tactics that would have tipped the balance of defeat towards victory...*

For revolutionaries a key part of the task of penetrating the advanced layer of militants *is through engaging in joint activity with those militants who are in the Communist Party or still look to it for guidance. We have to be prepared to offer them programmes of action with which they can agree, but which lead them into opposition to the vacillations of the left trade union leadership and its backers in the CP...*

In the present situation the revolutionary organisation can draw to it a few thousand workers – large compared to the present size of the organisation but small compared to the class as a whole, or even compared to the number of shop stewards (300,000). But a few thousand militants can affect decisively the outcome of a number of key disputes. They can begin to prove in practice the relevance of our ideas to broad layers of workers whose own experience is already driving them to the left of the Scanlon-Jones elements...

Why have we traditionally taken this position? The answer is clear: for some years now IS has argued that the trade union bureaucracy, including the 'left' leaders, would become increasingly unable to deliver even the traditional goods, in terms of trade union militancy and the significant gains it can win. In the face of this failure, we have said that the objective need of the class is clear: a national organisation of rank and file militants and this means mainly shop stewards and convenors, because these are the people who are so situated in the class struggle that they can offer leadership on the shop floor, at the point of production.

Of course, this does *not* mean that we cannot or do not recruit young, inexperienced workers. Indeed, we recruit them somewhat more easily than we recruit seasoned militants. And they play a vital role in that, through joining or working with IS (instead of the Communist Party or Labour Party), and agitating for IS policies younger workers act as an important pressure on their elected representatives, forcing them to question their social-democratic allegiances and ultimately to join IS themselves. But we cannot see the recruitment of these young workers as the *main task*.

At a meeting recently in East London, Chris Harman attempted to answer this last point by saying that our perspective was to train these younger comrades to *replace* their shop stewards and convenors. This of course can and does happen, particularly in the traditionally less militant industries, but yet again, as a central perspective, it is just not on – for two reasons:

Firstly, we must take very seriously the length of time it takes to become an experienced, credible leader of workers – a *"militant of some standing"*, to quote the Perspectives document. Many young IS members, catapulted to positions of leadership in the course of one or another dispute, have shown an impressive flair and talent for filling that role without much previous experience. But flair and talent, essential as those qualities are, do not equal and cannot replace trade union and political *experience* and the credibility and trust of workers who know a comrade has, through many struggles, argued and fought in their interests. If we are seriously considering a perspective of replacing militants, this means replacing not just their positions, but their standing amongst those they represent. Clearly the groundwork needed to do this would necessitate setting back our perspective for building the party by a further 10-15 years.

But there is a far more positive reason for concentrating on the advanced militants: it isn't just that we cannot replace them, it is that they are in fact the people we wish and need to recruit. Among the current effective leadership of the working class, these militants are the most advanced, the most class conscious; they consider themselves socialists of one sort or another. And it is because of this that we can recruit them... It is a long, arduous process but there is no substitute for this work... we must now put *all* our resources into building the rank and file movement in the only way it can be built, by the setting up of local groups; by the production of local and national bulletins which begin *now* to capitalise on the serious contacts made at the first Rank and File Conference; and by the active attempt to attract to the Rank and File Movement the advanced militants with a view to recruiting as many as possible into IS.

Ruth Nelson
Hackney IS

Platform of the IS Opposition

I shall prick this bloated bladder of lies with the poniard of truth
Aneurin Bevin

This document is the platform of the IS Opposition. It is not the preparation for a split and it sees the fight around its main planks as the reconstruction of IS as a democratic centralist organisation. We stand upon the IS tradition of maximum possible internal democracy and maximum unity in action. We see as central to the task of party building, serious work in the rank and file movement, the extension of factory branches, and the mutual development of the branches, districts and fractions of IS.

We stand unashamedly on the IS tradition of worker leadership at all levels in IS and for practical steps to make this possible. We believe that IS, by tradition, politics and experience is uniquely placed to build the party in Britain today. We strongly believe that current organisational moves from the centre, the downgrading of central political leadership are counterproductive to the essential tasks.

This document does not exhaust all the criticisms, its development will take place, and we hope constructively, in the process of genuine discussion. At the end of each section we outline resolutions containing specific proposals for the conference. At the end of the document we list the eight general points of our platform. We urge all those who support our main criticisms, proposals and determination to fight for IS politics, within IS, to contact us to join the faction, and to fight wherever possible within IS for its programme.

Democratic Centralism

Democratic centralism is not a luxury but an indispensable principle of internal organisation in the struggle to build a revolutionary socialist organisation. By democratic centralism we mean that every IS member should be involved as deeply as possible in the discussions and the decision making of the organisation. This is no easy matter. It requires a serious and consistent education programme, a frequent discussion of the relationship between the party and the class and the development of a mutual trust between the leadership and the membership. Only with trust will self-discipline through commitment of the members develop. This is the only kind of discipline that helps in the building of the organisation. Any system of orders from above by a Central Committee will reduce the members to sterility, irrelevance or apathy.

The development of genuine, thorough-going democratic centralism requires a healthy internal life. Duncan Hallas summed it up perfectly in his introduction to *Party and Class*:

> Such a party cannot possibly be created except on a thoroughly democratic basis; unless in its internal life, vigorous controversy is the rule and various tendencies and shades of opinion are represented, a socialist party cannot rise above the level of a sect. Internal democracy is not an optional extra, it is fundamental to the relationship between party members and those among whom they work.[1]

The truth is that in the past two years IS has at best been operating only partly on these principles and at worst has degenerated into a bureaucratic centralism worthy only of a sect. This came to a head last year with the sackings from *Socialist Worker*. The response from the members showed their concern: more than eighty resolutions from branches expressed concern to the May National Committee. That National Committee censured the Executive Committee for its neglect of the internal life of the organisation. This was reinforced at the last conference when a similar resolu-

---

1. Op. cit., p. 21.

tion from Harlow was carried. But since that conference the spirit and the letter of the resolution have been largely ignored. And more recently the members' rights have been seriously threatened. The current rationalisation for the clamp-down is basically efficiency and security. Take the question of security. Nothing that we can reasonably do will avoid the attentions of the Special Branch. As long as we maintain an organisation of any recognisable kind we will be the subject of successful attempts to learn our internal affairs. Modern technology makes it unnecessary for the state security agencies to infiltrate IS, although we have no doubt that they do. Every meeting held in public halls, and some held in private, can be overheard by electronic surveillance. Of course, we must be acutely conscious of the need for security and take every precaution. But security should mean extreme care over names, financial and administrative detail. It should not be used as a basis for restricting political information from the members, including political divisions among the leadership. In the end, the best kind of security we can have is the protection of the organised working-class movement against state attacks. That will best be won by an informed membership building our base in the working class movement.

The threat of a state clamp-down and repression of the revolutionary left is not one that we take lightly. But we do say that one of the preconditions for survival and effective work in semi-legal conditions is an informed, educated membership able through political understanding to operate with the necessary degree of independence. The plans set out by the Executive Committee in no way measure up to the needs of IS if the leadership's dire predictions come true. There is no alternative system of communication; national, district and local leaderships are not shadowed by substitute leaderships. There is no suggestion of safe houses, no letter drops and, most important, there is no plan for alternative printing facilities. One thing is clear: the latest organisational proposals are at best irrelevant to security and will deny both the members and the leadership the concerted discussion that will adequately prepare us for attack.

If the argument on security is overdone then we are left with the question of efficiency. This raises a point of some significance: is efficiency the rapid conclusion of debate by a restricted number of people who will agree with one another? Surely it is the case that revolutionary efficiency is accomplished by the development of the greatest number of members who have a firm grasp of overall politics and who will work for those politics? Current proposals for the banning of visitors to conference and for one delegate per thirty members elected on a district basis will have the opposite effect. It is argued in the document of the Organisational Commission that IS conferences are more akin to rallies, with demagogy and crowd-pleasing from floor and platform. A small conference dealing in depth with key questions in splendid isolation from the distraction of IS members would, the Commission says, be a great advance.

The truth is that the form of the discussion and whether it deals with key questions is a function of the agenda and the quality of the pre-conference discussions. It is within the power of the central leadership to deal with both of these items but they have shown no discernible inclination to do so. The Internal Bulletin has contained no documents that would enable anyone to orient around a clear political discussion. The degree of demagogy at any meeting is not related to its size but to the quality of the speeches and the speakers. The conference is a part of the life of IS. If properly organised it can be a positive inspiration to the comrades. Under the current ground rules it will become the object of suspicion. With the new proposals on district discussion and election we enter the area where the word "gerrymander' seems not inappropriate.

We are not opposed to district organisation, quite the opposite, we believe it will be very important in the development of IS, bringing together the best experiences of an area for other comrades to build from. But the few districts that already exist and function well have been built step by step from discussion, experience and learning how to adapt the organisational form to the local situation. There can be no national formula, it will fly in the face of our few successful attempts if we try to railroad the idea through artificially. What is more, if it is forced on us before conference the district aggregate will be the victim of all the ills that are alleged to afflict our national conference to date. Demagogy and verbal intimidation are implicit within the scheme. During the discussion two years ago on the introduction of factory branches, one of the great merits claimed for the proposal was the fact that factory branches, as opposed to factory cells, would enable the worker members to be better represented at conference. The latest idea will jettison this desirable objective into the same old geographical electoral base. Further, the highly restrictive adoption of the one in thirty rule will mean that most districts will have only two or at the most three delegates. District organisation must be developed as we grown in numbers and when the political preconditions for such a method of organisation in any given area exist. It cannot be imposed from above in the hope that by declaring districts we will in reality create them.

The proposal for a new Central Committee of nine full-time organisers and a two-monthly advisory National Committee is making a bad situation worse. Over the years there has been a problem of how the National Committee of forty meeting once a month can effectively control an Executive Committee of ten full-time IS organisers. National Committee members have tended to see themselves as rubber stamps, only occasionally asserting themselves, particularly if the Executive Committee was divided. However, in the last analysis, a committee with the majority of its members with their roots in the working class was able to prevent some of the worst errors of the full-time leadership. The new proposals will remove what control there is, and make the full-time Executive Committee even less accountable to the members.

The real problem is the construction of a worker leadership. Far from assisting this, the Executive Committee proposals fly directly counter to worker involvement at national level. Past and current practice has been for the National Committee to act as the passive recipient of the 'line' produced by the Executive Committee. National Committee members are not involved in actually making policy but in rubber-stamping or occasionally rejecting what is put before them. The obvious need is for the worker members (indeed all the National Committee members) to be involved at a much earlier stage in the process of policy making. This is not at all impossible. National Committee members should be distributed among various commissions that deal with all the organisational and political areas of group activity. Quite obviously it is not possible to bring worker National Committee members down to the Centre twice a month. A solution would be that the National Committee should meet every two months and that in the 'non National Committee' months the commissions should meet mandatorily for at least a day to prepare their report for the next National Committee.

The commissions will require support from the centre for efficient circulation of documents concerning meeting and submitting reports to the National Committee. Unless the National Committee through its commissions can develop the worker specialists in every facet of group politics and activity, the most immaculate Central Committee will be rudderless. The Executive Committee proposals for a purely consultative National Committee is no substitute for a properly involved and experienced worker leadership with real power to effect the direction of policy.

If this procedure seems cumbersome, we can only say that the alternative is not just contrary to the IS tradition and the often stated need for worker leadership, but is in fact the reverse of efficient and a device that denies the leadership almost as much as it denies the members.

Throughout this document we make specific proposals in resolution form for the running of IS. We are aware that the resolution in itself will not solve the problem, but we do believe it shows the right emphasis and given the correct spirit, can begin to restore the practice of democratic centralism to IS. One thing is clear: continuation of the present trends to more secrecy, more centralism and less democracy, will lead to a growing cynicism among a dwindling number of members.

This conference believes that it is vital for IS to base its internal life on genuine democratic centralist principles. It further believes that while security is important, it should not be used for restricting political information to members. Conference affirms that while changes to the existing structure will in future be both necessary and desirable, they should not be imposed from above, hurriedly and without discussion. It therefore believes that until the next conference the following points must be adhered to in the running of the organisation:

1. The National Conference is the supreme policy making body of the group. Its decisions are binding on all sections of the organisation. Only in an emergency will the National Committee be empowered to change a conference decision.

2. Delegates to conference will be elected by branches on the basis of one to fifteen, or majority of fifteen members. In workplace branches with a majority of manual workers the basis will be one to five.

3. Visitors to conference will be encouraged. Problems of security will be dealt with by credential issue and strict gate security.

4. Conference will elect an National Committee for forty members which will be the leading body of the organisation between conferences. The National Committee will elect an Executive Committee as at present.

5. The National Committee will consult the members where possible in making its decisions. To this end, National Committee members will be allocated to branches/districts/fractions and must engage in regular two way discussion.

6. Full National Committee minutes with voting records will be circulated to branches, with a full summary appearing in the Internal Bulletin (security sensitive items omitted).

7. The Internal Bulletin should be published monthly and supplied to all members. All major documents shall appear in the Bulletin, articles from members will be encouraged.

The conference recognises that these points on their own will not guarantee the practice of democratic centralism in IS. It believes that this can only be developed by a mutual trust between the membership and the leadership. It therefore calls upon the incoming National Committee, Executive Committee and all full-time workers to develop this over the coming year.

On Perspectives

The aim of perspective writing is not merely to produce an accurate description, but to draw a clear picture of the world in which we operate and to orient the cadre towards revolutionary activity and the construction of the party. This is central and indispensable and it is in this sense that we would criticise the perspectives set out by the Executive Committee.

We agree that there is a crisis of capitalism internationally. We agree that Britain has been able to avoid the worst rigours of unemployment and slump due to the large influx of petro-dollars. We accept fully the rightward drift of the trade union bureaucracy. We agree that the phenomenon of 'Bennery' is not an expression of a left wing; we would go further and say that it is an expression of state capitalism as a model for reviving British capitalism.

We do have a less catastrophic view of the likelihood of the oil deposits disappearing from the city of London (for the good and sufficient reason that the Arabs have only New York as the alternative site for their deposits – a place that has distinct politi-cal disadvantages for them), but we certainly agree that there is a degree of crisis and instability in British capitalism that must give some sleepless nights in the upper echelons of the system.

Having agreed with all this, we are still dissatisfied. Our com-plaint is that the broad sweep of the perspectives is not accom-panied by a serious attempt to fit the activity of the group into the perspective. The class analysis is missing. For example the IS Journal and Internal Bulletin contain a passing reference to the possibility of a centrist split in the Labour Party. Such a possibil-ity should not be idly floated. It requires some discussion of the experience in the localities to test out the idea, and if it were seen as a possibility, definite proposals for IS activity should have been forthcoming orienting our work on the Labour Party. We do not think there is a possibility of a centrist split, but give the example as one of many where the perspectives are left as vague generali-ties. A further example occurred at the March National Commit-tee. The suggestion was made by a leading Executive Committee member that the prospect was for the Arab oil deposits to be withdrawn within the next six months. Such a possibility carries with it certain political conclusions flowing from the collapse of the pound sterling, if not the entire system itself.

Government of national unity and all manner of splits and dif-ferentiations in conventional parties would be on the cards. That is something that has certain conclusions for our activity. The only one drawn at the National Committee was that there was no time for lengthy discussion before the crash. Perspectives are not general statements, but should link in very definitely with how to develop our activity.

Our differences are not in the general analysis but in the disconnection between the generalities and the specific course of action proposed. This can be summarised at the leadership's adoption of perspectives and methods that assume or, more accurately, require a continually-rising level of struggle in the class. With this goes the assumption that the tasks of members are essentially apolitical – to sell more papers to people who are waiting eagerly for our line and to recruit people who only need to be asked. This results in disillusionment, with members left unprepared for the hard political slog.

The IS case is not argued in detail in the paper, merely stated with the appropriate amount of force and conviction. The *Socialist Worker* Perspective article appears to say that there is really not much we can do until the prediction eventually comes true, so it follows that clarity about the present period is not all that important.

The general struggle would create a worker leadership for IS and our intervention would provide the answers to disputes without the need for the "luxury" of internal debate, and the rising tide would sweep non-IS people into the rank and file movement and remove the need for special efforts to avoid IS dominance.

Where the real world has forced itself on the leadership it has not led to any questioning of the method. The response to disillusionment is the demand to 'think big', to *do* more, ignoring the fact that mindless activism is almost as destructive as inactivity. The response on the paper is the ad hoc insertion of political articles that have no consistent theme. The response on perspectives is to admit the error and propose a strategy that is essentially to do whatever will keep us going until the original view comes true.

The response on internal organisation is two-fold; on the one hand to propose the new delegate basis that was originally conceived for a situation with strong districts based on leaderships tested in the expected struggles, and the Central Committee which was designed in the same way; on the other hand to indulge in the security frenzy as a new gimmick to get the members committed to an organisational structure they do not understand and will probably dislike.

The response on the Rank and File is similar to the response to disillusionment: multiply the circulars, the resolutions and the demos in a desperate attempt to gain the initiative and capture the people we have failed to bring in.

In reality we have moved into a far more complicated area of diffuse and localised struggles from the mass actions of last year. Unemployment, shot time and the prospect of large-scale redundancies are the external signs of the crisis and they are the reason for the less ready acceptance by workers of militant activity and slogans. It is no longer possible to recruit on the basis of a generalised strike offensive.

Politics become the key question in terms of recruitment and the maintenance of the members and the building of a cadre. As another manifestation of the crisis we get new possibilities – as at Imperial Typewriters – to make consistent politics a reality to numbers of workers. At Leyland and Chrysler we have opportunities for bringing the question of combine organisation and action to the fore and to politicise a whole new audience. We have a number of possibilities in the unions and in the factories if we take the trouble to actually elucidate serious political policies. The vital need is to reaffirm the development of factory branches, and the strengthening of the trade union fractions. This has to be seen as an integral part of our work to develop the rank and file movement. However, these steps cannot happen accidentally. The work of the IS centre in clearly outlining priorities after much discussion with IS members and giving consistent support and attention to the fractions and factory branches, has been lacking. Around the issues of redundancies, short time working, attacks on the trade union organisations, health and safety at work, our factory branches and trade union fractions could be active, so allowing the development of our work in the rank and file movement on a far more serious basis.

The perspectives, if they are to be more than annual ritual, have to actually guide the members in their activity in the real world. That means a serious attitude to the developments in the Labour Party and the government. As the capitalist crisis deepens the pressure will inevitably build within the Labour Party and more importantly among working class Labour voters. The danger will be that, as with Bevanism in the 1950s, Bennery will represent for a new generation of industrial militants a new, and more attractively populist, left wing. The workers cooperative idea has obvious attractions for workers living with redundancy as a real prospect. We have to oppose this with a clear statement of nationalisation under workers control without compensation. This will not be easy. There is a real and entirely justified reaction against bureaucratic nationalisation. But we do have the capacity to organise a campaign that will have nationalisation as a central part together with opposition to health, welfare and education cuts. In such a campaign we could mobilise a much wider, more political periphery than we have at present. *Socialist Worker* can once more become an important focus of consistent activity, with features, background and reports. Such a campaign will pay off in terms of membership and influence far more than the ill-conceived and adventurist Walsall by-election comedy.

The politics of working class life now contain arguments on political issues such as nationalisation and the nature of welfare. This means that the trade unions are once again an arena for political discussion that transcends simple trade union militancy. The relationship between capitalist failure, Labour political failure, the social contract, inflation, welfare cuts and how society is organised are now open questions that can be the subject of a far more specifically political treatment by revolutionaries. The perspectives fail to even show any appreciation of this fact.

Of even more concern is the fact that the perspectives document has practically nothing to say on the Rank and File Movement. What was for the last three conferences a central part of the task of party building has been down-graded to a single paragraph that tells far less than the low level of existing activity.

The real indictment that we level at the present leadership is that it is unable to connect either the perspective with the members or develop the leadership that could do so. The changes in the line that we have seen over the last period seem more concerned with the internal situation in IS than in the real world outside. Perspectives are written to the IS conference calendar, not to the objective needs of the political operation of the members outside. *Socialist Worker* episodically and fitfully, attempts to fill the gap made by the disconnection of the leadership from the members. Leadership never was the issuing of instructions – it should be a mutual process of development. Unless those links are restored and strengthened the prospect is for more disputes, more mistakes and a steady loss of comrades.

This conference believes that the perspectives document produced in *Socialist Worker* and the March Internal Bulletin is a barely adequate description of the development within capitalism and the Labour Party, and is grossly inadequate in failing to guide the members to serious work in the next period. Apart from the Rank and File Movement, there is no serious prescription for activity. The very effect of the crisis is to give a spurious left credibility to Benn and to foster the illusions in Labourism in that very section of advanced workers among whom IS should presently be gaining influence and members. It is therefore necessary for the group to develop a total critique of Labour and to campaign nationally on our own distinctive policies.

The main elements of such a campaign, in addition to the work already being done on the social contract should be:

> **1.** Nationalisation without compensation under workers control.
>
> **2.** Government cuts in education, health, welfare, etc.
>
> **3.** A centralised and properly monitored struggle in the unions and industry for a militant stance on pay, redundancy and unemployment, to both expose the union bureaucracy and to indicate the need for a rank and file movement.

The details of this wide campaign to be worked out and submitted to the members at district and regional aggregates within one month of the May conference. Special reference should be made to utilising *Socialist Worker* as a central feature of the campaign with supporting articles, reports, etc.

Rank and File Movement

To make clear our criticism of the IS record on the Rank and File Movement, and to point to the necessary first steps to begin to set things straight, it may be helpful to say a few words about the theory behind rank and file work. In so doing we may also throw a little light on the nature of transitional politics.

The rank and file cannot be conjured up at the whim of the revolutionary movement. It is not a timeless formation merely requiring the initiative of revolutionaries to exist. The partial success and tremendous potential of the Minority Movement in the 1920s was based on a number of necessary factors:

1. The post-1918 decline of British capitalism.

2. The attack on workers' living standards and conditions.

3. The inability and unwillingness of the official trade union machine to provide a solution to workers' economic problems.

4. The existence within industry of a large number of militants developed in the rank and file struggles that occurred between 1910 and 1922.

5. The existence of a small but overwhelmingly working class revolutionary party in the Communist Party (the Communist Party membership of the time numbered 3,000–4,000 members).

The crisis in capitalism and the inadequacy of the trade union bureaucracy are necessary preconditions. The weakness of the revolutionary vanguard and the political grip of trade union and social democratic reformism make the rank and file movement the ideal vehicle for the transition from economic to political struggle and from mass reformist politics to revolutionary politics. It is in this sense that the rank and file movement is "the bridge to the revolutionary party".

But the rank and file is neither the substitute for nor a section of the revolutionary organisation. Its main thrust is militant trade union struggle. In so far as the crisis in capitalism makes struggle inevitable it will require and acquire political objectives that a consistent revolutionary organisation will be able to supply.

It follows from this that the Rank and File Movement that is not independent, that is both in appearance and in fact a front will never become anything of significance in the workers' movement. It is also true, and history confirms this, that the initial impetus for the movement must come from revolutionaries. Having established the framework, the task is to work tirelessly to make it independent. The Rank and File Movement, unlike the revolutionary party, has to represent the highest common factor of trade union struggle. It cannot be this nor can it be any sort of bridge if it does not with reasonable speed go beyond the capacity of a small revolutionary party to control it. No matter how hard it is to swallow, you just cannot have a worthwhile movement that performs any useful let alone revolutionary function that is the passive creature of IS or any other group.

The situation in Britain is different from that in the 1920s, but there are important similarities. If the nature of the crisis is different, there is nevertheless a crisis that afflicts the economic, political and industrial life of the country. There is the long standing and apparently endless pressure on wages. In the 1920s the ruling class had sufficient strength and confidence to defeat the trade unions. Today they have to buy, cajole and convince the TUC and the bureaucracy. The trade union bosses, despite the power of the movement, despite the absence of defeat, nevertheless are convinced of the need for passivity because they can see no other solution within the context of capitalism. By politics, their own function and tradition they cannot go beyond the boundaries of capitalism. It is part of that dilemma they cannot even adequately perform their modest trade union role. It is then abundantly clear that at least the first three conditions for the Rank and File Movement are fulfilled.

But what of the other two vital conditions? There is not a layer of militants with a common reference to a heritage, such as the syndicalist-influenced rank and filers of the 1920s. There is however within the factories and workshops a highly developed, if insular, system of worker representatives and shop stewards. The more politically inclined are often to a greater or lesser degree influenced by the Communist Party. In consequence their notion of generalising beyond the individual factory is too often seen through the trade union machinery, with the preoccupation on elections and vote gathering. But it is from this layer, the one whose numbers actually lead in the factories, that the rank and file movement must be built. It is for this reason that we see the argument about the audience to which *Socialist Worker* addresses itself as vitally important. It is because of the Communist Party influence in the broad movement that we see the question of the independence of the Rank and File Movement as of more than secondary importance.

As the crisis deepens, as unemployment, redundancies and prices creep upwards, capitalism itself will provide the generalising experience that cannot be answered either within the individual factory or the trade union machine. The Labour left and the Communist Party will not have an answer. If we make our politics clear and indicate their relevance and coherence we will have a great deal to gain. If we orient our cadre correctly in industry and the trade unions the Rank and File Movement has a great future.

But of course IS does not have the far more favourable social composition of the early Communist Party. It has even less the wide periphery of workers schooled in ten years of shared struggle, and it does have the opposition of a Communist Party entrenched in a number of important areas where we need to succeed. The situation then is much more difficult for us, but is it impossible? If it is impossible then we should, with the least fuss and as discretely as possible, wrap up the whole enterprise. A body that holds periodic conferences with declining credibility is a dubious asset that will rapidly become a millstone.

We do not believe that it is impossible to carry out the necessary tasks. We believe that by theory and politics IS is ideally and uniquely situated to perform them. But to do so it will have to learn from its own past errors and omissions. First it has got to organise real roots in the localities. Because of the diffuse nature of the movement, the work will often be at a low level of target and performance, but a start has to be made. If all that can be achieved is for single IS militants to meet one other non-IS steward to agree on some preparatory steps to build something perhaps not even a local Rank and File committee but the production of a rank and file bulletin that goes beyond one factory, then we have started something that can grow. Far more ambitiously, we do have a cadre, in one or two big combines to initiate moves for combine stewards' committees and for the production of combine newspapers. That work is tremendously important and requires more than the rather feeble efforts put in it by the centre to date. Between both of these upper and lower limits there are a number of levels of activity that members can usefully work in. But unless we attempt a general, carefully planned and monitored pro-

gramme of activity, whatever successes we have in combine newspapers and committees will not build the Rank and File Movement if there has not been consistent work all over the country at
every level possible. There has to be organic growth or there will
be nothing but an IS financed and sustained shell that will stand
in the way of future attempts to build in the rank and file.

The record of IS during the past twelve months of the Rank
and File Movement has not been one to justify the high hopes of
the founding conference in March 1974. The need to take the initiative granted by that first conference was not grasped. The requirement for independence was not understood or was ignored.
The Organising Committee was staffed by IS members whose
qualifications were more their IS cards than their ability to lead in
their workplace. The clear need to bring non-IS militants in was
seen as subversive of IS control. At the March National Committee we had the ludicrous suggestion put forward by Executive
Committee members (written down in the Organisation Commission report) that the worker members of the National Committee
should be put on the Rank and File Organising Committee. The
members must be made to learn, or to remember, that the Rank
and File Movement is not nor should be the property of IS into
which it can decant leadership from above. Either the leadership
arises from the worker militants in or out of IS who agree with
the programme and are capable of fighting for it in their unions
and factories or the Rank and File Movement does not exist except as an extension of IS's propaganda effort. The accusations
levelled frequently by the Communist Party and other hostile
groups that the Rank and File Movement is an IS front become
more and more difficult to contradict.

The essence of the theory and practice of a genuine rank and
file movement is not that it is an auxiliary arm of IS or any revolutionary organisation, but that by its independent, autonomous
existence it provides the arena in which workers can fight more
effectively. This is the fact that, in the midst of capitalist crisis,
will bring new and tested worker members to the party. Even now
it is not too late to make amends for the lost time and opportunities over the past year, but the work has to be put in hand as a
matter of urgent priority.

The role and importance of the Rank and File movement is not developed in the political perspectives document. There needs to be a careful examination of the experience with the National Rank and File Movement and what it can do in the future.

1. Factory branches, and a serious concern to develop them, have to be re-emphasised. They are an integral part of our work to build the Rank and File Movement.

2. The present crisis creates possibilities for IS members to initiate rank and file activity at many levels, from the development of combine newspapers to the drawing together of factories in a locality to fight common problems of wages, conditions and redundancies. These possibilities have to be encouraged.

3. The way the centre supports and gives attention to rank and file activity so that initiatives can be taken up needs more coordination.

4. This, of course, does not mean that the Rank and File Movement has to be preserved. But on issues to which IS can give a good deal of support, if there is adequate preparation and attention, for example the Health and Safety School, then IS should clearly put a major effort into such activity.

5. The ability of the Rank and File Movement to implement policies is related to its strength at local level. Attempts to call for actions which the National Rank and File Movement cannot play some part in implementing can only serve to discredit it. Therefore we should be looking far more to initiatives which can develop the movement's credibility rather than to grandiose calls to action.

Socialist Worker

The decline in the political influence of *Socialist Worker* and the sharp fall in its sales are a major concern. The paper no longer provides a clear and consistent political lead for members and readers. Politics is no longer an integral feature of the paper but is reduced to the occasional exposure of a leading Labour politician. Worse, the paper's coverage of industry is restricted to strike reports and ritual attacks on the union bureaucracy without a clear set of policies and programme to direct the work of our industrial members and our close supporters. The paper's attitude to the Labour government has opened a dangerous credibility gap between IS and those militants who still have illusions in reformism. Twice yearly attacks on the phenomenon of Wedgewood Benn that merely accuse him of political dishonesty and crudely make no distinction between Benn and the Prentice/Jenkins wing strengthen militants' support for Labour rather than weaken it. As we have noted, Benn represents a state capitalist solution to the problems of the British economy, but his solutions are cloaked in left phrases and he is under constant attack from the Tory press. Workers will be won from 'Bennery' towards revolutionary politics only by a sensitive critique of Benn's politics and the workers' cooperative experience and a clear exposition of our alternative of nationalisation under workers' control.

The paper must be a two-way transmission belt between the leadership and the members. Strike reports by themselves are an inadequate alternative to real analysis and guides to action. Security considerations aside, the paper must direct to a large extent IS's industrial work. This means not only directives and programmes for our trade union members but reports of our successes and failures and some honest accounting of our difficulties.

The paper's current style flows from the debate a year ago when a majority of the Executive Committee promised a rapidly rising circulation if the paper abandoned its concern with 'hard' politics and its orientation on experienced militants. The new audience was to be traditionless but rebellious younger workers who, it was patronisingly assumed, would not read 'boring' political articles. Two journalists were removed from the paper for daring to disagree with this departure from traditional IS politics. The result has been no major shift in the paper's orientation – there is nothing in it specifically to attract younger workers – just a rapid retreat from politics, an over-compensation with "exposure' and corruption articles and proliferating strike reports that lack analysis and fail to offer cohesive advice to our members and industrial supporters.

Education – a vital part of the revolutionary paper – has been reduced to the occasional snippet buried at the back of the paper. But historical articles on the failures and successes of previous workers' movements can inform current practice and prevent the repetition of mistakes. Similarly, the need for a revolutionary party needs argument, analysis and historical back-up, not just slogans tacked on to news items.

A change is urgently needed if the paper's decline is to be halted and reversed. *Socialist Worker* must be the political expression of IS, analysing and directing our members' work. Regular non-IS readers should be able to grasp IS's distinctive political style and content.

The paper should continue the education of members and their overall development of the work. The paper should be the mainstay of the group and its advance guard in the factories. The old dispute about a 'paper for workers' or a 'workers' paper' is not the question at issue. A workers' paper is not necessarily written by workers; it is one that generalises revolutionary ideas so that it has a relevance to a wider audience than would otherwise be possible. *Socialist Worker* is not such a paper. It must be transformed into an IS instrument for intervention in the class struggle.

Conference, concerned at the declining sales and influence of *Socialist Worker* and the paper's drift from a coherent political analysis, affirms that:

1. *Socialist Worker* must be the political expression of IS providing a consistent political analysis that determines the activity of our members and supporters. In industry especially, the paper must present programmes and policies that direct the work of our members in the trade unions. Work that in turn should be reported and critically analysed in the paper. Strike reports and attacks on the 'bureaucracy' do not by themselves arm the membership.

2. The paper must intervene in the politics of the Labour movement with a sensitive and regular coverage of the Labour Government. Twice yearly exposes of 'Bennery', a crude lumping of rights and lefts in the Labour Party, or blurring of the class differences between Labour and Tory politicians divorces the paper from militant class conscious workers whose lingering illusions in reformism are strengthened, not weakened by the paper's attitudes.

3. There must be a return to regular educational articles on the history and development of working class and revolutionary movements, both national and international. Such articles are a badly needed antidote to the increasing voluntarism of the paper at present. The need for a revolutionary party requires argument and analysis, not the ritualistic slogan tacked on to the end of every news item.

4. While every effort must be made to expand sales and support, *Socialist Worker*'s main thrust must be towards the advanced militant in industry and the trade unions, the essential cadre of the revolutionary party.

Women

IS can and must recruit working class women. We must see our main aim as developing women cadres to lead struggles in their workplaces. Last year's conference voted for a monthly *Women's Voice* and a full-time worker to edit it and organise around it. We have the monthly paper and editor but there are no perspectives that seriously link women with our general economic and industrial perspectives and as a result there are no guidelines for women's work in industry. The predicted upsurge in women's struggles around equal pay is not happening. The idea was based on the belief that equal pay year would act as the same trigger to widespread action as threshholds did in 1974. This perspective ignored the effect of the social contract and the threat of unemployment. It also ignored the complexity of equal pay compared to the straightforward demand for a threshhold payment. In this situation, a Rank and File Conference that was a result of the mistaken perspective needed to be adapted to the reality of the situation. In fact any value that such a conference could have offered has been forfeited in the way it has been sprung on members with only five weeks to organise women worker delegates, who face more problems than other workers in attending national conferences. Then with three weeks to go branches received a desperate plea for observers for the conference.

In this situation, members can have no confidence in the outcome and will not be willing to do the necessary hard work to get delegates and observers. And the details of the conference have not been accompanied by any industrial perspective for branch work.

We believe there can be no national blueprint for work around equal pay at the present time. The emphasis must be on local intervention, especially by factory branches and *Socialist Worker* groups. The women's sub-committee should produce a national worksheet outlining the stated positions and activity to date of the major unions, the employers' loopholes developed over the past five years, and instructions to branches on what to find out to ensure they understand their local situations so they can intervene and argue a principled line. The woman full-timer should coordinate this work.

The single issue worrying most women workers at present is the threat of redundancies and our militants must be armed with principled arguments about women's right to work. This cannot be approached as a separate issue. It must be at the forefront of all our propaganda about unemployment. In situations such as Imperial Typewriters, where women are among those affected by the closure, our intervention must consider the needs of women. But though similar situations will undoubtedly occur, we cannot base our perspectives solely on them. More common will be the pamphlet on unemployment with a major section on women's right to work, showing how women's position in society and women's wage rates are connected to the idea of 'women out first'. *Socialist Worker* must arm our militants with relevant and down to earth arguments and each factory branch or groups must thrash out their attitudes and how they are going to argue. All IS meetings on redundancies should have a local woman trade unionist on the platform and speakers' notes should be produced by the women's sub-committee.

Non-industrial work has been an equally startling omission. This stems from a narrow perspective that sees women only as workers and fails to realise that women workers often have to face their problems as women at the same time as they confront their problems as workers, such as the problem of looking after children while maintaining a 24 hour picket. It must also be recognised that although the best male class leaders are inevitably in industry, the same cannot necessarily be said about women. Due to family responsibility, many may temporarily be out of these positions but they can be drawn back into struggle over a whole number of issues where women fight to protect their standard of living – prices, housing, education and so on. The importance of these issues is to show that the crisis is affecting all aspects of working class life and campaigns around them will help expose the Labour Party and the social contract. We need to work out the issues that will give rise to struggles, give a lead in how to organise campaigns and link them with the relevant groups of workers, drawing on what our members are already involving themselves in, such as the campaign against education cuts in Richmond, Surrey.

Branches need detailed help on how to inject politics into community campaigns. We have some relevant experience already but it needs collating and generalising. *Women's Voice* is unlikely to be used constructively as a monthly paper while the group lacks leadership in women's work. The paper has changed its whole orientation without discussion with the areas that use it most. IS women have different experiences of whether *Women's Voice* is more successful with its main emphasis on trade union matters (as at present) or more of a balance between work and the issues that affect women as wives and mothers (as was the case until the end of 1974). The paper needs more time to be tried as a monthly organiser and more discussion is needed with members, but whatever emphasis proves most successful, there should be a shift back to a paper written by working class women rather than being produced mainly by teachers, journalists and full-timers at Cottons Gardens. The appointment of Sheila MacGregor as the women's full-timer is also unsatisfactory. The woman appointed to this job should be someone with experience of and sympathy for work with working class women. Comrade MacGregor has argued on the National Committee for the past two years, and in her branch, against a separate women's paper, and until recently she also argued against the need for any kind of women's work in IS.

A monthly *Women's Voice* with the right editor/organiser could advance our work with women rapidly but, as with all aspects of IS work, it needs to be linked with a comprehensive perspective that is capable of being operated by the membership. The crisis will mean additional hardship for working class women. It will affect all aspect of their lives. Just stabbing at unrelated aspects, as at present on abortion, in search of a campaign will not on its own inspire our members or impress the women we should be organising and recruiting.

Conference considers that IS's work with working class women should take account of the fact that their problems as women are inextricably linked to their problems as workers.

> **1.** Our main perspective should be to develop working class women cadres to lead struggles in their workplaces, and IS militants must play a leading role in this by intervening wherever women go into struggle over the right to work, Equal Pay etc. In our work with women workers we must also attend to the concrete problems that affect their ability to struggle – child care problems, domestic responsibilities.
>
> **2.** If we are to recruit working class women we must intervene in struggles outside the factory which illustrate the wide-reaching nature of the crisis – education, welfare, rents, prices etc. Such issues are important in the consciousness of women workers as well as housewives, and can develop confidence to fight at work. They are also significant in the attempt to expose the Labour Government and the Social Contract. Our growing strength in the unions – teachers, health workers etc, should link up with such struggles.
>
> **3.** Conference welcomes the implementation of the decision to appoint a full-timer for women's work and to produce a monthly *Women's Voice*. It considers, however, that the comrade appointed should have experience of, and sympathy for, women's work, rather than someone who has consistently opposed having a separate women's paper.
>
> **4.** Whilst recognising the vital importance of local initiatives, conference believes that because of the lack of IS's experience of women's work the leadership must begin to include an analysis of women's position in society with general perspectives, and must lay down clear guidelines for resulting work.

The Women's Sub-Committee should produce worksheets for factory branches/groups on Equal Pay, and speakers notes on women's right to work. An updated pamphlet on unemployment should be produced with a major section on women, showing how the idea of 'women out first' is directly connected to women's wage rates and role in the family – and outlining principled but down to earth arguments against the idea.

What is to be Done

We believe that the issues before us are the credibility and viability of IS as the future revolutionary party. This issue is raised sharply by the developments in the world and the course of the current IS leadership. These are issues of considerable importance and we are prepared to fight as hard as necessary to defend the past traditions of IS and its future revolutionary prospects. We invite your support for our factional programme and your participation in this much needed and long overdue work.

Our platform can be stated as:

1. For genuine democratic centralist organisation.

2. For a worker leadership that actually leads and does not perform a purely symbolic function.

3. For a consistent policy of Marxist education in IS.

4. For a central leadership that informs the membership and is informed by them, with an administration that assists and directs this mutual process.

5. For a serious perspective that relates IS politics to the practical activity of the members, worked out in conjunction with the fractions and groups of members concerned.

6. For a drastic reappraisal of the work in the Rank and File Movement, with the intention of ensuring the existence of a strong, independent movement.

7. That *Socialist Worker* should be transformed into a paper that consistently puts over IS politics, with particular appeal to advanced industrial workers but including the popular exposition of historical, theoretical and contemporary political questions.

8. For an end to arbitrary and ill-thought-out schemes for reorganisation that effectively reduce the rights of the members.

Reply to Duncan Hallas by the IS Opposition

Duncan Hallas's reply to the *Platform of the IS Opposition* makes a number of points and several assertions. In so far as it addresses itself to our substantive criticisms, it denies their substance. At the end we are left with the impression that the IS Opposition is a collection of dedicated malcontents, united only in opposition to the Centre. This reply to Duncan Hallas will take up, in turn, Hallas's points and, we hope, effectively answer his criticisms.

DH1: The IS Opposition have politics no different from IS and do not disagree with the general thrust of the perspectives document.

The first half of this assertion is true, the second part is half true. Of course we stand four square on IS politics, it is no accident that we call ourselves the IS Opposition. We stand for IS tradition and theory, for rigorous political analysis, for full membership participation and discussion, for worker leadership and serious perspectives. We do find it difficult to disagree with the extreme generality of the perspectives document. We claim that the perspectives are descriptive not prescriptive. They do not orientate the comrades to fruitful activity. A measure of the inadequacy of the perspectives is that they have to be supplemented (in the April *Internal Bulletin*) by documents called: 'EC Discussion Documents'. These afterthought additions to the pre-conference discussion are certainly more detailed but almost as useless. To take the first of these: 'The Labour Party, Benn and Centrist Developments' – it goes on, in some detail, to tell us what might happen on the one hand and then tells us what might happen on the other hand and in the end tells us nothing we have not heard at the last three conferences. It is vaguely interesting as an academic exercise, mildly informative but not at all satisfying if we are serious about building a 'combat' party.

The document, in the same series, on the Rank and File Movement, presents us with the thought that our intention is to reach the stage where the Rank and File Movement detaches *"most of the organised workers from the control of the reformist TU leadership"*. Now this may just be an example of careless wording but if it is not it represents a fundamental misunderstanding of the theory behind the chances of building a Rank and File Movement. We are not building a dual union. We cannot expect to mobilise the majority of workers before the revolution. The Rank and File Movement is directed specifically toward those who lead at rank and file level. The Rank and File Movement can be the bridge to the party for numbers of rank and file workers because it carries out the trade union task that the TU bureaucracy will not and cannot perform. It must do that within the existing movement and it will almost by definition be a minority within that movement. The Rank and File Movement document for the rest is general in its attempt to apply theory to the work of our own cadre. In its reportage of the last year's work it does not evaluate the two National Conferences of the Rank and File Movement.

When it discusses work in the localities the report indicates that what happened was either unconnected with the Rank and File Movement Organising Committee or, if it was, it was as a result of a preexisting strike situation, from which nothing remains. Building a movement, as we said in our Platform document, is first of all the task of directing and monitoring the work of all the IS industrial cadres on whatever small or large task they can perform in the localities. If the Rank and File Movement is not based upon real roots in the localities, all the worthy campaigns on Chile and Shrewsbury will not be a substitute. We need also many small time, duplicated bulletins in factories and workshops. We need on whatever small scale to push the local struggle a little further beyond the individual factory wall.

If, as the document says, "*Within the British working class the pos-sibility of building a revolutionary party is closely linked to building a genuine Rank and File movement*", then it really is time we stopped pretending that what we have today can by the same methods as we have used in the past be built into such a "*genuine Rank and File Movement*". To utilise all the latent possibilities of the IS indus-trial cadre to this task would be to make a breakthrough into real industrial and trade union work. It is work in a situation where direct political demands can be raised with some practical applica-tion, political demands not just on the Labour leaders but on the TU bureaucracy as well. Which leads on to Hallas's second point.

DH2: The IS Opposition are divided among themselves on the ques-tion of the Common Market and on Labour Party perspectives. There-fore, on the first they remain silent and on the second produce a grab all statement, which signatories with differing views can sign.

We should look at these two items with a little more care. They really amount to an accusation of: 'an unprincipled bloc'. It is true that members of the IS Opposition disagree on the Com-mon Market. At aggregates up and down the country Executive Committee spokesmen have made much of this point. Why? Apart from the obvious one of, any stick to beat a dog, there can be no reason at all. As Hallas knows – far better than most – it is quite possible to be in general political solidarity without agreeing on everything. The IS Opposition is not a tendency with monolithic unity on all questions. If we were we would be a party within a party and that we refuse to be or to contemplate.

On the Common Market there is certainly a substantial agree-ment among comrades of the IS Opposition and it is this. The IS record on the Common Market has not been entirely consistent over the years. For years we were abstentionist on the question, before Heath took Britain into the Market we were anti. After Britain actually entered, an National Committee motion was car-ried unanimously, moved interestingly enough by Hallas and sup-ported by all the Executive Committee, that once in there was no merit in calling for withdrawal! Since then the National Commit-tee has changed its mind that it is quite within its rights to do so.

It would, however, and on this Opposition comrades absten-tionist or anti all agree, have been far better, more instructive and useful for the newer comrades, who know nothing about the past, to have actually discussed this allegedly crucial question with the membership. We are for full membership discussion and participation on major policy changes, we are not at all ashamed of our own disagreements on the Common Market issue.

Now to the business of the Labour Party and, in Hallas's document, it is a complicated one. Hallas confesses that he does not know whether there will be a centrist split in the Labour Party, there are too many imponderables in the equation, he says. In terms of certainty neither do we. The point that we are raising, and Hallas raised in both the *Internal Bulletin* and *ISJ*, is that a Labour Party split perspective is not one that should be raised as an interesting speculation. Either we have sufficient confidence that would enable us to work for that desirable objective or we have not.

In other words we need to discuss and work out with the members the concrete consequences of such a split. Equally we should have detailed perspectives for the Labour Party if this does not occur. Our complaint is that the political perspectives or Hallas's article do neither.

Let us try to make the position of the IS Opposition clear. We are neither committed to placing a comprehensive list of demands on the Labour Government based on the 1938 *Transitional Programme* as does the Militant for example, nor do we believe that IS can ignore the existence of the Labour Government or the collaboration between the TU leaders and Labour leaders; nor the existence of the Labour Left and their relationship with the rank and file in the labour movement. We are in business to expose the inability of any of these groups to solve the crisis or to offer a real alternative. The best way to do this is of course to campaign on a number of points which both relate to the needs of the working class and expose the inability of the Labour leaders or the Labour Left to meet these demands. In the 'Platform' and in our resolution on perspectives we point to the need for an integrated campaign in the labour movement on (a) nationalisation without compensation under workers' control; (b) opposition to health, welfare, education and housing cuts; (c) the struggle in industry against redundancy, short-time working and the social contract. Of course in this kind of campaign demands must be made on the Labour Government and the Labour and Trade Union Left.

Every demand must have an agency to carry it out, if you are making a political demand for nationalisation under workers' control that agency is the Labour Government. The essence of transitional politics is to develop a strategy which starts from where the struggle is now and advances that struggle by moving workers into action, and in that process raises their political consciousness by exposing the reformist path. The truth is that until recently the danger in IS has been that we have been ignoring transitional politics. Instead we have had a style of politics which suggests that struggle by itself or at best connected to an abstract set of politics will advance the movement.

This is certainly the impression that *Socialist Worker* gave until recently. The Executive Committee it seems has begun to notice this, partly we believe as a result of our criticism. We gather they are now proposing a national campaign against cuts in public spending. While welcoming the change in emphasis we believe that a single issue campaign like this is fraught with dangers. We believe that in the present crisis the battle on nationalisation cannot be separated from the fight against redundancy and the social contract of the fight against cuts in public expenditure. To campaign solely on the cuts has dangers of fostering reformist illusions that the cuts can be restored under capitalism. The campaign needs to be cast firmly in a political context. Not as Hallas suggests, by orientating on the Labour Party alone but, more usefully, by raising in the trade union bodies the issues of nationalisation and workers control, health and welfare cuts. We can do this as IS, and if it were more than it presently is, through the Rank and File Movement. The Executive Committee and Hallas should also realise that a campaign is not just a series of meetings with 'star' speakers (the failure of the Autumn/Winter Campaign and the Social Contract Campaign should have taught us that). A campaign is the mobilising of the members around the issues and directing them in the work of the branches, districts and fractions. Therefore our disagreement with the Executive Committee on perspectives towards the Labour Party is that they are not specific enough to orientate our members for the battle in the Trade Union and Labour Movement.

An interesting example of this vagueness was demonstrated in another area at the April National Committee on the question of

Ireland. No doubt because Ireland receives barely a mention in the political perspectives, the Executive Committee proposed a resolution on Ireland. This suggested that for a whole number of reasons the question of Ireland was likely to become more important over the next year and that comrades in the districts should therefore raise the issue in a manner appropriate to their area. It required an IS Opposition National Committee member to move an amendment to make specific what demands we should be raising in the localities, namely troops out, an end to repression, repeal of the anti-terrorist laws, self-determination for the Irish people. It is this kind of programme that orientates members to fight in the working class movement. It is this kind of perspective that we should be developing towards the Labour Government, Labour Party and left Labour and Trade Union leaders. Instead, all we have from Hallas is a restatement of our two year old Trade Union Programme.

DH 3: The IS Opposition while complaining of the current IS regime suggest that the existing structures, through which the current leadership emerged, should be kept intact.

In its own small way this last accusation raises even more interesting questions. Does Hallas believe that the existing leadership will change under the new Central Committee structure? The very description of the requirements for the Central Committee are in fact a description of the existing Executive Committee.

If as Hallas says the (two or three monthly) National Council will have complete control over policy, on what qualities will the Central Committee be elected – administrative and organising ability? If so there will have to be a few changes made. But is it true that the National Council will hold political control? Executive Committee speakers, apart from Hallas, have at different aggregates made clear that the National Council will be advisory. In fact as it is suggested it could be nothing else. How can a large committee with shifting membership – delegacies from districts and fractions will not be fixed and can be substituted – or elected from each meeting, have any control over policy. It will exaggerate the weaknesses of the existing National Committee. At least the present arrangement does have the power, and occasionally uses it, to curb the worst excesses of a full-time executive.

Hallas does not address himself to the solution, the practical solution that we offered in the Platform. For National Committee commissions meeting and initiating and directing policy between National Committee meetings, which would probably then have to be two monthly. That we believed to be a practical solution to the problem of actually utilising the experience of the worker National Committee members. It may not be perfect but it is a great deal better than the Executive Committee's proposals which will effectively exclude the workers altogether. We are not wedded to any particular organisational form but we are wedded to the notion of worker leadership in IS, at all levels.

It is bizarre but true that if the Central Committee and National Council proposals are carried then we will get not, as Hallas suggests, an increase in democracy but a reversion to federalism. Indeed it is now clear from the contributions of Executive Committee members at district meetings that federalism is what they are saying they want. *"We don't need workers' leaders at the Centre, let them lead in the districts"*. Whether they actually desire this or whether they wish to run the group nationally with an Executive Committee of 'professional' full-timers without interference is not clear. Either way we believe there are great dangers for IS in having a small full-time Central Committee unchecked by any other body and without its roots in the labour movement.

Our suggestion for a development of the existing structure is not bloody-mindedness. We are not prepared to say that because the National Committee/Executive Committee relationship may prove difficult we should dispense with the workers at national level.

We are not against strong districts in IS, we are wholeheartedly for them. We do not believe that strong districts can be built by Diktat or the passing of a resolution. The credibility gap between the desire and the actuality is not automatically filled because we wish it so. A strong National Committee with clear powers, seriously involved in the evolution of policy can be the spearhead of a drive to build districts. A small overworked Central Committee alone will not do the job, we will just get more well-intentioned resolutions less and less related to the facts of life in the districts.

One final point on Hallas's reply. He claims that the disputes of last year and the censures of the Executive Committee have been heeded. He also claims that since then there have been no restrictions on the rights of members. This is really rather surprising since it was Hallas who at the May '74 National Committee (when the last Executive Committee was sacked and he rejoined it) moved a long and detailed resolution setting out some of these rights. That resolution was unanimously endorsed by the 1974 conference which also called on the incoming Executive Committee/National Committee to carry out the spirit and the letter of Hallas's motion. Hallas's resolution, since clearly he needs to be reminded of it, contained a number of important points.

1. That the National Committee shall be the supreme body between conferences.

2. That the National Committee will consult the membership where possible in making its decisions.

3. That the membership is kept informed and security is not used as an excuse for restricting information.

4. That full National Committee minutes and voting records are issued to the branches.

Every one of these points has been reversed by the current Executive Committee with Hallas's support. In addition, of course, the members have recently been deprived of the right to attend National Committee meetings as visitors, to attend conferences as visitors, and indeed the numbers attending conference as delegates has been halved. How Hallas can claim that these are not restrictions on members' rights is beyond us.

In this context it is interesting that a supporter of the Executive Committee organisational proposals, John Molyneux, should write quite sharply on this question in the same *Internal Bulletin* as Hallas's reply. *"For some time"*, he says, *"we have had a situation in which the membership learns of differences in strategy and approach among the National Committee only through vague rumour and in which open debate takes place only after crucial decisions have been taken. Branches are presented with a fait accompli and can only protest impotently"*. Comrade John Molyneux cannot be described as a born factionalist or a tired ex-functionary but he makes an effective point on these organisational proposals. Two months before the conference the members are presented with a fait accompli. They are expected to accept it without debate. If they do dissent they are accused of ignoring the politics. There is no good reason in objective reality why the members should be railroaded in this way. If, as has been argued by Executive Committee spokesmen, the new organisational proposals are a product of the new situation we presently face, we cannot believe it. These actual proposals were raised over two years ago by Comrade Tony Cliff, and regularly raised ever since. Justified most often with references to Lenin and the Bolshevik conferences, they were small, lengthy and very businesslike. It is also true that the conferences were in Western Europe and the members in Russia. A situation that makes free access very difficult.

It is also the case that any party member, who could prove his membership, was not excluded from the Bolshevik conferences.

But bent precedent and persistence have found their reward. The argument used last year to alter the basis of delegacy to 1 in 15 of an ever growing membership cannot apply this year with static membership. Instead we get the nonsense about 'rally atmosphere' and 'demagogy'. The truth is that the new proposals are very old mouldy proposals and thoroughly bad ones, they should be rejected out of hand.

While we have the opportunity we would like to answer one last point, not raised by Hallas but by some of his own faction. This concerns the allegation that the Platform of the IS Opposition is merely a vehicle in which certain ex-members of the Executive Committee will ride back to high office in IS. We will, of course, put up a slate for whatever elections are held but that is not the main point of the exercise – in fact we have not as yet chosen the slate. Our concern is with IS, not with jobs for the boys. Cottons Gardens is not IS for us. IS is the members in the fractions and branches who deserve a great deal more than they are getting for their work, devotion and dedication to IS. We are concerned that IS will not grow and we want it to grow. We are very worried about the loss and potentially greater loss of valued comrades. We are more than sorry at the impossibility of raising political differences without calling down a stream of abuse and vilification, and organisational manipulation. The members do have the chance to set them right, we can once and for all settle the question and then start to build IS on the solid ground of an informed and united membership. That is what we mean by the IS tradition. Ignoring that tradition will condemn IS to a slide into sectarian irrelevance, another quirk of revolutionary history that did not come off.

Glossary

AFL - *American Federation of Labour*
ASE - *Amalgamated Society of Engineers*
ASTMS - *Association of Scientific, Technical and Managerial Staffs*
AUBTW - *Amalgamated Union of Building Trade Workers*
AUEW - *Amalgamated Union of Engineering Workers*
CARD - *Campaign Against Racial Discrimination*
CND - *Campaign for Nuclear Disarmament*
CPGB - *Communist Party of Great Britain*
CPSU(B) - *Communist Party of the Soviet Union (Bolshevik)*
ETU - *Electrical Trades Union*
FLN - *National Liberation Front (Algeria)*
GDR - *German Democratic Republic*
GPU - *Gosudarstvennoye Politicheskoye Upravlenie ('State Political Directo-rate')*: A section of Stalin's secret police.
ICFI - *International Committee of the Fourth International*
ILP - *Independent Labour Party*
IMG - *International Marxist Group*
IRA - *Irish republican Army*
IS - *International Socialists*: Forerunners of the UK Socialist Workers Party.
ISFI - *International Secretariat of the Fourth International*
ISJ - *International Socialism Journal*
ISL - *Independent Socialist League*
ISO - *IS Opposition*
IWGB - *Industrial Workers of Great Britain*
IWW - *Industrial Workers of the World*
KPD - *German Communist Party*
LLOY - *Labour League of Youth*
LPYS - *Labour Party Young Socialists*
MNA - *Algerian National Movement*
NALGO - *National Association of Local Government Officers*
NCLC - *National Council of Labour Colleges*
NUM - *National Union of Mineworkers*
NUT - *National Union of Teachers*
NUTGW - *National Union of Tailors and Garment Workers*

NUWCM - *National Unemployed Worker's Committee Movement*
POEU - *Post Office Engineering Union*
RCP - *Revolutionary Communist Party*
RFM - *Rand and File Movement*
RSDLP - *Russian Social Democratic Labour Party*
RSL - *Revolutionary Socialist League*
SDF - *Social Democratic Federation*
SLL - *Socialist Labour League:* Healyite group, forerunners of the WRP.
SPD - German Social Democratic Party
SPGB - *Socialist Party of Great Britain*
SRG - *Socialist Review Group:* Forerunners of the UK International Socialists and Socialist Workers Party.
SSWCM - *Shop Stewards and Workers' Committee Movement*
STLA - *Socialist Trades and Labour Alliance*
SWP - *Socialist Workers Party*
TGWU / T&G - *Transport and General Workers' Union*
UMS - *United Mineworkers of Scotland*
UPW - *Union of Post Office Workers*
USFI - *United Secretariat of the Fourth International*
WFM - *Western Federation of Miners*
WIL - *Workers' International League*
WPA - *Works Progress Administration*
WRP - *Workers Revolutionary Party*
YCL - *Young Communist League*

Index

Blake in Cambridge

Ben Watson

ISBN: 978-0-9568176-8-6
Published: Apr 2012, 168pp

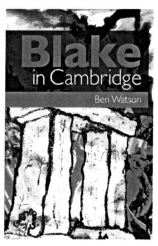

Blake in Cambridge was written after reading William Blake's visionary epic *Milton* during extended bouts of childcare in Coram's Fields in the summer of 2010. *Blake in Cambridge* is the Marxist critique of Eng. Lit. Christopher Caudwell was meant to write, but screwed up due to a CPGB sociology which denies literature the chance to answer back. In Marx's polemic, the jokes of *Tristram Shandy* and *Don Quixote* became weapons in class struggle. This, argues Watson, is how Blake can and should be used.

The **Association of Musical Marxists** says: A revolutionary party would not be paranoid about its members' proclivities. It would not try, like the Lindsey German-era SWP, to insulate members from avant garde extremes and bathe them, infant Cleopatras, in a dilute milk of inoffensive, politically-correct culture – soggy crumbs from the bosses' table. We need to pierce the veil of moralism and fear which protects the bourgeois racket. Blake for the masses! Start here…

1839: The Chartist Insurrection

Dave Black and Chris Ford

ISBN: 978-0-9568176-6-2
Published: Apr 2012, 268pp

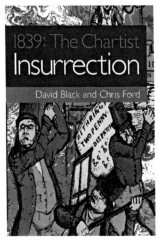

"With its meticulous attention to detailed sources, its comprehensive scope and its exacting research, this book doesn't just address the neglect of this important and interesting episode in Labour movement history, but more importantly it also challenges us to think again about the revolutionary potential of the British Labour movement."

John McDonnell MP, **Foreword**

In retrieving the suppressed history of the Chartist insurrection, David Black and Chris Ford have written a revolutionary handbook. Without romanticism or condescension, they track the difficulties of unifying local revolts without selling out to the 'representative politics' favoured in the parliamentary charade. As today's anti-capitalism faces the problem of anger without organisation, the lessons of the Chartists become crucial. Dialectics is not something to be derived from pure philosophy: by looking at the political problems of an insurgent working class, Black and Ford resurrect the true One-to-Many dialectic.

Association of Musical Marxists

The Struggle for Hearts and Minds: Essays on the Second World War

Ray Challinor

ISBN: 978-0-9568176-1-7
Published: Sep 2011, 128pp

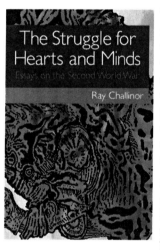

This book of essays is a shocking read, but the shocks arrive from the history itself, not sensationalist writing. We've been told that the Second World War was a war against evil waged by the goodhearted and true. The spectre of Hitler and Nazism is invoked every time NATO bombs are aimed at a defenceless country.

In his scathing account of ruling-class fears, plans and allegiances, Ray Challinor shows how much their every move was governed by competition and self-interest – and anxieties about popular reaction. His evidence shatters the comforting national myth which has been spun around the cataclysm – and shows that people, working-class people, do not like killing each other, they had to be cajoled and manipulated into doing so.

"Read Ray Challinor's, The Struggle for Hearts and Minds, *to learn the truth, not just about the Second World War, but of the eternal truth about war: They were bombing Iraqi villages in 1923."*
Sharon Borthwick, **Unkant**

Happiness: Poems After Rimbaud

Sean Bonney

ISBN: 978-0-9568176-6-2
Published: Sep 2011, 128pp

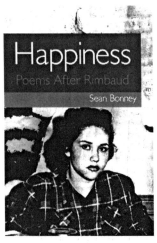

It is impossible to fully grasp Rimbaud's work, and especially *Une Saison en Enfer*, if you have not studied through and understood the whole of Marx's *Capital*. And this is why no English speaking poet has ever understood Rimbaud. Poetry is stupid, but then again, stupidity is not the absence of intellectual ability but rather the scar of its mutilation.

Rimbaud hammered out his poetic programme in 1871, just as the Paris Commune was being blown off the map. He wanted to be there. It's all he talked about. The *"systematic derangement of the senses"* is the social senses, ok, and the *"I"* becomes an *"other"* as in the transformation of the individual into the collective when it all kicks off. It's only in the English speaking world you have to point simple shit like that out. But then again, these poems have **NOTHING TO DO WITH RIMBAUD**. If you think they're translations you're an idiot. In the enemy language it is necessary to lie.

Adorno for Revolutionaries

Ben Watson

ISBN: 978-0-9568176-0-0
Published: May 2011, 256pp

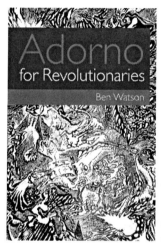

Starting with the commodity form (rather than the 'spirit' lauded by everyone from Classic FM retards to NME journalists), Adorno outlined a revolutionary musicology, a passageway between subjective feeling and objective conditions. In *Adorno for Revolutionaries*, Ben Watson argues that this is what everyone's been looking for since the PCF blackened the name of Marxism by wrecking the hopes of May '68. Batting aside postmodern prattlers and candyass pundits alike, this collection detonates the explosive core of Adorno's thought.

The **Association of Musical Marxists** says: Those 'socialists' who are frightened of their feelings can go stew in their imaginary bookshop. For us, great music is a necessity. To talk about it is to criticize everything that exists.

"For those who have the ears to hear I strongly recommend Adorno For Revolutionaries *as a substantial and very readable effort."*
Dave Black, **Hobgoblin**

Lightning Source UK Ltd.
Milton Keynes UK
UKOW05f1046210713

214119UK00001B/6/P